The United States in the Asia-Pacific since 1945

In a fast-moving and incisive narrative, Roger Buckley examines America's close and continuous relationship with the Asia-Pacific region from the end of the Pacific War to the first days of the presidency of George W. Bush. The author traces the responses of the US government to the major crises in the area through the Cold War decades and the initial post-Cold War years. He demonstrates how the United States sought to maintain its dominant regional position through a series of security alliances and its own political, military and economic strengths. Roger Buckley examines the subject from geopolitical perspectives to provide a gateway to the understanding of a complex region certain to be of global importance in the twenty-first century.

Roger Buckley is Professor of the History of International Relations at the International Christian University, Tokyo. His publications include *Japan Today* (3rd edition) (1999), *Hong Kong: The Road to 1997* (1997) and *US–Japan Alliance Diplomacy, 1945–1990* (1992).

To
Ian Nish and Hosoya Chihiro,
without permission, with gratitude

The United States in the Asia-Pacific since 1945

Roger Buckley

International Christian University, Tokyo

CAMBRIDGE
UNIVERSITY PRESS

CAMBRIDGE UNIVERSITY PRESS
Cambridge, New York, Melbourne, Madrid, Cape Town, Singapore,
São Paulo, Delhi, Dubai, Tokyo, Mexico City

Cambridge University Press
The Edinburgh Building, Cambridge CB2 8RU, UK

Published in the United States of America by Cambridge University Press, New York

www.cambridge.org
Information on this title: www.cambridge.org/9780521007252

First published 2002

A catalogue record for this publication is available from the British Library

National Library of Australia Cataloguing in Publication data
Buckley, Roger, 1944– .
The United States in the Asia-Pacific since 1945.
Bibliography.
Includes Index.
ISBN 0 521 80964 9.
ISBN 0 521 00725 9 (pbk).
1. United States – Foreign relations – Asia. 2. United
States – Foreign relations – Pacific Area. 3. Asia –
Foreign relations – United States. 4. Pacific Area –
Foreign relations – United States. 5. United States –
Foreign economic relations – Asia. 6. United States –
Foreign economic relations – Pacific Area. 7. Asia –
Foreign economic relations – United States. 8. Pacific
Area – Foreign economic relations – United States.
I. Title.
327.7305

ISBN 978-0-521-80964-1 Hardback
ISBN 978-0-521-00725-2 Paperback

... it seems to me that my friend Lee Kuan Yew of Singapore was right when he said, a couple of years ago, that the least distrusted great power in this part of the world is the United States.

Helmut Schmidt, Tokyo, 29 October 1994

Contents

Maps

Preface

I must thank the International Christian University for kind assistance over the past decade. Despite bewilderment that a student of diplomatic history could so obviously belie his job description, my colleagues have displayed both unwarranted good will and rare tolerance. My appreciation of them and of the support from Ms Marigold Acland and her team at CUP Melbourne is exceeded only by my thanks to Emeritus Professors Ian Nish and Hosoya Chihiro, the doyens of international history in Britain and Japan respectively. Their scholarship and friendship has kept me from wandering too far and too frequently from the straight and narrow. I am well aware that this text does not approach their own high academic standards.

Abbreviations

ANZUS	Australia, New Zealand and the United States Defence Treaty
APEC	Asia-Pacific Economic Cooperation forum
ARF	Asia Regional Forum
ASEAN	Association of South East Asian Nations
ASEM	Asia–Europe Meeting
CCP	Chinese Communist Party
CIA	Central Intelligence Agency
FTAA	Free Trade Area of the Americas
GATT	General Agreement on Tariffs and Trade
GHQ	general headquarters
IMF	International Monetary Fund
KEDO	Korean Peninsula Energy Development Organization
KMT	Kuomintang
LDP	Liberal Democratic Party (Japan)
MITI	Ministry of International Trade and Industry (Japan)
NAFTA	North American Free Trade Area
NAM	Non-Aligned Movement
NATO	North Atlantic Treaty Organization
NLF	National Liberation Front (Vietnam)
NSC	National Security Council (USA)
NVN	North Vietnam
ODA	Overseas Development Assistance (Japan)
PLA	People's Liberation Army (PRC)
POWs	prisoners of war
PPS	Policy Planning Staff (USA)
PRC	People's Republic of China
ROK	Republic of Korea
SAR	Special Administrative Region
SCAP	Supreme Commander for the Allied Powers (USA)
SEAC	South-East Asia Command (UK)
SEATO	South-East Asia Treaty Organization
WTO	World Trade Organization

Introduction

That afternoon the Observatory had hoisted the typhoon warning cone before we had even foolhardily left the jetty. The choppy waters forced the coxswain of the Marine Department launch to make a couple of dummy runs before he could put us alongside the pitching wooden ladder of the grey-hulled warship. With collection tins around our necks, my mother and I jumped. Seconds later we clambered on board to be promptly greeted by the officer of the watch on what must have appeared a quite ridiculous mission. His frigate had only just anchored in Hong Kong's outer harbour and already he and his crew were being pestered by European expatriates for contributions to local charities. Explaining that the sailors carried nothing but US dollars made no difference to my mother. I was instructed to pin the small paper flags in the lapels of the men, who, I realize now, doubtless thought that to protest overmuch might greatly impair their chances of going ashore at Wanchai pier. It was November 1950, the first autumn of what would prove to be the lengthy and costly Korean War, and my own introduction as a young boy in the Far East to both American hospitality and American power.

What follows is a survey of American foreign relations with the Asia-Pacific region from the end of the Pacific War in August 1945 to the first hundred days of the George W. Bush presidency in April 2001. It is written for undergraduates and the general reader who may be curious to learn how the United States first became involved and has long since remained at the centre of this vast area. The text is a product of lecturing at the chalkface in Tokyo, though it attempts what is the near impossibility of going beyond its author's domicile and nationality. Since I invite my students to discard their passports at the start of each term, the least I can do is attempt to follow my own advice. It may be that an outsider in both Asia and the United States stands a slightly better chance of viewing events in the round. I suspect, however, that Asian audiences may regard my views as too complimentary to the United States and American readers may see my approach as overly critical of their nation's performance.

One additional word of caution is in order: historians loot. It is their task to excavate and examine selected material in the pursuit of knowledge of the past. Since no one individual can hope to dig up more than a few trowels-worth of artefacts on his own, I readily plead guilty to the public exploitation of earlier studies. The text rests very largely on the exertions of others. I have incorporated their scholarship and mixed it with a sprinkling of personal findings from presidential and state papers in an attempt to straddle the gap between diplomatic history and international relations.

It is, however, hard to avoid the risk any historian faces of letting the documents dictate his story for him, and the alternative danger that the international relations specialist encounters of rushing to describe the picture in over-generalized, theoretical terms. It should also be stressed that since contemporary history is based on fragmentary and contradictory sources, most of my conclusions are tentative at best. Supposedly confident assertions on, for example, the continuities in future US policy towards Asia or what Stalin said to China in the hours before Mao Tse-tung (Mao Zedong) launched his attacks on UN forces in Korea in October 1950 deserve to be taken with a pan of salt. Given that all governments prefer to restrict access to sensitive state documents and all Asian governments are particularly unwilling to allow anything but the circulation of their version of events, there are instances where we may never know for certain. Potential readers may wish to refer to the short bibliography to see how others in various disciplines and with varying viewpoints have tackled portions of the subject on offer here. I apologize in advance for mangling their arguments and purloining their evidence without due attribution.

A second word of warning on methodology is also necessary. Throughout the book I have endeavoured to demonstrate that the United States' objectives in the Asia-Pacific region (defined simply as those parts of Asia that are adjacent to the Pacific Ocean from the Russian Maritimes to Indonesia) are hierarchical in form. The claim is that for most of the postwar era, successive American administrations have regarded political and security considerations as of the greatest importance, both during the Cold War decades and in the yet untitled years since the collapse of Communism in the Soviet Union and Eastern Europe. It follows, therefore, that the establishment and maintenance of security alliances, particularly today in Northeast Asia, but a generation and more ago in Southeast Asia, took near automatic priority over economic, financial or cultural affairs. The result, to adapt the remarks of Edwin Reischauer, the distinguished Japanologist and ambassador to Tokyo during the 1960s, was that in both American and Asian eyes, US military commanders were seen to outrank diplomats. These officials in turn stood above expatriate businessmen, and all these gentlemen (very few women ever got a look-in) could claim seniority over the assorted academics, journalists, clerics and resident eccentrics at the bottom of the pile. Naturally Reischauer, who had been born in Japan of missionary parents, felt that as a Harvard professor he was deserving of greater respect, but, his complaints not-withstanding, that was the order of things.

Wars and rumours of war are central to my story. This is a tale more of high politics between major armed powers than the low politics of trade and finance and the still novel politics of cultural diplomacy and human rights. For two generations fears of Communism, either in the shape of a monolithic Sino-Soviet bloc or in its several national components, have prompted the United States to intervene repeatedly in Asian affairs. Time and again US presidents have had to remind domestic audiences that the Pacific War, the Korean War and the Vietnam War were fought to uphold American national interests and honour in the region and to underline the United States' position in the wider international system. The collapse of the Soviet Union and frequent predictions on the end of the Cold War system in the Asia-Pacific region in the 1990s have yet to radically alter such strategic premises. However, watching President Clinton, on a sweltering summer's day in Honolulu, take the salute to commemorate the fiftieth anniversary of VJ Day, it was difficult not to wonder if the American era in the Pacific would endure much longer. The presence in August 1995 of regular units marching with the jubilant veterans on their last parade was designed to reassure doubters on that score. So too was the sight of units of the Pacific fleet assembled off Diamond Head and the Stealth bombers and F-16s flying in close formation across the bluest of skies. It is less certain whether the huge crowds would have been quite so impressed had they known that each of the classified Stealth bombers, shaped like back-to-back boomerangs, came with a price tag of over $1 billion.

Six months before these extensive Honolulu ceremonies, the US Department of Defense had released the so-called Nye Report on regional security, in an attempt to answer those critics of what might be termed 'continuing commitment'. The document argued the case for US involvement in the Asia-Pacific in order to engage the People's Republic of China (PRC) from a position of greater strength, in conjunction with a renewal of the US–Japan alliance structure. Indeed, Joseph Nye would note in a brief reassessment in February 2001 that the growth of Chinese military strength means that 'China is likely to look more intimidating to its neighbours, and its enhanced capabilities will mean that any American military tasks will require greater forces and resources than is presently the case'. Provided, however, that the United States is prepared to remain in the region in strength, the author felt confident that regional changes, particularly with regard to the Korean Peninsula, could be managed and the prospect of future interdependence even welcomed.

For all the determination of the Clinton administration to campaign under the banner of geo-economics, there is little evidence to suggest that the United States' first post-Cold War president was ever contemplating a reversal of established policies in the Asia-Pacific. Trade mattered, as it has always done, but even at the most confrontational moment of economic 'warfare' with Japan, the basic premise of US strategy in the region did not shift. Clinton's predecessor, George Bush, emphasized this reality when noting after protracted and bitter negotiations that had eventually led to the signing of a major trade agreement with Tokyo, how first and foremost the United States and Japan shared close strategic ties. Bush explained with satisfaction in April 1990 that the new arrangements would 'strengthen our security relationship and enhance the US–Japan global partnership, while simultaneously facilitating the solution of outstanding economic differences'. Remarks of this nature are deeply embedded in the current thinking of the United States towards Japan, South Korea, and other Asian nation-states. Such attitudes, it will be argued, have persisted for the past half-century.

The Cold War, indeed, proved to be the catalyst for the extraordinary economic reconstruction of first Japan and then other pro-Western states in Asia, as the United States deployed its technological and financial muscle to encourage their rapid growth. Such material assistance by Washington to promote sound economies was premised on the strategic value that Japan, South Korea and later the Southeast Asian countries held for the United States. While no one would wish to claim that the United States alone was responsible for the unanticipated hyper-growth of the region, it is doubtful if progress could have been made and then sustained without sure access to American funding and markets. The richer such Asian societies became, the closer, it was felt, would be their overall ties to the United States and the weaker the prospect of domestic turmoil or subversion. It should be noted that the Cold War and the associated 'hot' wars in Korea and Vietnam proved to be a major boost for the Japanese economy, much as Tokyo's earlier wars against China, Tsarist Russia and its actions in the First World War had played important roles in propelling Imperial Japan forward from 1894 to 1918. American procurement orders to Japanese industry in the early 1950s helped stoke the fires of growth, just as the presence of free-spending servicemen on US bases in South Korea and the Philippines would also contribute to other regional exchequers.

Sceptics, however, have long questioned both the desirability of the American presence in the Pacific and its specific priorities. Yet the historian, unlike the analyst or commentator, is obliged to accept the evidence in front of his eyes and recall the combat of the past and the high troop levels and associated host nation support of the present.

To date, the picture remains one of military commitment and alliance cooperation that undoubtedly leaves many critics within the United States and in the region disappointed. Chalmers Johnson, for example, argues that the continuation of what he sees as expensive and short-sighted policies is unsustainable. Perhaps the only brief response is to note that numerous American politicians, generals and executives have long thought otherwise and held that the consequences of withdrawal would be too damaging to American power and prestige, both in the Asia-Pacific and the wider world. Any American attempt to quit Asia would likely produce regional confrontation and conflagration, mass migrations and widespread misery, as well as the more prosaic factors of the loss of markets and capital investment.

If the policies of the past fifty years were discarded and the region were to be left to its own devices, it is difficult to see how governments traditionally friendly to Washington could avoid moving increasingly into the orbit of the People's Republic of China. A severe power imbalance is surely unavoidable without a substantial American commitment to the Asia-Pacific that is designed to continue to reassure friends and discourage possible foes. Contemporary attention to the globalization of goods, services, peoples and information does little to alter the unpleasant realities of force in international relations, particularly as the proud sovereign state gives few indications of withering away in Asia. The internet may serve as a battering ram for the new economy, but fear of neighbouring nations is a far stronger phenomenon than dot.com cooperation and the promise of sharing overseas markets. Tensions remain high. The European Union model of creeping federalism is a non-starter – the letters USA are not about to stand for the United States of Asia. Governments continue to require the reassurance of visible foreign military support on or near their borders, while the supertankers and bulk carriers of international trade still require the hidden hand of naval power to sail unencumbered through contested and piratical waters. Attempts to move beyond the suspicions of history to the assumed salvation of Asian multilateralism have a long way to go. The possibility of the Asia-Pacific even agreeing to work in concert towards a less antagonistic series of political, military and economic measures is far from likely in the medium term. It is hard to envisage how a contem-porary Asia that still relies heavily on the United States for the main-tenance of its stability and economic prosperity can easily shift gears. Attention to regional or subregional cooperation is unlikely to bear fruit, unless the United States is first convinced that it too wishes to give such initiatives its blessing. To discuss security practices in the Asia-Pacific or to envisage a zone of peace and prosperity without reckoning with the probable reactions of Washington is to ignore contemporary realities.

Hopes for the future should rest on an accurate perception of what present-day policy-makers are obliged to face, before jumping to the easy pleasures of recommending how the region ought to behave in an imaginary tomorrow of happier days.

One final caveat. Given the extended time-span and the breadth of this survey, it will be immediately obvious that events have had to be severely truncated and short paragraphs made to stand duty for what could easily serve as the basis for an entire chapter in a more specialized monograph. Yet students have to begin somewhere and I can still recall the inappropriateness of being presented as an undergraduate with a closely typed, dozen-page bibliography on the day that I signed up for a basic course in early American history. Since my knowledge of the subject was zero, I could only think that, doubtless, well-intended, transaction to be a combination of the theatre of the absurd and the theatre of cruelty. Perhaps this brief guided tour will prove slightly less intimidating and a little less painful.

1   Postwar: Asia-Pacific, 1945–1950

After the people who have come under the domination of Japan's armed forces are liberated our task will be that of making the Pacific and eastern Asia safe – safe for the United States, safe for our Allies, safe for all peace-loving nations.
>   Memorandum for Secretary of State Cordell Hull, 18 April 1944

Nowhere, even in Europe, is there greater possibility of future difficulties that may involve the United States in serious friction or even in war than in the Far East.
>   Dr Arthur Young, American adviser to the Chinese Ministry of Finance, Washington, 2 April 1945

Our material might was exemplified by the atomic bomb; our moral might is exemplified by General MacArthur. I am confident that when the hour of decision comes, the Japanese people in the light of these exhibits will elect to become dependable members of the world that is free.
>   John Foster Dulles, Tokyo, 22 June 1950

The Rise of the USA in a Contested Asia

The ending was abrupt. The dark age of carnage across the Asia-Pacific region ceased suddenly with the Imperial Japanese government's belated decision to surrender unconditionally on 14 August 1945. While Allied commanders prepared for the complex business of disarming entire Japanese armies across a still vast empire, rival politicians and diplomats from victor and vanquished states alike scrambled to make plans for the new Asia. Yet the welcome prospect of peace after years of battle brought few guarantees of stability to the demoralized peoples of a devastated continent. The defeat of Japan obviously spelt the demise of the brutal titan but provided few clues to what might follow beyond the near certainty of political change and the pressing challenges of economic reconstruction. The formal surrender proceedings of 2 September underscored, however, the central power reality of the newly transformed

Asia-Pacific region. By virtue of the American war effort against Imperial Japan, the United States was in a position immediately to influence the fate of much of the region. In a brief ceremony on borrowed British chairs under 16-inch American guns, and with Commodore Perry's ensign on display as a reminder of an earlier US encounter with Japan, General Douglas MacArthur spoke of his wish for a better world. Allied generals, crew members and journalists watched in silence from the crowded decks and turrets as the senior Japanese representatives boarded the battleship USS *Missouri* in Tokyo Bay to sign the instrument of surrender. After Foreign Minister Shigemitsu Mamoru and General Umezu Yoshijiro had committed the Japanese government and the imperial forces to its terms, the Pacific War was finally over.

In his remarks MacArthur had stated his conviction that mankind needed to transform itself or face an atomic Armageddon. Yet MacArthur's statement went unheeded, since there was little prospect of either the winners or the losers immediately considering the spiritual revolution envisaged by the newly designated Supreme Commander for the Allied Powers (SCAP) in occupied Japan. (Later MacArthur would certainly alter these views and during the Korean War urged that he be permitted to deploy tactical atomic weapons. He was also most careful to censor information on the consequences of the Hiroshima and Nagasaki bombings to prevent the Japanese public from gaining a full picture of the horrors of the attacks on their cities.) The speed with which events moved during the next few weeks left the region's leaders at the mercy of a succession of fresh developments. There had been little opportunity to think beyond the immediate horizons of ending the war and devising some approximate schemes for the future of the war-wracked region. Inevitably, this led to improvisation and imprecision. Hasty decisions that might have been subject to greater scrutiny or even cancellation slipped easily through the bureaucratic net. Exhausted men made a series of hasty responses and obvious mistakes that were to have massive consequences. President Truman, for example, complained to his secretary of commerce Henry Wallace that faced with having to read 'a million words', he was suffering 'bad headaches every day'. Equally, senior members of the newly formed Labour government in London found themselves continuing with the same punishing schedules they had already been subjected to from their lengthy war years in the coalition cabinet.

The concluding scenes of the Pacific War followed with perfect logic from the manner in which it had long been conducted. Even before the start of hostilities, it had been widely recognized among the powers that any major anti-Japanese war in Asia would prove to be an American-dominated business. Winston Churchill and Chiang Kai-shek, for example, both rejoiced once it had become apparent immediately after the attack

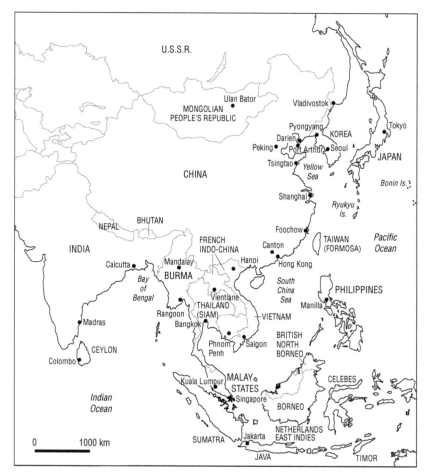

The Asia-Pacific, September 1945

on the Pacific fleet's key naval base at Pearl Harbor that the United States would commit itself whole-heartedly to the defeat of Imperial Japan. The destruction on 7 December 1941 of portions of the American fleet in Hawaii's 'battleship row' by Admiral Nagumo's carrier-launched aircraft left Britain and China in far stronger positions. Chiang declared war on the Axis powers on 10 December, stating that China too was involved in the common struggle, following Japan's 'dastardly and treacherous' assaults on the Americans and British. He added for good measure on 15 December that 'Chinese resistance and the world war against aggression have now merged into one conflict', where 'we find ourselves allied to other friendly countries in a common cause'. Churchill might express his sentiments in different style and admit privately to holding very different perceptions of China than those popular in the United States, but the Prime Minister was enormously relieved that the United States was at last committed to fighting with its friends in a world war. Germany's gratuitous declaration of war on Washington, in support of its Asian semi-ally, ensured that Britain would no longer have to struggle on alone. 'So we had won after all' was Churchill's famed remark after Pearl Harbor, but as the war progressed he would have to stomach a growing inequality in the Anglo-American relationship. For his part, President Roosevelt reckoned that whatever global strategies were to guide the Allied war effort, 'Europe first' was both his and, of course, Churchill's preference. He possessed the priceless advantage of knowing that revenge for Japan's day of infamy was indelibly stamped on the national consciousness. 'Remember Pearl Harbor' would remain a rallying cry in the troubled years ahead.

The leaders of Britain and China were fully aware that it would require the might of the United States to crush Tokyo and compel it to disgorge its newly acquired empire. Only by a huge concentration of American resources and manpower in the Pacific could the British and Chinese hope to see the deliverance of the region from Japanese imperialism. Since the Pacific War was so overwhelmingly an American war, it necessarily followed that the fate of post-surrender Japan would be largely decided by the US government. General MacArthur, for example, was appointed to his new post in Tokyo and instructed on his duties by the US government after only perfunctory discussion with British officials. MacArthur, although grandly titled as Supreme Commander for the Allied Powers, was answerable in reality only to Washington. He insisted on conducting business on a very long leash with, in the first years at least, little more than the occasional nod in the direction of his nominal superiors.

Yet no American viceroy, however self-confident and secure within occupied Japan, could afford to ignore the wider changes taking place in the Asia-Pacific. The Soviet Union, much to the dismay of the Truman administration, had greatly strengthened its hand in the last days of the Pacific War. This was the direct result of Stalin's commitment to President Roosevelt that the USSR would enter the war against Imperial Japan three months after the end of the war against Nazism in Europe. It had been agreed at the Yalta conference of February 1945 that the Soviet Union would end its long-standing neutrality pact with Japan and join forces with the United States and Britain in exchange for what it had lost after the humiliations of the Russo-Japanese War of 1904–1905. The price that Stalin extracted for this arrangement was high and has remained controversial ever since its secret annexes were revealed to the American public, but something comparable had, of necessity, to be granted to gain Soviet cooperation. The results went according to plan. Once Soviet tanks had rapidly driven back the less than effective Kwantung divisions of the Imperial Japanese army, Stalin was legitimately entitled to claim his prizes in Manchuria, Sakhalin and the Kuriles. It needs also to be underlined that the Soviet action had an immediate and vital impact on the thinking of the inner Japanese war cabinet and its belated road to reluctant surrender. The USSR's declaration of war on Tokyo left the Imperial Japanese government quite friendless in world politics. When combined with the dropping of the two atomic bombs by the United States, it led to the fateful and evenly balanced cabinet decision to admit defeat.

The principal victor remained, of course, the United States. Since the Pacific War had been the greatest overseas conflict in the republic's history, Washington could be expected to dictate terms both to the vanquished and to the lesser powers who had never played more than secondary roles in the prolonged Asia-Pacific contest. Japan was required to accept the ignominy of unconditional surrender, while the United States' allies had little option but to swallow their pride and acknowledge the emerging new American order in increasing portions of the region. The fact that the opinions of wartime friends of the United States were frequently disregarded when American policies for Japan were being prepared underlines emphatically where power in the Pacific lay. MacArthur promptly proceeded to conduct his occupation indirectly through the agencies of the Emperor and the Japanese bureaucracy. He quickly disregarded the views of those who had called for the installation of a republican form of government, and by punishing few but ex-military figures made it apparent that he was already expecting a transformed US–Japan relationship. MacArthur broadly followed the recommendations of those on his staff, who saw, a mere month after Japan's surrender, that in 'the long run it is of paramount, national importance that Japan harbor no lasting resentment'. They felt that 'American long-range interests require friendly relations with the Orient based on mutual respect, faith and understanding'. Much in international relations would soon turn on these sentiments.

The Divisions of Postwar Asia

Any assessment of the international politics of the Asia-Pacific in August 1945 must begin by underlining the military and economic superiority of the United States. Its troops were preparing to land in Japan, Korea and parts of China; its officials were in place to command operations not only throughout Japan proper but also in Okinawa, the southern parts of the Korean Peninsula, the Philippines and across the Pacific. The dropping of the world's first atomic bombs on Hiroshima and Nagasaki, coupled with the extraordinary economic and financial strengths of the United States, were further reminders of America's newly acquired power. Roosevelt's wartime arsenal of democracy now had the fresh task of supporting an uncertain and suspicious world that badly required assistance to even begin to remake itself. In the late summer of 1945 the United States stood watch over large portions of a devastated Europe and a newly liberated Asia-Pacific region. The Pacific was indeed an American lake and the Japanese home islands represented a particularly valuable prize which were about to be occupied and controlled very largely by US forces.

While the United States' predominant role in the defeat of Imperial Japan was beyond dispute, the broader issue of how to manage the future of post-surrender Asia was both more complicated and more contested. Not surprisingly, it had been the subject of considerable international debate during the Second World War. At a series of major international conferences from 1942 to 1945, there had been extensive discussion over the question of the future of the Japanese empire and the possible divisions of Allied responsibility within the Asia-Pacific region. Yet despite talks among the Great Powers and additional secretarial soundings, relatively little had been accomplished by the time of Japan's defeat. The Yalta Conference had established a very approximate division of labour among the Great Powers in the Asia-Pacific region. Yet since these discussions among the leaders of the wartime coalition were taken against the backcloth of the imperative to first crush the Axis states, the arrangements were piecemeal and subject to later change. President Roosevelt for one appears to have approached Yalta with a degree of casualness that may have been the result both of increasing ill health and of his predilection for conducting business without prompting from State Department briefing books. The results, too, hardly correspond to the construction of an international system with mutually understood rules and penalties for non-compliance. It is doubtful if the word 'system' appears even once in the official British and American documents on Yalta.

On his arrival back in the United States after the Yalta conference in the Crimea, President Roosevelt went out of his way in public to accentuate the positive. He stated, in words that have been quoted against him frequently in the years since Yalta, that international society could look forward now 'to the beginnings of a permanent structure of peace'. The successes of Yalta, Roosevelt maintained, presaged a new era that ought to see the final elimination of 'the system of unilateral action, the exclusive alliances, the spheres of influence, the balances of power, and all the other expedients that have been tried for centuries – and have always failed'. In their place Roosevelt intended to offer 'a universal organization in which all peace loving Nations will finally have a chance to join'. Clearly the President was talking up the Yalta summit in order to ensure American acceptance of greater internationalism once the war against fascism had been won. He was determined to see an end to isolationism and an active American voice in the new organizations required to guarantee political and economic security in the future. Roosevelt's recollections of Woodrow Wilson's failures undoubtedly prompted the former junior member of the Wilson administration to work carefully to build on public support for interventionism.

In the last months of his life President Roosevelt concentrated on foreign policy. Given the vast issues of winning the wars in Europe and Asia, while working simultaneously to gain Anglo-American-Soviet cooperation after the defeat of the Axis powers, this was only to be expected. Since the war against Nazism ended three months before VJ Day, and it had been widely felt that any immediate surrender of Japan was unlikely before an amphibious invasion of the home islands in 1946 at the earliest, events in Europe took centre stage. Yet increasing difficulties with the Soviet Union over the highly sensitive question of the future of Eastern Europe quickly boded ill for any sustained continuation of Allied wartime cooperation. Major differences over the composition of the new government of Poland were followed by what can only be described as the gradual 'Sovietization' of Central and Eastern Europe. Unfortunately, Roosevelt died before the war in the Pacific had ended. His efforts to secure a lasting partnership between the Big Three nations, to which he insisted on adding China in the expectation that it might in time prove to be one of the leaders of Asia in tandem with Washington, had not borne much fruit by April 1945.

His successor, however, was decidedly less prepared to adopt a conciliatory approach towards the Soviet Union and what most of his cabinet saw as its perceived goals in Europe and beyond. President Truman feared that unless he stood up to Stalin there was the distinct danger of a repetition of the events that led to the successes of Nazism in the 1930s. Yet the American administration could offer little but defiant rhetoric to place in the path of Stalin's conquest of Eastern Europe. The continent was parcelled up along the traditional lines of international politics: where the conquering armies halted would largely determine the boundaries of the new occupation zones. It followed, therefore, that Stalin could expect no role in Italian affairs and that Poland would be his exclusive playground. The splintering of the continent from the Baltic to the Adriatic that Winston Churchill would soon decry in his 'iron curtain' speech at

Fulton, Missouri, in March 1946 was to be a fait accompli once Prague fell to Communist subversion two years later. Under these circumstances the United States and its Western European friends saw the urgent necessity of shoring up their portion of the continent through political, economic and military measures that became identified under the generic term of containment. At the heart of the issue was the long-term future of Germany, where neither the United States nor the USSR was prepared to countenance any loss of control over its own sphere. The Truman administration was committed by September 1946, following Secretary Byrnes' Stuttgart speech, to the immediate economic reconstruction of its zone and had promised a speedy return of sovereignty to what would soon become West Germany as a pro-American bulwark against the advance of Communism in Europe. American foreign policy was radically transformed by the Truman Doctrine of 1947, which committed the United States to support non-Communist regimes in the region, and by the generous economic assistance associated with the Marshall Plan and the establishment of NATO as the basic security system for Western Europe in 1949. The United States quickly showed its resolve in Europe and was rightly seen as the undoubted leader of the Western alliance. Yet it was different elsewhere. The clear-cut international rivalries that fractured Europe and left the war-wracked continent at the mercy of two armed and ideologically opposed power blocs dominated by Washington and Moscow had a cruel simplicity that was singularly absent in Asia.

All that had been established at war's end in the Asia-Pacific was a rudimentary series of arrangements that divided the region into four rather approximate spheres of influence. The United States would impose its will on defeated Japan. Equally obviously, Washington would be responsible for the future of its newly liberated colony of the Philippines, while Britain would concentrate on the reconstruction of Southeast Asia, in keeping with its campaigning during the Pacific War to retake Singapore and Rangoon. It was also apparent that the Soviet Union was intent on returning in triumph to Northeast Asia, where, under the terms of the Roosevelt–Stalin agreement made at Yalta, the recent conqueror of Manchuria was fully entitled to remain. The Soviet Union did not, however, venture seriously beyond these Yalta limits. Stalin, it is true, would chance his arm briefly in mid-August and demand of President Truman that Soviet troops occupy the northern portion of Hokkaido, but once rebuffed by the White House, the Red Armies halted. Within weeks Stalin would complain to Ambassador Harriman in Moscow that the USSR was being treated like a piece of furniture by his government on all matters Japanese.

No one, however, could make more than intelligent guesses over what might happen to China. It was highly probable that the ending of the

Pacific War would lead to a resumption of the Chinese civil war that had been fought intermittently during the anti-Japanese era, but the eventual outcome was far from certain in the autumn of 1945. Roosevelt, Churchill and Stalin, of course, had long held their individual preferences for what each imagined would occur in China, but the countries they represented would quickly discover the limits of this influence. The Great Powers of the region might be generally secure in their own spheres but each would have to summon up varying degrees of patience and wait on events elsewhere. The fate of postwar China would soon be seen to depend in the last resort on its long-suffering peoples. China's sons would choose sides in the contest, sensing that an end had to be put to the demoralization, despair and near exhaustion of a once proud and powerful nation. When combined with the political rivalries between the Nationalist government and its Chinese Communist opponents led by Mao Tse-tung, China's immense size and dislocations after years of warfare and rampage made for near chaos. Families were reduced to eating grass and drinking polluted water across huge stretches of the countryside. Starvation stalked the land and the cities offered no better alternative. Unless, as the United States hoped against hope, a political settlement could be brokered between the two warring political parties, it was difficult to see how to avert a renewed contest to the death to determine who should rule in Beijing.

The American Occupation of Japan

No government could claim to be prepared for the speed with which Japan threw in the towel. The United States, however, was less unprepared than the rest, who had merely reckoned that Tokyo's determination to fight to the last man would require both the large-scale invasion of western Japan and then bitter house-to-house combat until Tokyo could be seized. It was calculated that it might well not be before 1946 or even 1947, if past experience of the bitter resistance on Okinawa was any sort of guide, before Japan would surrender – assuming, of course, that the archipelago still possessed an effective government able to determine policy. The shock of the twin atomic bombings of Hiroshima and Nagasaki, when combined with the rapid push by the forces of the Soviet Union southwards through Manchuria, fortunately aborted any further hopes that the beleaguered Japanese cabinet might have had of prolonging its unwinnable war. Faced with naval blockade, near starvation and ruined cities, the Japanese state reluctantly saw that the game was up and that its leaders would be held accountable to the Allies for their misdeeds.

The United States had played the largest role in gaining Japan's unexpectedly swift surrender. The butcher's bill for the most bloody overseas war in American history was the loss of 100 000 servicemen, though this huge figure was dwarfed by the millions of Japanese military and civilian casualties. Once Washington had taken the Japanese surrender, it rightly claimed its prerogative to determine the arrangements for the subsequent occupation. Beyond the possession of troops on the ground, the victor in the Pacific conflict held two cards that were to prove crucial in the years ahead. First, the civil and military bureaucracies in Washington had managed, even when faced with the pressures of organizing the myriad demands of total war across the Pacific, to think seriously about what should follow from Japan's eventual defeat. Second, President Truman had moved quickly to appoint General MacArthur as SCAP in Japan. Truman had no great personal respect for MacArthur (he confided to his diary in June 1945 that the general was 'Mr. Prima Donna, Brass Hat, Five Star MacArthur'), but he sensed that the domestic political consequences of not employing MacArthur were too dangerous to contemplate. MacArthur's dynamic leadership over a nation where the United States was determined to prevent rival Allied zones on the divided German model, together with the possession of detailed pre-surrender planning on what the United States's objectives ought to be in occupied Japan, quickly proved highly effective. Yet no American commander, however gifted, would have been able to gain the cooperation and consent of postwar Japan if there had been months and months of wretched slaughter up the Japanese islands until Tokyo had been captured and resistance elsewhere eventually quelled. In this sense one can speculate that the dropping of the atomic bombs probably 'saved' a great number of Japanese and Allied lives and also made possible the relatively benign occupation that followed on from the Imperial Cabinet's decision to surrender in August 1945. Although of absolutely no consolation to those who would continue to mourn the deaths of tens of thousands of family members, the destruction of Hiroshima and Nagasaki had the indirect consequence of making possible an entirely new US–Japan relationship. The swift ending to the Pacific War prevented the widely expected scorched earth tactics and hand-to-hand combat which would only have prolonged the inevitable and would have resulted in the bitterest of memories and encouraged vows of revenge. The atomic bomb, while deployed to end the war and in fact inflicting fewer casualties than the daylight conventional bombing raids on an unprotected Tokyo in March 1945, had a perverse role in starting the peace.

Once MacArthur and his ever zealous staff reached Tokyo, serious attention began almost immediately over the probable long-term consequences of the American occupation on the international relations of the region. MacArthur's military secretary had written to his superior after Japan's surrender, cautioning him over the dangers of a vindictive approach, while MacArthur himself assumed instinctively that American values would prove an effective substitute for the discredited Imperial ideology for the exhausted and hungry Japanese. MacArthur might claim defensively in reply to a question on the philosophy of the occupation that 'history will clearly show that the entire human race, irrespective of geographical delimitations or cultural traditions, is capable of absorbing, cherishing and defending liberty, tolerance and justice', but what he really had in mind was something slightly less universal. He stated to the same correspondent that the 'pattern of my course in the occupation of Japan lies deeply rooted in the lessons and experience of American history' and that what had been successful for the United States must fit the new Japan. His own nation's exceptionalism, the fact that MacArthur's father had served briefly as military governor in the first months of the American occupation of the Philippines, and the driving ambition of his son were all factors that contributed to the determination to remake Japan. The United States, MacArthur modestly instructed his questioner from Brooklyn, possessed 'a spiritual and material strength never before equalled in human history'.

MacArthur's total self-confidence worked to his nation's advantage. The occupation, as both Japanese and non-American observers in Tokyo could hardly dispute, was run by the United States, and the exercise would clearly remain in place until its government had determined that Japan deserved a peace treaty. The occupation was an American show. It proved to be a far lengthier process than the staff officers in MacArthur's General Headquarters had initially expected in their surveys of evolving American–Japanese relations, but these delays did not greatly alter the probable position of Japan in any future regional political framework. The occupation was certainly protracted, but this did not seriously impair the initial policy goals of establishing a reformed Japanese polity prepared to work in close cooperation with the United States. These aims were finally realized in the San Francisco peace settlements of September 1951, which required of Japan that it side openly with Washington and reject the normalization of relations with its Communist neighbours.

From the outset the United States had no intention of abdicating from what it held to be its vital objectives in Japan. Memories of Pearl Harbor and the bitter fighting in the Pacific ensured that the American government alone would very largely determine Allied policy and would require that the future of Japan and its relationship to the Asia-Pacific region should be carefully crafted to American national objectives. Policy-makers certainly appreciated that there would be finite limits in due course to the degree of American control over Japan's subsequent behaviour, but the determination to guide and monitor Tokyo's every move and strenuously influence its probable course of action rarely wavered. Secretary of the Navy James Forrestal, during his first visit to Tokyo in July 1946, noted that 'Japan will need the most careful study by the United States to be sure that when the Americans get out her position as a nation is sufficiently clear so that she cannot be led in some other direction'.

This intent was made considerably easier through two self-evident factors. First, it was undeniably the case that the rest of Asia viewed Imperial Japan's recent barbarism with near total revulsion, and therefore if Japan were to have any prospect of a future in Asia it would have to be under the auspices of the United States. By the autumn of 1945 Japan had lost both its empire and its international reputation. The only way back would have to be through close cooperation with the United States, since it alone was Tokyo's only potential friend in the world. Japan's pariah status left it with few options but to put its trust in the United States and conform at least outwardly to its design. The second restriction on Japan's freedom to manoeuvre was the parlous state of the Japanese postwar economy. The harsh realities of daily life in its blitzed cities and overpopulated villages were obvious to all. As the nation began the struggle to improve its desperate situation, no one but the United States was prepared or able to exhibit the slightest charity. Japan's lengthy bid for Asia-Pacific dominance had ended up destroying not only its own cities but large portions of the region's infrastructure as well. This fact, unfortunately, tended to be all too quickly forgotten within Japanese society as its people dug themselves out of the ruins and began the dreary search for food and shelter. No one in Tokyo or Osaka, though, was blinkered enough to imagine that Japan could improve its material lot without American assistance. All were aware that scarce emergency food supplies were landed at Yokohama and Kobe thanks to the intervention of General MacArthur. Every Japanese child knew and practised the English phrase 'give me chocolate' whenever GIs were spotted in the neighbourhood. Their parents, who patronized the thriving blackmarkets to sell off family heirlooms for meagre quantities of substandard rice mixed with barley, were in equally little doubt that any rudimentary recovery for Japan in the future was dependent on American financial and economic aid.

The occupation years clearly established the framework for new political and economic philosophies in postwar Japan. The role of the United States as the vital instigator and the response of many (though certainly far from all) Japanese to a multitude of reform programs and experiments ensured that at the very least the nation's future would be immensely different from its past. The confusions, contradictions and switches in occupation policies deserve note, but the overall scale and determination behind the reform programs were unmistakable. Conservatives did indeed complain bitterly over MacArthur's actions, yet their protests were testimony both to the effectiveness of the American-instigated schemes and disappointment at the enthusiasm with which whole sections of Japanese society embraced previously suspect ideas of parliamentary democracy, vigorous public debate and extensive trade unionism. Some of the new converts to an open political system would admit later that the American-led process was uncomfortably the creation of outsiders. The internationally acclaimed film director Kurosawa Akira stated with customary honesty in his autobiography that 'the freedom and democracy of the post-war era were not things I had fought for and won; they were granted to me by powers beyond my own'. Equally, the first union organizer at Tokyo's important Shinagawa railway depot would tell the BBC forty years on that he had begun his activities with only the vaguest of ideas of what the occupation officials expected of him. It is to Mr Shimada's credit that less than four years later in 1949, he would be dismissed for his very successes as a union activist, once US policies had taken a decidedly conservative shift to accommodate occupied Japan to a harsher domestic and international environment.

Critics of MacArthur tended to adopt two stances. The first suggested that he had insufficient understanding of the inherent realities of Japanese society and that his actions were unintentionally preparing the way for more radical shifts in domestic affairs that risked leading to a Marxist state. Sir George Sansom, the leading British authority on Japan, wrote in January 1946 when visiting Tokyo that he was 'not sure that the Americans realize what they are doing in their enthusiasm for freedom. It would be an ironical outcome of the occupation if Japan should be pushed into the arms of the USSR'. Sansom reckoned that 'many of the young officers at GHQ (not the professionals but men drawn from civilian life) have Communistic leanings, and these are visible in their work'. Others, however, adopted the opposite position and claimed that SCAP was insufficiently hostile to the old guard within the political and bureaucratic establishments. In fact MacArthur saw his job as providing leadership and reassurance to a confused nation by implanting new values more akin to those of the United States, in the hope that portions at least might survive the inevitable twists and turns of policy that would follow any eventual peace settlement. Despite his bombastic public statements, MacArthur frequently confided to British officials in Tokyo that the best to be expected of Japan's behaviour in the future would be to operate under at least the semblance of a democratic system. He had few illusions about the totality of his handiwork surviving much beyond the end of the occupation era.

Yet prospects for close United States–Japan ties were favourable because most of the occupation era saw conservative politicians in positions of power. The astute, abrasive and at times indolent former diplomat

Yoshida Shigeru was Japan's prime minister from May 1946 to April 1947 and again from October 1948 until the last weeks of 1954. His lengthy tenure as premier served to cement the Pacific relationship. Yoshida, in truth, an Anglophile whose fits of temper at American reform could get the better of him, was a realist. He saw with considerable clarity that his country had perilously few options after its surrender in August 1945. This no-nonsense approach to international affairs had earlier landed him in trouble with the wartime authorities, and his views on Japan's desperate situation in the last months of the Pacific fighting had ensured that he be subjected to house arrest.

Yoshida never disguised his very considerable reservations over what he frequently insisted were thoroughly un-Japanese constitutional, political and economic reforms imposed needlessly on his nation. He bitterly resented, for example, the demotion of the Emperor from his earlier position at the centre of the Japanese polity. Yet he saw dispassionately that occupied Japan simply had to conform to American orders and preserve its latent strength for the distant day when recovery might be at hand. Any future salvation would only emerge, however, by working with the United States, which alone could assist both Japan's economic recovery and support its re-entry into the wider world. Yoshida certainly enjoyed baiting the American eagle and gained domestic popularity from letting it be known that he regarded MacArthur's GHQ as standing for 'Go Home Quickly', but he had to acknowledge Japan's dependency on the United States. The perilous state of his country ruled out the politics of neutrality or autonomy. There could be no manoeuvrings to play off both sides in the ideological battles of the Cold War or any misguided thoughts of a return to past glories. Little was to be gained by refusing to reckon with the fact that post-surrender Japan was now merely a third-rate power whose limited prospects rested on the goodwill of the United States. To cooperate was the sensible goal that might lead eventually to a generous peace settlement and a modest future as a competent trading nation, trusting for its security in the protection of the United States.

The United States had entered Tokyo in the autumn of 1945 with considerable ambivalence towards newly defeated Japan. General MacArthur had quickly begun to formulate constructive policies, but domestic opinion within the United States was decidedly unsympathetic; the polls indicated overwhelming support for the hanging of the Emperor and the avoidance of American aid for the bereft Japanese economy. MacArthur assured US journalists on 21 September that Japan 'never again will become a world power', and his insistence that the Emperor be summoned to call on him brought home to audiences everywhere the extent of Japan's humiliation. The cautiously positive response of the Japanese establishment and the public at large therefore contributed to a welcome reduction in tension and the transition to a more amicable set of dealings. The rapid rotation out of Japan of American troops who had fought in the Pacific theatres certainly further eased what might have been a disastrous opening to the occupation. The impracticality of Chiang Kai-shek's wish to station Chinese forces in Japan, thereby avoiding almost certain clashes between Imperial Japanese veterans and Kuomintang (KMT) soldiers, was an additional piece of good fortune that helped get the occupation era off to a satisfactory start.

For the Japanese people, the priority of feeding themselves left little time or energy for careful scrutiny of MacArthur's herculean bid to reform their nation root and branch. Food was also the inevitable centre of much of the political debate, where mass demonstrations organized by the Left would display huge posters of the Emperor guzzling at a full table while the proletariat starved. General MacArthur needed no reminding of the potential disruption that food riots might cause to the success of his regime and he took pains to gain extra grain and staples from elsewhere in the region and beyond. He also impressed on his many overseas visitors that the difficulties of feeding the Japanese worker played into the hands of what the more conservative elements on his staff saw as malcontents and rabble-rousers. The alternative was also held to be true: if adequate food, clothing and fuel were provided, it ought to be possible to stave off criticisms from the Left and press ahead with at least the initial stages of Japan's economic reconstruction. It followed that the more that rudimentary improvements could be shown to be in place, the greater the likelihood that the occupation might succeed. Japan might then look forward to some distant prospect of limited prosperity under a radically different political structure, where parliamentary democracy, thanks to the hybrid American-scripted 1947 Constitution, had the opportunity at last to sink deeper roots.

Yet there remained throughout the next six years of occupation two major issues that acted as brakes on American aspirations for a democratic, stable and secure Japanese state. The first was the controversial question of economic reform, particularly in the light of the complaints of some influential figures in the United States that Japanese business enterprises were being severely hampered through excessively liberal measures. The second was the related question of how to design adequate American–Japanese security arrangements in a changing and increasingly difficult international context. Once it was apparent that the ending of the Chinese civil war would inevitably lead to the installation of a Communist state with ties to the Soviet Union, many in Washington felt the time had come to shore up Japan as a potential ally. Tokyo could thereby dispense with any further attempts at what critics at least held to be excessive economic reform that weakened management in its frequent clashes with newly organized trade unions. These twin problems were harder to solve than the continuing implementation of a far-reaching range of political, social and industrial reforms. These measures, un-popular with many conservatives, clearly had enthusiastic support among farmers, teachers and blue-collar workers, who had never previously experienced more than marginal influence within Japan. By 1949 it was apparent that the Truman administration was reconsidering MacArthur's handiwork in Japan. The growing antagonism between the United States and the Soviet Union that had emerged shortly after the end of the war in Europe was now being widely felt in the Asia-Pacific region. Japan, much to the bitter disappointment of the many reformers in MacArthur's headquarters, could no longer be isolated from global international realities. The emergence of the Cold War in Asia did not destroy the bulk of the occupation's sturdy reforms but it most certainly prevented any further experimentation. Japan had to begin to live within its means and ask itself how it might cope with a harsher external environment. American planners now reassessed their earlier attempts to leave Japan as little more than a disarmed rump state off the Asian mainland. In the same manner that Washington had earlier worked to transform what rapidly became West Germany, Japan found itself being taken much more seriously in American regional schemes. The United States now wished to ensure that Japan was secure militarily and politically from any pros-pect of future Soviet aggression, intimidation or subversion. While the changes do not, in truth, constitute what the Left immediately decried as a total 'reverse course' in the conduct of the occupation, the new thinking undoubtedly gave heart to Japan's conservative, pro-capitalist groupings. As in West Germany, these elements would accept, however reluctantly, the need to align Japan with the United States in a divided region.

Japanese Peace-Making

General MacArthur would frequently declaim that he had done all he could to alter Japanese institutions and attitudes within his first two years of arriving at Atsugi. By the spring of 1947 he had already told his own government and indeed the entire world that he considered that occupied Japan had kept to its part of the bargain implicit in the surrender terms and should therefore be rewarded with the earliest possible peace treaty. He preached this pet sermon to all his guests from abroad, who rarely got an opportunity to say a single word during his interminable luncheon monologues. He insisted that the longer the occupation was allowed to stagnate, the more difficult it would become to ensure continuing Japanese friendship and cooperation. The United States, MacArthur complained, was obsessed as always with European affairs and Washington had better concentrate on United States–Japan ties both for the sake of the bilateral relationship and for the value of Tokyo in the wider regional context. By March 1948, for example, MacArthur was already beginning to show signs of doubt over the efficacy of the occupation. The drearily familiar issues of economic revival and a peace settlement had certainly by then begun to engage much closer scrutiny from his nominal masters in Washington, but the result had been to postpone rather than accelerate any final day of reckoning. He told the State Department's George Kennan, the author of the original containment thesis, that 'if we accomplish this mission, we might fundamentally alter the course of world history', but the qualification in his statement would have been out of place twelve months earlier. In the spring of 1947 MacArthur had been at the zenith of his power; a year later and it was apparent that his conversations with Kennan and submissions to higher authorities in Washington were merely a single part of a broader picture. By 1948 MacArthur was only one of many voices that the Truman administration had to listen to as it gingerly thought through the fundamental policy implications of a Japanese peace settlement.

Not surprisingly, the longer the occupation was allowed to continue, the greater became the involvement of the US administration in considering and coordinating the mass of factors relating to Japan's future. Termination, though, was dependent more on what was happening outside the hothouse of occupied Japan than on the domestic good conduct medal being won by the Japanese nation. MacArthur was relegated to a back seat in this great debate. Instead of being openly courted and consulted, he found himself gradually marginalized as the same planning institutions that had reckoned during the war with post-surrender Japan started to prepare the way for the post-occupation era. The State Department and the military at last began to cooperate, while MacArthur had to perform a taxing holding operation on the ground as the Japanese government anticipated an improbably early end to the entire occupation.

Repairing the civil/military divide within the US government was only a fairly simple part of the more complicated whole. First there had to be cooperation between General MacArthur's staff, the State Department, the Treasury, the Army, the Joint Chiefs of Staff and the White House, but there remained the broader issue of how to gain a peace treaty with Japan that had at least a modicum of support from other powers in the region. For the United States alone to make peace with Japan would have been a fairly ludicrous pastime. The specific mechanics of the peace process proved to be protracted and arduous. While it shared this feature with the occupation that it intended to replace, the main difference between the United States' unilateralism in Japan and the eventual peace settlements was the need to take fully into account the views of America's allies. These consultations, headed by a patient but insistent John Foster Dulles, required simultaneous diplomatic offensives on both domestic and overseas fronts. Ambassador Dulles had to negotiate with rival bureaucracies in Washington, while attempting to listen sympathetically to General MacArthur, Prime Minister Yoshida and the leaders of all Allied states with a stake in Asia-Pacific affairs. Given the inevitable conflicts of interest between so many parties, it remains surprising that the United States was able to gain at least a degree of agreement among these nations, though the results should not be overstated. The eventual text signed at San Francisco in September 1951 was far from the liking of many in the region. Major nations, such as the Soviet Union and the People's Republic of China, refused to have anything to do with the American-led settlements, while others gave only grudging pro forma support and made no secret of their reservations. Although Washington was able to pack the peace conference with its Latin American friends, it was careful not to draw the world's attention to the fact that not a single Asian state had a gracious word of welcome on the return of Tokyo to the international fold.

The final ceremonies were less than triumphant. Probably little could have been done to bring the largest Communist nations on board, but even the Philippines, the traditional supporter of American power in the Pacific, noted that the peace arrangements appeared to be particularly generous to Tokyo. This, of course, was not how Japanese commentators then (or now) generally viewed San Francisco. Most had long felt that the occupation had outgrown any possible justification and many were decidedly anxious over the security arrangements, which were clearly a quid pro quo for the formal end to the occupation. The fact that Prime Minister Yoshida alone signed the text on behalf of Japan and then slunk back to Tokyo was indicative of the mood within his nation. Opponents immediately claimed that the agreements whereby the United States was granted permission to retain its military bases on the archipelago ensured that in reality the occupation was continuing. The alleged American kindnesses to Japan that were so readily identified by nations such as Britain, Australia and the Philippines were seen in Japan in a very different light within all but diehard conservative ranks. While the British government disliked the forthcoming economic competition it would have to face from post-occupation Japan, the substantial American financial and technological assistance already in evidence had increasingly been taken for granted by Tokyo. Dulles certainly worked energetically to sponsor Japan's entry into the pro-Western club, but it was one membership that many in Tokyo held the nation could have done without as the Cold War intensified.

What disturbed the Japanese government was the extent of the commitment that the United States now required of its new associate. The annual subscription appeared over-expensive and the corresponding benefits decidedly limited. Yet Yoshida, for all the unpopularity that his signature brought him, had again taken the correct decision. He saw, as he had at the inception of the occupation, that the least bad option was to remain aligned to the United States. Despite widespread anger at American extra-territoriality (the Meiji state had taken half a century to overcome the same issue after the forceful 'opening' of Japan by Commodore Perry) and Washington's freedom to deploy its troops at will both inside Japan and throughout the Far East, Yoshida was prepared to be branded as a collaborator. It was always an uncomfortable position and would have become doubly so if his opponents had known that in August 1950 the United States reckoned it had 'the right to maintain in Japan as much force as we wanted, anywhere we wanted, as long as we wanted'. Those looking for a succinct definition of imperialism could hardly ask for a more telling statement.

Anti-Americanism was fuelled by disappointments at the new roles required of Japan in the peace settlements. By 1951 Japanese public opinion saw as almost irreconcilable the initial support of a strict constitutional definition of pacifism in the early days of the occupation and recent blatant pressure on Yoshida to rearm. Even defenders of the security treaty argued that the numbers of troops required, the costs to be incurred, and the political repercussions within Japan were excessive. The disappointments that Japan had to accept can be seen clearly in the contrasting remarks of General MacArthur, who naturally enough was reluctant to abandon his constitutional handiwork. In March 1947 MacArthur had argued publicly for a peace treaty in which the Allies should 'undertake to guarantee the neutrality of Japan, with the view to the transfer of such undertaking to the stewardship of the United Nations, where the responsibility properly should rest'. By December 1949, in the light of discussions with the Truman administration, MacArthur had had to reckon with 'the granting of a limited number of bases in Japan to the United States, with a total force not exceeding, say, 35,000 men'. He then insisted, however, that US forces in Japan should be 'entirely self-supporting and would have no right of interference with the prerogatives of the Japanese Government. In any event, the granting of bases should be for a limited period of time only'.

Allied Differences and the Postwar Region

While the role of the United States in handling the fate of defeated Japan was rarely challenged openly, the broader issues of how to deal with post-surrender Asia had been the subject of considerable international debate during the Second World War. Given the speed with which Japan had finally capitulated after months of warfare where it had appeared that Tokyo would rather fight to the last man than give up, there was an inevitable hiatus of confusion. With so few existing Allied agreements, there were obvious opportunities for each victorious state to press its claims to the limit. Intemperate messages between Allied commanders on the ground symbolized the difficulties their masters were having in the rarified atmosphere of foreign ministries and cabinet offices. Generals Mountbatten and MacArthur, for example, jostled each other over what should constitute the exact boundaries of their commands and then argued on the minutiae of surrender ceremonies. Yet the issues were often more serious than their schoolboy jokes about keeping one's pants on and ensuring that MacArthur took Hirohito's off might suggest.

What is equally noticeable is the general lack of American consultation with its Allies over its intentions in Northeast Asia. The distinction between the leadership readily expected of Washington by its friends and the United States' determination to exclude others from anything beyond a token role was to remain pronounced during the Japanese occupation era and long after it ended. The burden of controlling Japan had been eagerly assumed by the United States in August 1945 without much ado about consulting wartime Allies and in near total disregard of their entitlement to a voice in the conduct of policy. Nations such as Australia felt badly let down by the United States' monopoly on power, while Britain continually had to balance its wish to influence events in Japan against its dependence on American support for domestic reconstruction and the imperative of designing new security structures for Western Europe.

Yet much the same criticism of the United States' 'go it alone' behaviour in Japan could also be made of Britain and the other returning metropolitan powers in Southeast Asia. British archives are bursting with material on schemes for the economic reinvigoration of Malaya and at least tentative thoughts on political reform for all of its colonies in the region, but scant attention appears to have been given to possible American reactions. If the American drive to control Japan unilaterally caught the Foreign Office unprepared, similar lapses can be seen within the State Department over the future of Singapore and Kuala Lumpur. The difference, however, between the relative strengths of Britain and the United States had already ensured that vocal elements in the American administration, Congress and the press felt entitled to offer sharp criticisms of the European record in Southeast Asia. Many, from President Roosevelt downwards, would argue that those nations shoved ignominiously out of Asia in 1941–42 either did not deserve a postwar future or, at best, their return ought to be conditional on substantial change leading to eventual self-government and independence without exception for territories under foreign sway. While the President enjoyed making particular sport of the French record in Indo-China, he could also be outspoken on the subject of Hong Kong and the alleged British wish to plant the Union Jack on every unclaimed speck of land around the globe. Not for nothing did GIs dub SEAC (South-East Asia Command) as 'Save England's Asian Colonies' and voice their anger at island-hopping strategies that seemed to take them campaigning from one British territory to another on the long road from MacArthur's initial headquarters in Melbourne to journey's end at Tokyo.

Despite vocal disputes and public disagreements, wartime and postwar relations between the United States and Britain were to prove far closer than Washington's ties to the Soviet Union and China. If the Anglo-American alliance had its share of bad-tempered ministerial meetings, it did prove to be something stronger and more cooperative than the mere 'quasi-alliance' suggested by some later students. Since this relationship in the region had been unequal at least from the days of the Manchurian crisis of 1931, it was only to be expected that the United States felt entitled to claim a role in Southeast Asia that was quickly to involve considerable political and military commitments. American assistance to returning Dutch forces in the Netherlands East Indies is one early example of American interest in the region, which would expand rapidly by the 1950s, particularly with regard to Indo-China. Although there would be occasions when British officials might deplore the activities of the United States, it was rarely the case that postwar Southeast Asia was seen as a region under exclusively European control. Postwar economic restraints, limited domestic concern for the fate of colonial territories, and the overwhelming necessity of retaining American goodwill simply derailed any remaining dreams that some in Britain, France and the Netherlands might have had of putting the clock back to 1941. It could not be done. Imperial Japan's successes in conquering the region had encouraged indigenous nationalism and the military and economic might of the United States made it apparent that all the colonial governments would be required to look over their shoulder and evaluate American reactions before making policy. Powers in decline, for all their displays of anger at infringements of their sovereignty, usually know better than to disparage in public friends whose active support they may require. Western European nations badly needed the United States and would rarely consider crossing her over any but the highest matters of national interest.

The China Question

In the Asia-Pacific region the United States had long wanted Stalin to commit the Soviet Union to entering the war against Japan. While this had become less pressing by the time of the Yalta conference in February 1945, President Roosevelt was still eager to have the Soviet Union join in the fight. Although American troops were inching nearer to Tokyo, any assistance from the Red Army in Northeast Asia would undoubtedly make the GIs' job less onerous. Naturally Stalin named his price for this intervention, and equally unsurprisingly Roosevelt was prepared to go some considerable way to cement the bargain. It soon appeared that almost anything that speeded up the ending of the Pacific War and thereby cut the terrible list of American casualties was seen as fair game. President Roosevelt consented to Stalin's list of demands without apparent compunction. In doing so, Roosevelt conveniently ignored the fact that it would be Chinese sovereignty and territory that would be grabbed in an effort to get the war over quicker.

It is also worth recalling that Roosevelt and his officials made similar demands of the British and thought nothing of recommending the establishment of postwar international trusteeships for territories that were not American responsibilities. Lengthy shopping lists of strategic bases on Allied soil had also been prepared by the US military as suitable requirements for the projection of its new global power. The critical point from the American point of view was Stalin's promise to enter the war against Imperial Japan within three months of the defeat of Germany. In exchange, Roosevelt agreed to what Stalin had demanded. Moscow got the transfer of the Kuriles and Southern Sakhalin from Japanese hands and the lease from China of Port Arthur, with special rights in the key railway lines of Northeast Asia and over the port of Darien. The arrangements turned back the clock to the era of Russian pre-eminence in the region and wiped out the dark stain of humiliation left from surprise defeat in the Russo-Japanese war of 1904–1905.

No decent excuses can be made for the Far Eastern sections of the Yalta conference. While it is true that some American officials had begun to question the Soviet military imperative by January 1945, this remained a minority view. Equally, to point out that much was subject to the approval of Chiang Kai-shek ignores the weakness of his position vis-à-vis the American President. Yalta's secret eastern protocol underwrote the new position of the Soviet Union in the region. The bear was back. There was, of course, little that the United States could do to prevent this reality. There were no American forces in the area that might have deterred the Red Army from moving through Manchuria, the Korean Peninsula and the island chains off Hokkaido. It is also the case that the Yalta accords were scrupulously observed by Stalin and that his troops would shortly halt halfway down the Korean Peninsula as US–Soviet agreement insisted. Yet for the United States to secretly consent to an arrangement that contradicted much of what the Roosevelt administration was attempting to achieve in international relations must remain hard for even the most sympathetic observer to defend. Criticism also falls on Winston Churchill. He too signed the arrangements, against the advice of his senior officials, in the expectation that it might facilitate a larger British role in the Asia-Pacific region. Yalta could only make it less likely that the British Empire would face the possibility of dismemberment under pressure from the United States.

President Roosevelt's detractors have had additional ammunition from his handling of Chinese affairs during the war. The military demands of encouraging Chiang Kai-shek to engage the Japanese, as we have seen, took priority over commentary on the corruption and incompetence exhibited frequently by Chiang and his supporters. It remains the case too that despite placing less emphasis on China's contribution to both winning the war and running the peace as Imperial Japan edged slowly towards surrender, Roosevelt never disowned Chiang. He may well have appreciated that, for domestic political reasons as well as the hope of having the one Asian state long befriended by the United States recognized as a Great Power after the war, there was no alternative to supporting the KMT's leader. His 'thinking about China', his friends claim, has been 'imperfectly understood'. By concentrating on China's postwar role, they insist, Roosevelt aimed to gain an Asian and global partner that would be able to stand with the United States. It was not a view that has had many adherents in the years since his death. Churchill, for one, had long felt that the President's perceptions of the true worth of China were extraordinarily naive, while many of those Americans who had worked with Chiang Kai-shek wrote scathing and entertaining commentary on China's supposed leader.

The weaknesses of Chiang's claims to be in control were widely discussed in official circles. Sections of American public opinion, however, greatly respected what they perceived as Chiang's wartime successes against Imperial Japan and saw the Generalissimo and his attractive US-educated wife as true friends. Well aware of both Chiang's failings and his popularity as the embodiment of an earlier China where US merchants and missionaries had thrived, Roosevelt preferred to ignore Chiang's defects. He hoped that the KMT might be prevailed on to form a coalition with its Communist rival and that this hybrid might form an effective barrier to Soviet ambitions in the region. Yet for all his alleged political sophistry, Roosevelt was tied to Chiang. The KMT leader surely gained the most from the arrangement, since neither Roosevelt nor his successors in the White House for the next generation were prepared to cut the knot. Strenuous American commitment to the concept of 'Free' China under Chiang was to be a most uncomfortable legacy of the Roosevelt era; in time it would prove to be the Achilles heel of postwar US foreign policy in the entire Asia-Pacific region.

By 1947 officials in the British Foreign Office were expressing in private their relief that China was no longer Britain's responsibility. Yet it had been apparent from the Yalta conference and indeed earlier that the United States could not determine events in China. Roosevelt might cavalierly give away Chinese rights to the Soviet Union, confident in the certainty of later gaining Chiang's consent, but no American president could shape China's future on the ground. The United States might land its marines in northern China and continue to subsidize the KMT, but these acts were marginal to the contest between the Nationalists and Communists. Only after lengthy and bloody civil war on the subcontinent was the issue finally decided in favour of Mao Tse-tung. The realities of Chiang's performance could not have escaped Roosevelt for a moment. The President asked critics for their views on both the KMT and Chinese Communist Party (CCP) and he sent observers to the region knowing full well that their findings would make for unpleasant reading. Representative Mike Mansfield, for example, agreed that Chiang in January 1945 was 'the *one* leader in China' responsible for its status as a Great Power. Yet he concluded in a telling commentary on present weaknesses that 'China used to be able to trade space for time but now she has very little space and not much time'. Mansfield doubted if Chiang would be prepared to cooperate with the Communists. He warned that the outcome of the failure to gain intra-Chinese agreement would be catastrophic. He predicted that 'the seeds of dissension will only continue to grow and the eventual harvest will be of such a nature as to make the Taiping Rebellion of the last century a minor revolution in comparison. It might even mean the intervention of a Great Power in the Chinese internal situation'.

With the ending of the Pacific war, the Sino-American quasi-alliance began to unfold. China found itself immediately subject to what it quite legitimately resented as imperialistic incursions from its supposed wartime colleagues. Territories widely recognized as being part of China proper and those it had long claimed on the borders of the state were suddenly at risk. Instead of enjoying the prospect of a wider international role, Chang Kai-shek faced fresh challenges within and without. It would have required superhuman skills to succeed under these circumstances, and for the KMT leader it proved to be an impossible task. Chiang could not simultaneously prepare to defeat the Communists and project Chinese power overseas. The best he could do was garner support from those powers that for their own reasons might assist the KMT. Aside from the tried and trusted link to the United States, he was obliged to look to the Soviet Union. For both Chiang and Stalin, opportunism motivated one of the strangest arrangements in postwar international politics. It was premised on the simple fact that both leaders for their own reasons had much to fear from an emerging Communist challenge to the KMT. For Chiang the domestic threat from an emboldened CCP was obvious. For the Soviet Union an alliance with Chiang would consolidate Moscow's recent gains in Northeast Asia and reduce the risk of a strong, Marxist China standing vigilant on Russia's vast eastern borders while preaching its own brand of ideology to fellow Asian converts.

The discussions in Moscow between the Chinese and Soviet governments proved long and bitter. After the announcement of the eventual Sino-Soviet treaty of friendship and alliance on 14 August 1945, Chiang Kai-shek could only tell US Ambassador Hurley that he was 'generally satisfied with the treaty'. This was hardly a ringing endorsement of a text which the Chinese government in Chungking supposedly felt demonstrated Stalin's support for the Nationalists' control of a united and strong China. While Soviet diplomats might speak disparagingly of Mao's men as 'margarine' Communists, the Sino-Soviet treaty did little to assist Chiang in organizing effective opposition to the CCP in the looming Chinese civil war. What the Sino-Soviet treaty clearly illustrated instead was the weakness of Chiang's position and his need to grab what crumbs he could from the Great Powers' table.

The Moscow accords could hardly prevent Stalin from deploying military force in Manchuria as and when the Soviet leader determined. What they did do was merely bind the Soviet Union to an international agreement to behave in a specific and limited manner over Manchuria and Outer Mongolia. In this sense the parallel between President Roosevelt's arrangements with Stalin at Yalta and T.V. Soong's at Moscow is striking; though this, of course, was of little practical consolation to Chiang Kai-shek. At Moscow he merely gained Stalin's word that the Soviet Union would only assist the KMT and, as the Generalissimo told Ambassador Hurley, help 'create a strong, united, democratic government'. This, in retrospect, would appear to be a particularly empty vessel, but recent scholarship has seen Chiang as exulting over the American and Soviet promises obtained at Yalta and Moscow. The Chinese leader apparently felt sufficiently encouraged by these twin Great Power endorsements to press ahead with his own agenda. Chiang after Moscow was confident that he could rid China of those under Mao whom he defined as non-Chinese Yenan Red elements, who persisted in refusing to recognize the position of the KMT as the rightful government of the state.

Chiang's difficulties did not end with the near certainty of approaching civil war. In addition to facing the CCP, he had still to gain an enhanced external presence for his nation. By the autumn of 1945, however, the glow of international prestige that had surrounded Chiang and his wife at the Cairo conferences of November and December 1943 had long faded.

The endless saga of incompetence and corruption within the KMT had sullied China's name, while the idea of an American president closeting himself with Chiang to draw up a detailed program for the future of the Asia-Pacific region was by now inconceivable. Chiang's reputation was such that no Allied leader in 1945 was likely to welcome China's bid for a share of the spoils from the Japanese empire or warmly endorse its presence on the international stage.

Chiang quickly discovered these new postwar realities. The determination of the United States to conduct almost unilateral diplomacy with Tokyo over the surrender terms it wished to impose on Imperial Japan was a brutal taste of what would follow. China's fall from grace as an active member of the Big Four Allied nations continued immediately afterwards when it failed to prevent both the return of Hong Kong to Britain and the reoccupation of Indo-China by France. After years of amicable negotiations with the United States on their supposedly mutual need to redraw the map of Asia, Chiang found himself little short of humiliated. American wartime professions of sympathy and friendship for China's predicament had not been translated into action against the Europeans. The Generalissimo's personal links to Roosevelt had not served him half as well as he had hoped. While Roosevelt had deliberately excluded Britain from private talks with Chiang at the opening of the Cairo conference, by 1945 the boot was on the other foot. By this time it was China that had to submit to similar treatment to that meted out to London in the middle of the war. Despite initially encouraging a sceptical Chiang to consider his nation's involvement in an international trusteeship scheme for Indo-China, the President gradually modified his views. Rather than form firm policy plans, he preferred to play for time. On New Year's Day 1945 Roosevelt wrote bluntly to Secretary of State Hull, instructing him that 'I still do not want to get mixed up in any Indochina decision. It is a matter for post-war'. Yet to postpone decisions was to make the repossession of Indo-China by France increasingly probable. Such measures had long been supported by the British government as part of its moves both to re-establish European rule in Southeast Asia and to give credence to Anglo-French aspirations for a potential power bloc to counter Washington and Moscow.

By the time of his death, President Roosevelt's stance on Indo-China was already undergoing change and his successor made it quickly apparent that he had no patience with anti-colonial measures in Asia that would undermine the urgent reconstruction of Western Europe. Since Chiang had never cared particularly for Roosevelt's approaches over Chungking's involvement in an international trusteeship for Southeast Asian territories, he lost little from the scuppering of such schemes. Much more serious was Allied policy towards the Korean Peninsula and

Japan proper. Here China found itself abandoned by others, at least in part because of faults of its own making. The opportunity to play a significant role in Northeast Asia was to be defeated by both the actions of China's erstwhile ally, the United States, and the singular inability of Chiang Kai-shek to commit a single KMT soldier to the military occupation of Japan.

Korea Divided

Four-power trusteeship for Korea had been agreed on before the surrender of Imperial Japan. At Yalta Roosevelt had spoken with Stalin over the composition of such a body for postwar Korea, and at the prompting of the Soviet Union the President had reluctantly agreed to Britain's membership of a fledgling international body which Churchill had instinctively loathed from its inception. Given China's traditional role in Korean affairs, this was seen by Chiang and his ministers as an issue of considerable importance, yet the initiative invariably rested with the United States. It was Chungking that deferred to American diplomats and meekly requested information on what precise policies the Truman administration intended for the divided peninsula. China had supported an *émigré* grouping in Chungking during the war that termed itself the Korean Provisional Government, but this entity feared getting left behind as myriad individuals and organizations across the political spectrum attempted to establish themselves on the peninsula. Chiang Kai-shek expressed particular concern to the United States in late September 1945 that Communist elements on the ground in Korea had already gained sponsorship from the Soviet Union. Yet the prospects of the four-power trusteeship council acting either swiftly or in concert were already fast disappearing. The initial ad hoc arrangement of dividing the Korean Peninsula at the 38th parallel for military surrender purposes quickly congealed into two separate zonal areas under the United States and the Soviet Union respectively. Chief of Staff Marshall did indeed admit to General MacArthur on 1 October 1945 that the provisional divide was 'highly artificial and that for many reasons a single administration for the whole of Korea would be preferable'. Yet the interim period of civil affairs administration by the United States and the USSR was gradually extended. Trusteeship never materialized because of Soviet–American rivalries; by early November 1945 Secretary of State Byrnes had to acknowledge to Ambassador Harriman in Moscow that 'the 38 degree parallel has become in reality a closed border'. Chiang might call for 'the speedy achievement of independence for Korea' and argue that the region was 'watching the fate of Korea' but Great Power rivalries quickly froze out all remaining hopes of a role for China.

The political skills immediately deployed by the Soviet Union and its supporters in Korea surprised and disconcerted the United States. American commanders on the ground feared that Communist activity south as well as north of the 38th parallel threatened the long-held Korean goal of national independence. By December General MacArthur concluded that 'the US occupation of Korea under its present condition and policies is surely drifting to the edge of a political-economic abyss from which it can never be retrieved with any credit to US prestige in the Far East'. MacArthur warned that 'there is growing resentment against all Americans', who appeared to the Korean public to be responsible for the divided state of their newly liberated land. He saw the position as almost untenable and noted that the 'word pro-American is being added to pro-Jap, national traitor, and Jap collaborator'. MacArthur's pessimism, which was fully shared by the State Department and the Joint Chiefs of Staff, led him to caution that any introduction of an international trusteeship scheme would prompt revolt. He reckoned that the only solution might be for Moscow and Washington to agree jointly to wash their hands of the entire peninsula. Under these circumstances MacArthur coolly advocated the 'complete separation of Korea from Japan in the minds of the press, the public, the State and War Depts and Allied Nations'. Sensing endless political storms, MacArthur wanted nothing further to do with the place. His instincts were to be proved correct over the next five years, since events on the peninsula would indeed destroy both his career and much of his reputation.

General MacArthur's report to the Joint Chiefs of Staff was an accurate and concise statement of the issues. He rightly argued that the erection of the border ruled out Korean unity for the foreseeable future and would only perpetuate bitterness. His view that the 'Koreans want their independence more than any one thing and want it now' was, however, impossible to reconcile with the fear that Communist groups were capable of destabilizing any government in South Korea that was seen as functioning under American auspices. Eventually, at the Allied foreign ministers meeting at Moscow in late December, it was agreed that a four-power trusteeship would decide within the ensuing five years how an independent Korea might be established. This quickly proved to be an impossible aspiration. Koreans in the south, as MacArthur had warned a month earlier, were angry. Kim Koo, head of the Korean provisional government, responded initially by deploring the Moscow accords and vowing immediate non-cooperation. Vapid cables from Eisenhower to MacArthur serenely suggesting that decent publicity would persuade the majority of Koreans that trusteeship was still the appropriate policy underlines the considerable gap between Northeast Asia and Washington. Patient explanations by American officials would apparently solve resistance to the Allies' familiar trusteeship schemes. They did not. Koreans on both sides of the 38th parallel might be divided ideologically and politically, but they were most certainly united in rejecting the concept of external control. The American acting political adviser in Seoul warned the State Department that 'all Koreans want their country to themselves in their life time and will not have any form of foreign tutelage to attain an alien standard of nationhood'.

By the end of 1945 the US government had begun to alter its stance towards Korea. While some still entertained hopes that there might yet be Soviet–American cooperation, as envisaged at the Moscow foreign ministers conference, the Joint Chiefs of Staff had begun reckoning with equipping South Korean civil police detachments and considering the creation of national armed forces. While there was still no clarity over US policies, there was at least the beginning of recognition that if the two Great Powers were to fail to agree on the future of Korea then American unilateralism in the south was at least an option. In the next two years a shift gradually occurred as a 'double bipolarity' evolved both within Korea proper and in the wider international arena.

Britain and Southeast Asia

It was the United States and the Soviet Union that wrestled uncomfortably with the highly complex Korean question. Although the situation would certainly alter later, it is apparent that both Britain and China played insignificant roles in events on the peninsula from 1945 to 1950. For London the centre of its attention in the region was always understood to be Southeast Asia. If Britain were to remain a Great Power in Asia, it would have to be in the retention and reconstruction of its colonial territories. In domestic political terms this was bipartisan policy. Certainly Winston Churchill was renowned for angry denunciation of those who might poke their meddling fingers into the very existence of the British Empire, but his Labour Party successors in government were careful too in safeguarding their Asian inheritance. Attlee and Bevin might lack the oratory of Churchill but they had similar backbones when it came to defending all but the Indian portion of empire.

The challenges facing Britain in the region were formidable. There was opposition from its wartime Allies, doubts at home over the costs and validity of resuming London's prewar role, and muted questions on how those recovering from Japanese rule might respond to the sight of the old order. Yet the British returned determinedly not only to their territories but also as the sponsor of French and Dutch colonialism in Southeast Asia. Whether adequate resources, however, could be found to match the tasks set and the necessary bureaucratic coordination among civil and military officials would be forthcoming was far less clear. The cabinet's post-surrender decision for Britain to remain an effective actor in the Asia-Pacific region was automatic; to make it stick would prove much harder.

The inauguration of the postwar era began with Lord Louis Mount-batten's acceptance of Imperial Japan's surrender in Southeast Asia at Singapore on 12 September 1945. Mountbatten's remarks were curt and quite without any hint of the visionary that came naturally to General MacArthur. He noted that the British invasion of Malaya would have begun on 9 September 'whether the Japanese had resisted or not' and he stressed that 'the surrender today is no negotiated surrender. The Japanese are submitting to superior force, now massed here'. The con-trast between the defensive tone of Mountbatten and the universalism preached by MacArthur underlines the differing national perceptions of Japan. In the autumn of 1945 the United States saw itself as the virtually unchallenged hegemon of the Asia-Pacific region, while the British could not easily forget the ignominy of defeat in 1941–42 and the long years of struggle required to inch slowly back to Rangoon and Singapore. These memories of two very different wars against Japan would colour how London and Washington were to view post-surrender Japan for more than a generation.

Mountbatten's initial tasks were military. He had simultaneously to disarm Imperial Japanese troops and then re-employ large numbers of these same men for security duties throughout Southeast Asia. The British had neither the men on the ground nor the money to undertake the full range of responsibilities expected of them as liberators. To feed, house and clothe the region was a near impossibility in the initial months before effective trade and commerce could be started up again. Admin-istrative problems only added to the near confusion. The Europeans came back with a full range of political policies for the region that varied from the antediluvian to the progressive. There was, however, a general understanding that the returning colonialists would have to justify their role through good works and, at the very least, express an official willing-ness to guide their wards towards eventual self-government. The British Foreign Office instructed senior diplomats that ostentation on the prewar scale was forbidden, both because of its obvious inappropriateness and simply because the exchequer could not afford it. The colonialists would have to be on their best behaviour if there were to be any prospect of a mutually beneficial relationship.

Yet the scale of the immediate difficulties facing Mountbatten's South-East Asia Command was bound inevitably to leave the wider political and international issues in limbo. The pressure on overworked military and civilian staff was immense. Simply to organize security patrols, oversee hundreds of thousands of surrendered Japanese troops, discover where emergency rice and firewood might be purchased or bartered and begin rudimentary reconstruction devoured all available resources. The beginnings of a return to normalcy after the unpleasant years of Japanese occupation concentrated the official mind on the present. Only when the British military commanders in the region were prepared to transfer their responsibilities to civilian administrations in 1946 could the initial phase of reoccupation be said to be over.

The first months following what the British liked to term the liberation of Southeast Asia were to test all the returning colonial powers to the limit. Despite the wartime planning and the serious discussions that had undoubtedly taken place in Whitehall among rival ministries, it cannot be said that events in Asia after August 1945 bore overmuch resemblance to Whitehall's carefully weighed policy recommendations. The military, besides, were impatient with lengthy files and much preferred to improvise on the spot. Platoon commanders and their men might not be particularly sensitive over local Malay or Chinese customs but they could get trams running again and repair burst water mains. Efforts to stamp out piracy, curtail coastal smuggling and limit the settling of scores between collaborators and anti-Japanese elements obviously required deploying force in numbers. All this was a necessary precondition to the re-establishment of Public Works Departments and primary education programmes.

The centre of British administration was Singapore. It was from here that Mountbatten and his advisers attempted to eliminate anarchy and begin the lengthy process of rebuilding regional confidence. The SEAC commander had nominal control over 1.5 million square miles and was expected to feed a population of nearly 130 million people. Mountbatten's responsibilities were by any standard over-extended and his resources insufficient. In late September he could only write to Eisenhower, 'This place is hell!' The challenges facing SEAC compared unfavourably with those that SCAP had to tackle. MacArthur was fortunate to possess clearly defined, non-porous boundaries, inside which security very quickly became no more than a routine task for General Eichelberger's Eighth Army, while his staff could call on enviable American food reserves and congressional funding to help stabilize the situation in occupied Japan. Mountbatten, by contrast, had an absurdly large geographical region to administer and to aggravate his problems he had orders to assist with the early return of French and Dutch forces to reclaim their Southeast Asian territories. SEAC's mission was simply too vast for the limited human and financial resources at his disposal. It is surprising, at least in hindsight, that Mountbatten's men were able to accomplish as much as they did under these highly disadvantageous circumstances. Yet it remains the case that the failings were very considerable and that final responsibility for the general mismatch of over-ambition and limited power in the region lies with the new Labour cabinet at Westminster.

SEAC had to attempt simultaneously to begin the reconstruction of its reclaimed British colonies, while facing major political and military dilemmas with regard to Indo-China and what would soon be known to the world as Indonesia. Mountbatten would have more success with recolonization than decolonization, but given the tangled international issues associated with the French and Dutch ventures, this was to be expected. No other commander could have done much better with such a poor hand. The return to Singapore, Malaya, Borneo and Hong Kong allowed the British government to note that all of its prewar Southeast and East Asian empire had been brought back into the fold. Since Clement Attlee as Churchill's deputy had had to report the loss of these same territories to the House of Commons in the last days of 1941 and early 1942, it was with some relief that his postwar government could begin by announcing better news from Asia. Yet this relatively trouble-free end to Japanese rule in British territories was not followed by any such similar pattern in the Dutch East Indies or French Indo-China.

Nationalism in these areas was certainly not the invention of Japan. Tokyo however, carefully cultivated the support of local, often student, groupings in order to wreck any prospect of the Europeans re-emerging with credit after the war. It was a policy that had more than enough success, despite its questionable motivation, in forming a permanent chorus of self-congratulatory rhetoric in later Japanese history. For the next half-century conservative politicians and commentators would claim time and time again that Japan had deliberately fought its campaigns in Southeast Asia in order to liberate the region from colonialism. It is a myth that still endures today to conveniently slide over the destructive nature of Japanese imperialism. Yet it should not be denied that the Japanese authorities did undoubtedly encourage some Asian nationalists to prepare for at least quasi-independence in the chaotic final months of the Pacific War.

The Birth of Indonesia

Japan played its nationalist card best in the Netherlands East Indies. Thanks to its encouragement of anti-Dutch youth movements and the building up of an indigenous paramilitary force, local nationalists were able to hastily proclaim the independence of Indonesia on 17 August 1945. Given this remarkably swift move, it inevitably followed that Mountbatten's officers and the Dutch would be faced with immense difficulties. The central policy dilemma was how to accommodate the

British government's wish to support the re-establishment of Dutch rule with the hostile reception accorded to SEAC forces. Foreign Secretary Bevin's difficulties were further compounded by sharp criticism from among left-wing members of his own political party and the reaction of domestic public opinion to news of British casualties at the hands of the Indonesians. The end of the war against Japan was understood at home to mean the earliest possible repatriation of British troops; the idea of costly police action over Southeast Asian territories that had no links to London appeared politically unacceptable.

For Bevin to attempt to justify government policy was always difficult. He might tell the House of Commons that 'all the world is in trouble, and I have to deal with all the troubles at once', but this cut little ice with the families of servicemen sent to Indonesia or pro-nationalist backbench MPs who had no time for the Dutch colonial record. His twin objectives were incompatible: bringing back the Dutch and then insisting on using British good offices to encourage the setting up of round-table negotiations between the less than enthusiastic *ancien régime* and the equally suspicious youthful Indonesian leadership. The Indonesians had sufficient confidence in their cause and sufficient military might to thwart the British on the ground and in the conference room. By the time the British washed their hands of Indonesia in November 1946, there was little that SEAC could look back and review with any satisfaction.

Britain never had the ability to deploy sufficient military force to gain the initiative. Its local commanders were further hampered by policies from Singapore and London that tended to react to events rather than allow the man on the spot to press ahead with clear-cut objectives. From the start the returning Europeans were dogged by poor intelligence and the necessity of using surrendered Japanese troops for the enforcement of some approximate semblance to law and order in Java and Sumatra. Yet many of these ex-Imperial Japanese officers were wary of cooperating with General Sir Philip Christison, since they and their men would then risk being attacked by the very Indonesians who until recently had been groomed by Japan to take over the country. The situation was further exacerbated by Anglo-Dutch divergencies on the appropriate way forward, which could barely be papered over even when there was goodwill on both sides. The Dutch, rightly or wrongly, expected to resume their rule with relative ease, while Mountbatten's primary objectives were merely to take the Japanese surrender, locate and transport Allied POWs and civilian internees back to Europe, and then hold the ring until Dutch-Indonesian negotiations were under way.

Mountbatten had his own political views that greatly reduced the chances of the Dutch being able to resume their empire. SEAC warned Christison that he was 'in for a very sticky time' and may have told him that final responsibility for the sensitive Indonesian operation would fall on Christison's shoulders. What is clearer, however, is that Mountbatten from the outset wished both to limit British commitments and strongly encourage any tentative moves towards a compromise settlement between The Hague and Jakarta. SEAC worked hard to persuade the less conservative Dutch officials that there was no viable alternative to talking rather than confronting the emerging triumvirate of Soekarno, Hatta and Sjahrir.

The reluctance of the Dutch to flesh out their vague wartime promises of constitutional reform and the strengths of both the new Indonesian military and the local Japanese-appointed bureaucracy left the British in a perilous situation. They were never able to persuade either the Dutch or the Indonesians that an accommodation might still be achieved through debate. Yet each month that passed left British and Indian troops increasingly vulnerable to the captured Japanese weaponry of the Indonesian militias. The security situation rapidly became tense. To separate rival pro-independence groups and hold back inexperienced and headstrong Dutch marines was well nigh impossible. The murder of Brigadier Mallaby at Sourabaya in late October was confirmation of the near hopelessness of the British position. If the Dutch grumbled at even the mere hint of possible dominion status for Indonesia and the more extreme nationalist elements willingly disregarded the instructions of their nominal leaders, it was obvious that neither Mountbatten's forces nor British diplomats could do much to prevent chaos.

In the end the British left under the fig leaf of a Dutch–Indonesian political agreement. The Linggajati accord on federalism of 15 November 1946 marked the formal ending of British involvement, but the military phase had been largely completed earlier with the return of General Christison to Britain on 1 February. By then officials reporting to Mountbatten had long since tired of patching up temporary ceasefires and watching both sides break their commitments. The entire venture had been flawed from its inception. The low priority placed on the expeditionary force by the cabinet and the inability of a weakened third party to gain a compromise political settlement that satisfied neither the Dutch nor the Indonesians made for failure. It was an inglorious episode that would be repeated by the West elsewhere in Southeast Asia over the next generation.

Impasse in Indo-China

The British government was relieved to hand back its 'mandate' for the East Indies. Much the same sentiment also applied to its dealings with Indo-China. Certainly there were contrasts between Britain's views on the two vast European territories in Southeast Asia and considerable differences in the behaviour of the British generals on the spot, but it is the similarities that deserve our particular attention. In both cases the period of British responsibility was short and in both cases nationalists were quick to declare their independence in defiance of the returning metropolitan power. Equally, it proved impossible in the Netherlands East Indies and French Indo-China to build towards a viable political structure that even began to approach the recommendations of Mountbatten and his senior advisers. The stubbornness of the Europeans was matched by the determination of the Asian nationalists, resulting in predictable bloodshed and economic dislocation. Political solutions along the lines that the British recommended were stillborn, not least because their advocates were seen by all to be holding the ring merely for the short term. Since no government in London would have dreamt of delaying its promised postwar demobilization process for long or have been prepared to justify lengthy casualty lists, there appears to have been no political alternative to the road taken.

Mountbatten's men faced near-impossible tasks with limited resources. As had often been the case with British ventures in Asia, there was a huge element of bluff behind the over-ambitious enterprise, whereby little effective resistance could be offered when determined force emerged to challenge the supposed overlord. Where the Indo-Chinese case differs from that of the East Indies is in the greater military might of the French when compared to the returning Dutch. It was also an obvious international reality that French prestige and claims to the status of a major power would necessarily demand the retaking of its Indo-Chinese empire in the autumn of 1945. The French mission in Chungking had put this point unequivocally to its American counterpart in January 1945 by stating that 'France cannot admit any discussion about the principle of her establishment in Indochina'. The following month General de Gaulle had warned the American ambassador in Paris that 'we do not want to become Communist; we do not want to fall into the Russian orbit, but I hope that you do not push us into it'. French public opinion, as its own left-wing parties fully appreciated, expected that the empire would be swiftly retaken and then stoutly defended; any backsliding over Indo-China was widely understood to have serious implications for the future of Algeria and French North Africa.

There was little that Mountbatten could do in the face of such resolve. Indeed, through the personal initiative of General Douglas Gracey in putting down Vietnamese nationalist opposition to any political arrangement short of immediate independence, the supreme commander found himself defending a position that he most certainly disliked. Mountbatten was obliged to issue statements confirming Gracey's behaviour in sponsoring the continuation of French administration in Saigon. The work by Gracey was explained away as necessary to prevent the collapse of Indo-China into anarchy, but this disguises the fact that the British action, in effect, saved Indo-China for France. The speed with which British and Indian forces were able to leave the area was simply through the early arrival of French forces and was certainly no indication that there had been any success in implementing a political settlement acceptable to either the French or the Viet Minh.

Britain clearly failed in Indo-China. It could boast only of gaining its minimal goals of accepting the surrender of Japanese troops and the repatriation of POWs and civilian internees. It proved virtually powerless to engineer a compromise peace, and by favouring the restoration of French rule it bears a share of responsibility for what would result in a near decade of conflict between the French and Indo-Chinese nationalists. This vicious era finally ended with the surrender of Dien Bien Phu in 1954 and the virtual demise of French colonialism in the Asia-Pacific region. The likelihood of an outright conflict between the two sides was always high, as too were the chances of Great Power intervention. The fact that from the end of the Pacific War the United States was prepared to arm the assembling French troops and then provide their vital transportation back to Indo-China is evidence of important shifts in American policy. Roosevelt had ordered that the question of what to do with the French territories in Asia be put on ice till the postwar situation could be clarified; his successor appears to have had no such qualms. The view that an inexperienced President Truman meekly followed in the giant footsteps of Franklin D. Roosevelt is hardly sustainable in this particular instance. The State Department, for example, was instructing its staff from as early as 30 August 1945 that the US government 'had no thought of opposing the reestablishment of French control in Indochina and no official statement ... has questioned even by implication French sovereignty over Indochina'. The two caveats of neither assisting Paris in the use of force nor of backing the returning colonialists, unless they had the general support of the peoples of Indo-China, were to be widely ignored in the years ahead.

The situation in Indo-China was made more complex by the decision at Potsdam to divide the region at the 16th parallel. The result in the last months of 1945 was an impossible amalgam of competing Vietnamese, Chinese, Japanese, British, French and American interests. The region was awash with clandestine missions, political agents, underground units and military formations, all of which were eagerly conspiring to nudge events in their favour. Ho Chi Minh might formally declare the independence of his nation in Hanoi on 2 September 1945, incorporating passages from the American model of 1776, but this was more evidence of bravado than political reality, particularly in the south. Ho could assert that his nation 'has become a free and independent country', but the fact that he then returned to the platform to caution his compatriots that they must expect 'much more adversity and suffering' was unfortunately highly prophetic. Surely no one could have imagined the scale of the bloodshed that lay ahead for his audience and their families over the next three decades.

The British and the Chinese were the first to accept formal responsibility for the fate of Indo-China. Both, however, were quite incapable of fulfilling more than a small portion of their duties inherited at the Potsdam conference, and both were quietly relieved to slink quickly offstage. In the short interim, Britain and China singularly failed to make much impression on events. The French thought the British had not exerted themselves sufficiently to support the tricolor, while Vietnamese nationalists were equally convinced that the British forces were only there to put down their desperate bid for power. It was plainly a mess. Even to free the Allied POWs and internees required a military presence that was generally unavailable, unless uncooperative Japanese units could somehow be dragooned into action. The wish to uphold the slippery area of law and order and from there encourage all parties to negotiate soon failed. Once French demonstrators attacked Annamites in the streets of Saigon and Ho's men took their revenge in turn, the ever slight prospect of Franco-Vietnamese dialogue disappeared. Historians might later claim that different personalities on both sides and a measure of compromise might have redeemed the situation, but this appears improbable. Certainly the French could have been more astute at the outset and the nationalists might have been wiser to accept a gradual process to complete independence, but neither side had much patience with any such half-measures. Military solutions quickly became the order of the day. The French were determined to reassert their authority, while the Vietnamese nationalists felt they had waited more than long enough for the dawn of liberation.

The two regional powers designated to take the Japanese surrender and provide a semblance of stability in a deteriorating situation had both abandoned their positions by early 1946. It is hardly coincidental that the British formally left Vietnam by the end of January 1946 and that the Chinese concluded their own separate Sino-French arrangements shortly afterwards on 28 February. In both instances local commanders were relieved to be departing and in both cases they elected to negotiate with the returning colonial authorities rather than deal with Ho's embryonic Democratic Republic of Vietnam. From the start it had been apparent that neither Britain nor the Nationalist government of China had been able to deploy enough force or show enough resolve to make a sustained bid for leadership even remotely practical. It is surely chimerical to imagine that London was ever seriously interested in posing as the long-term protector and arbitrator of the entire region. The task was held to be beyond its limited resources and posed risks that were quite unacceptable within the changed domestic context of postwar British politics. The brave new world of the welfare state had shrunk horizons and would necessarily lead to calls for careful scrutiny of overseas commitments.

Return to Malaya

Elsewhere in Southeast Asia, however, the political situation was less threatening to the position of the metropolitan powers. When, for example, it came to ensuring the future of its own territories, the British government acted with considerable speed and a degree of skill. There was, not surprisingly, a far greater military and economic involvement than in the case of botched operations over Indo-China and Indonesia. An obvious priority was the attempted retention and reconstruction of a very mixed bag of territories, extending from Burma on the western margin to the pinprick of Hong Kong on the south China coast in the east. Yet there was little clarity on how individual colonies might be given greater political opportunities or their economies developed through some general policy statements. There had been few such rulings in Britain's Asian empire before the Pacific War, and officialdom had rarely been encouraged to think in regional terms until the Japanese attacks revealed the weaknesses of the piecemeal approach. Burma had a large and potentially disruptive nationalist movement and knew at first hand what self-government implied, while North Borneo, to put it charitably, had few assets and Hong Kong in 1945 possessed a totally unreconstructed administration run on thoroughly nineteenth-century Colonial Office lines. The areas to receive the greatest attention were Singapore and Malaya, where the government was eager to urge the valuable dollar-earning primary industries back into production. Although this might over time help the peoples of the region achieve a slightly higher standard of living, the urgency of the task was dictated by exploiting Malayan tin and rubber for Britain's benefit as it faced its own immense problems of postwar domestic reconstruction.

Before these extractive industries could be put back to work it was also necessary to tackle the political future of the entire Malay Peninsula. This proved to be a far harder and lengthier task than the wartime planners in Whitehall had envisaged before Japan's surprise surrender. Constitutional reform programs went through several changes before a Malayan Union was first proposed and then scrapped in the face of opposition from Chinese groups, who resented the manner in which the Malays had hung onto their privileges. Yet a far greater challenge to British rule emerged as cautiously revised changes began to be put in place. In June 1948 the assassination of three British planters in Perak heralded the start of armed insurrection on the peninsula. This so-called 'emergency' immediately threatened both to destabilize the Malayan economy and divide its peoples into those prepared to support the colonial regime and those willing to resist under the banner of international Communism. It quickly developed into bruising guerrilla warfare between the British administration and its Malay associates against the more politically radical Chinese. For Britain it marked the start of the Cold War in Asia.

Since Singapore and Malaya were intended to form the heart of British power in postwar Asia, the challenge from the Malay-Chinese was met with an iron fist. Troopships arrived with reinforcements, new propaganda machinery was installed and efforts were made to sway waverers with material incentives. The Attlee cabinet explained to the Australian government that any extension of the Communist insurgency on the Malay Peninsula had serious implications for the entire region and, by implication at least, far beyond. The strategic and political danger was presented as dire, with Malaya as the only place on the world map where 'we are actively fighting against Communism, and moreover it is territory for which we are responsible. Clearly we cannot afford to lose Malaya to Communism'. Thus appeared the domino theory, which would be taken over and evoked repeatedly by American politicians in the next two decades in defence of their own involvement in Vietnam. It was born, however, in Malaya by British leaders who wished to counter what they saw as the Asian portion of an insidious global Communist movement. If it were not stopped in Malaya, so the thesis went, the infection would spread rapidly and the West would suffer still greater hurt.

The US–Philippine Relationship

Gradual success in turning back the Malay Communists may have temporarily increased Britain's status in Southeast Asia, yet it had been apparent long before the ending of the Pacific War that the United States was the coming power throughout large parts of the Asia-Pacific littoral. Even within Southeast Asia, Washington had been obliged to exercise direct political responsibilities in the autumn of 1945. Its commitments to the Philippines were, of course, long-standing, though under the Tydings-McDuffie Act of March 1934 they were due to be terminated in 1946 under arrangements that would permit the United States to maintain military installations. President Truman had announced in 1945 that he and President Osmena were in agreement over both the maintenance of bases and 'special trade relations' for the future development of

US–Philippine economic relations. The manner in which the United States managed the transfer of its sovereignty over the Philippines provided an immediate reminder of American involvement on the fringes of the nominally British sphere of influence. It is also the case that the independence of the Republic of the Philippines on 4 July 1946, after nearly half a century of colonial rule, saw the United States sponsoring the first example of Western decolonization in the postwar Asia-Pacific.

Much of the groundwork for the eventual independence of the Philippines was put in place during the 1930s. Although it might have been subject to possible change in the wake of the severe dislocations of the wretched Japanese occupation, the United States honoured its promises and followed the existing timetable for the handover of power. It was a test case of American integrity. The result certainly enhanced ties between Manila and Washington, creating in the process a 'special relationship' par excellence. Many in Manila, however, sensed that America's limited financial contributions to the postwar reconstruction of the Philippines compared unfairly with the attention given to occupied Japan and its problems. It also perpetuated considerable political, military and economic dependence on the United States and in doing so inevitably weakened Philippine ties to the region. A similar process has long been observable in postwar US–Japan relations where American dominance and the legacy of war worked together until recently to minimize Japan's Asian diplomacy.

The United States worked out a series of political, economic and security arrangements with the Philippines that were far more comprehensive than anything the British or French were able to accomplish as their own Asian territories began to gain independence. London had hoped that informal political understandings and possibly even defence arrangements with the Indian subcontinent might have provided a precedent for continuing British ties to the region, but New Delhi had its own ambitions and a very different ideological agenda. Only the United States, helped by individuals sympathetic to maintaining Philippine friendship, demonstrated that the end of direct colonialism need not lead to the automatic sundering of links – as happened, for example, to the British over Burma and the Dutch in Indonesia. Certainly vocal critics inside and outside the Philippines would claim that this supposedly novel US–Philippine relationship was no more than the old, unequal sham cleverly displayed in new packaging, but this was not how the electorate interpreted events. The arrangements were endorsed and an independent Manila accepted both a continuing US military presence and a highly favourable trading arrangement that made a mockery of American professions of free unrestricted global markets. Protectionism under the United States continued in many different forms.

The US Position in the Asia-Pacific by 1950

In the immediate postwar years, Asia exhibited contradictory evidence over the approximate outlines of its future. The return to Southeast Asia of the prewar imperialist powers had been strenuously contested by the formidable twin forces of indigenous nationalism and the aspirations of international Communism. Admittedly these entanglements were to prove comparatively mild in comparison with the unfortunate situation in Northeast Asia where, as we shall see shortly, the world would witness terrible warfare as rivalries between the superpowers and their proxies turned the unfortunate region once again into the cockpit of Asia. Within the European sphere of Southeast Asia, however, there had been considerable resistance from nationalist groupings once foreign troops had set foot again in the region. This quickly placed impossible strains on the Dutch and resulted in their inevitable retreat. The French adopted a different strategy and accepted that only a full-scale military contest would determine their fate in Indo-China, while the British decided that they had little choice, if their key economic interests were to be safeguarded, but to pour scarce resources into the protection of Malaya from Communist subversion.

Amid these setbacks, the one vital consolation for the West was the continuing military strength and political resolve of the United States to maintain its power in parts of Asia and to offer assistance to its Allies. The fact that the Europeans could hardly have conducted operations in Southeast Asia but for US military aid and financial support was best seen by the return of Dutch marines to Java in American fatigues and equipped with American weapons. The US government had displayed a determination to remain on guard and a willingness to underline its position by conducting a remarkably lengthy and thorough occupation of Japan, while cautiously assisting its friends elsewhere. Those who portray the United States as having been reluctant to assume international responsibilities after the collapse of the grand alliance at the end of the war in 1945 may risk overlooking the alacrity with which Washington accepted burdens in Northeast Asia and established military bases throughout the Pacific. President Roosevelt did indeed assure Stalin that American troops would be withdrawn swiftly from Europe after Nazism had been crushed, but his successor approved already prepared plans for a comprehensive and professional occupation of Japan that remain an important, if neglected, part of the Rooseveltian legacy. This venture was clearly no mere reluctant improvisation or temporary holding operation.

There may, admittedly, have been only limited coherence to the United States' general approach to the region, but given the complexities of a changing environment and the military limitations the Truman administration faced while it looked on helplessly as its wartime armies quickly melted away, this was surely excusable. Certainly, later observers are correct to note the gap between the already firm positions being adopted in Europe against the Soviet Union and the hesitant shifts under way in the Asia-Pacific, yet even a fragmentary series of subregional policies sent reassuring signals to America's friends. The United States had not put in place anything in Asia comparable to its clear European containment-based policies, but it had undoubtedly increased its general responsibilities in the region by 1950. Tentative steps were at least being considered that took serious note of the unpleasant and seemingly near-permanent breakdown in relations between the United States and its Western European Allies and the Soviet Union and its Eastern European bloc. Communism had now to be considered as a global movement that threatened the interests of the United States not only in Europe but also in the Middle East and the Asia-Pacific. The success of Mao Tse-tung in gaining control of China from the US-backed KMT regime by October 1949 and the signing of the Sino-Soviet Treaty of Friendship and Alliance in January 1950 were obvious blows to the position of the United States in the region. Yet the implications of what appeared to be evidence of a stronger and more unified global Communist movement had still to be digested. The Truman administration, after all, had determined in 1949 to let the dust settle in China, since it knew the folly of attempting any massive military intervention on the ground in Chinese affairs. Suddenly in the summer of 1950, however, this comparatively benign picture was fated to change. Overnight the evolving postwar international realities of the entire Asia-Pacific region were put to the test. The United States found itself faced with the first great challenge of the Cold War era as a major conflict rapidly unfolded on the Korean Peninsula. The eruption of a seemingly obscure corner of Northeast Asia would quickly prove to have both profound and long-lasting consequences across the entire international spectrum.

2   War: Korea, 1950–1953

Were Japan added to the Communist bloc, the Soviets would acquire skilled manpower and industrial potential capable of significantly altering the balance of world power.

> Secretary of State Dean Acheson, 24 December 1949

The only possible explanation for the President's action is that he felt it was necessary to get rid of MacArthur so that Acheson would be free to make a deal with the Chinese Communists along the lines proposed by the British. We can now expect that the State Department will go ahead with its original plan of turning over Formosa to the Communists and of recognizing the Chinese Red government just as the British have been urging.

> Senator Richard Nixon, press release, 11 April 1951, quoted in
> Stephen E. Ambrose, *Nixon: The Education of a Politician, 1913–1962*
> (New York, 1987)

Korea does not really matter now. I'd never heard of the bloody place until I was seventy-four. Its importance lies in the fact that it has led to the rearming of America.

> Winston Churchill, 1953, quoted in Jon Halliday and
> Bruce Cumings, *Korea: The Unknown War* (London, 1990)

The Road to Conflict: Northeast Asia and the Powers, 1945–50

Following the United States' victory in the Pacific War, the Truman administration had moved quickly to promote its interests across the entire Asia-Pacific region. Once it had reasserted its hold on the newly liberated Philippines and its recaptured Pacific island territories, the United States placed priority on ensuring that its writ alone ran throughout the Japanese archipelago. At war's end it also commenced policies in Southeast Asia that would soon be seen to be considerably more extensive than London had either anticipated or welcomed. The United States was now the leading power throughout the region. President Truman's review of the might of the US Navy on the Hudson River in

October 1945 was a reminder of both the United States' accomplishments in the Pacific War and a clear message that it intended to retain its newly acquired status. The last time such an American naval display had been seen by New Yorkers was when Admiral Dewey had returned in triumph from Manila at the end of the Spanish–American War. The difference this time was that with the total destruction of the Imperial Japanese Navy, the entire Pacific Ocean now lay under the virtually complete control of the United Sates Navy. Within days of Truman's inspection of the fleet, the Senate Naval Affairs Committee was informed that the Navy envisaged the US policy objective as maintaining 'strategic control of the Pacific Ocean Area' through an intricate patchwork of naval and air bases. The Pacific Fleet, Admiral Nimitz reported to the Senate in May 1946, 'will have in active service an amphibious force adequate to lift a reinforced marine division, 7 carriers, 6 escort carriers, 2 battleships, 17 cruisers (8 heavy and 9 light), 72 destroyers, 39 submarines, 16 destroyer escorts'. In the face of such vast power projections across the entire Pacific Ocean, one Soviet naval commentator writing in *Pravda* was reduced to wondering, 'if this can be called "defense", what is "attack"?'

The United States also endeavoured to ensure that its changing objectives on the Korean Peninsula were met. The situation in Korea risked reflecting much of the Great Power confusion evidenced elsewhere in Asia, but thanks to a US–Soviet agreement there had been some degree of clarity over the initial division of international responsibilities. At the initiative of the United States, it was rapidly agreed that the Korean Peninsula should be divided into two approximately equal halves; the spoils were to be shared. The rationale for this splintering of the peninsula made no economic sense. Policy-makers in Washington reckoned, however, that a near halving was a more than reasonable compromise as the proposed demarcation line had the twin advantages of incorporating both Seoul and two-thirds of the Korean population into the American fold. Moscow was assigned control of the northern sector, where indeed its forces were quickly in place, while the United States would have similar responsibility over what eventually became South Korea. Yet, initially at least, this was intended to be no more than a temporary stopgap measure, pending supervised elections and the reunification of the entire peninsula under some form of national government. Although different groups claiming to represent the Korean people had long held very different aspirations on what should follow once the detested Japanese had been removed, it was widely reckoned throughout the peninsula that national independence could be realized after a suitably brief interim period. Unfortunately, the Allies' tripartite Cairo Declaration of 1 December 1943 had spoken only of Korea being entitled to its freedom 'in due course'. Furthermore, the Soviet Union, since it was not yet at war with

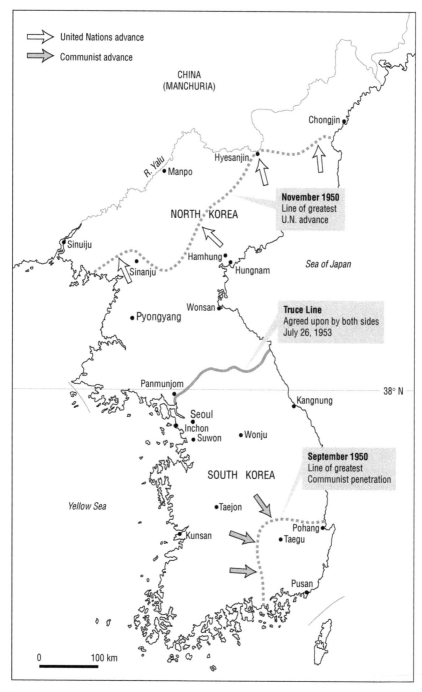

The invasion of North Korea, 1950
Based on US Department of State, Foreign Relations of the United States, 1950
(Washington, DC, 1976).

Imperial Japan, had not been a party to the American, British and Chinese agreement.

The general optimism within Korea was badly misplaced. Korean affairs quickly became an unholy mess, with the result that more than half a century later, the peninsula has yet to realize its long-held dreams of reunification. The deep divisions between and within the Korean people have still to be healed, despite the passage of nearly three postwar generations and periodic outbursts of euphoria. Korea remains the most militarized corner of the globe, where the seeds of conflict have grown into a pair of firmly rooted and hostile plants.

Yet the omens appeared favourable in August 1945. Temporary occupation by the United States and the Soviet Union was assumed to be no more than a short preparatory phase before the creation of a government of national reconciliation and the attainment of full sovereignty with the blessings of the entire international community. The fact that the line drawn across the Korean Peninsula at the end of the Pacific War by Colonels Dean Rusk and Charles Bonesteel in Washington should have persisted into the next century would have surprised the middle-ranking officials who hastily prepared these arrangements. As it was, the victorious Red Armies had the advantage of a four-week lead time over US forces, who only occupied Seoul on 9 September 1945, but Stalin kept firmly to his side of the bargain and made no move to cross unopposed southwards of the 38th parallel. Whatever can be said of later developments, it is apparent that the Cold War hardly started on the Korean Peninsula. Though his motives remain unclear, Stalin may have calculated that demonstrable goodwill over Korea would strengthen his bid for a role in the control of occupied Japan, or he possibly saw the Korean question as a lesser issue that could be safely postponed under pressure of more urgent matters. It may also be that the shock of the American use of the atomic bomb against Hiroshima and Nagasaki had the effect, whether intentional or not, of restraining Stalin's objectives in Asia. What is certain is that the bomb galvanized the Soviet leader into ordering a massive rearmament programme. Recalling events nearly half a century later, one Soviet scientist stated that his government's view on the news that the United States had dropped the first atomic bomb was stark and graphic. It was, Yuli Khariton felt, 'atomic blackmail against the USSR, as a threat to unleash a new, even more terrible and devastating war'. Stalin, it has been suggested recently by younger Russian scholars, may have wanted to wait until his scientists had made substantial progress on gaining the bomb before adopting a more assertive stance against the West. In the interim Stalin might be prepared to cooperate.

Yet whatever Stalin's immediate reactions may have been to what the Soviet embassy in Washington defined in late 1945 as the 'Anglo-Saxon alliance of atomic powers', the supposedly simple Allied scheme for Korea never worked. Within weeks it was apparent that neither side felt able to provide anything resembling the degree of cooperation envisaged for future reunification. Secretary Forrestal was informed that the differences in political and economic systems between the United States and the Soviet Union were intractable. The inevitable result was that both overlords quickly concentrated on creating as viable a zone as possible in disregard of their earlier professions of mutual goodwill. In this process there was an undoubted determination in both North and South Korea to craft a domestic political system entirely to the liking of their respective protectors. The process may have been more direct and overt in the north but there was considerable arm-twisting and violence among groups in South Korea as well. The result was a movement towards ideological orthodoxy on both sides of what was quickly regarded as the armed frontier between two antagonistic states rather than an inconvenient line between brothers eagerly anticipating their forthcoming family reunion.

In North Korea the process began and ended with the creation of an entrenched Communist state under the sway of Kim Il Sung. As the young leader of a resistance group to Japanese colonial rule, Kim's military credentials and his clear political stance earned him vital support from Moscow. The result was the installation of a pro-Soviet, anti-capitalist and vehemently anti-Japanese regime. Ironically, Kim could draw on the beginnings of heavy industrialization established – but thereafter, of course, unacknowledged – under Tokyo's earlier colonial auspices. The new regime in North Korea also had the good fortune and political sense not to work through Imperial Japanese forces. This was made possible because the Russians and their Communist sympathisers in August 1945 had at least the required manpower and resources to eliminate the reliance on Japanese troops and civilians that General John Hodge was obliged to accept in the south. Instead of employing Japanese officers and officials, the Russians and their North Korean comrades arrested those suspected of war crimes and then marched off into captivity the great bulk of the surrendering imperial troops. It would take the next decade before the fate of many of these POWs was established and relatives in Japan informed officially of their privations in the camps and hostile environment of Siberia.

Russia and North Korea began in the autumn of 1945 a close relationship that paralleled the ties between the United States and South Korea. By February 1946 the North Korean Provisional People's Committee had been established and in July the North Korean Workers Party quickly solidified the main Communist groupings. Given that the economic prospects for North Korea appeared somewhat positive and the domestic political situation was hardly subject to mass dissent, it was not impossible to envisage that North Korea with the support of the Soviet Union might be in an advantageous position in any moves towards national reintegration. A stronger economic and political base than its counterpart in South Korea, when combined with the opportunity to gain the upper hand in the determination of an interim all-Korean government, could hardly fail to concern the United States and its protégés in Seoul. Washington, however, could point out that the Soviet Union had refused to cooperate with measures introduced in the United Nations in November 1947 which called for pan-Korean elections to be held under the supervision of a UN Temporary Commission on Korea. Since the two superpowers could not agree, it had been hoped that the United Nations' agents might have replaced the American and Russian protectorates with an alternative road map to national unification and independence. Yet after the refusal of Moscow to consent to elections, and after bitter fighting within South Korea over the wisdom of unilateral polls, a general election was held on 10 May 1948. Unfortunately, the demonstrations and killings that accompanied the first South Korean attempts at representative democracy hardly augured well for the fledgling republic. The worst atrocities occurred on the small island of Jeju in the Korea Strait where, it has been suggested, perhaps 30 000 people were executed for alleged pro-Communist sympathies.

As the postwar era began, American commanders and diplomats in South Korea had undoubtedly found themselves in uncharted waters. Lieutenant-General Hodge is reported to have received neither firm directives from the Joint Chiefs of Staff nor adequate background briefings from US officials before his arrival on the peninsula on 8 September 1945. Although Hodge was to get a great deal of criticism for his handling of Korean affairs in the months ahead, it should be said in his defence that it was asking much of a regular soldier to be suddenly confronted with the acute and sensitive problems of conducting an occupation of a non-Western society without proper guidelines or sufficient forces to do the initial job. Few military organizations are designed to throw up a MacArthur and fewer still ever have the wish or opportunity to grant such far-ranging proconsular powers to any one individual.

Mistakes were made. The beginnings of American intervention were marred by bitterly resented announcements that the United States would work through the existing Japanese structure rather than by the imposition of direct military rule. Demonstrators were then roughed up by the police and little sympathy was shown to critics of the American over-reliance on Japanese officials and conservative Korean elements. Hodge and his advisers received a bad press over the initial months of the occupation and clearly displayed impatience towards those Koreans who thought immediate independence should be granted to coincide with the repatriation of the Japanese military. In truth, the United States quickly discovered, as it was also doing in MacArthur's GHQ in Tokyo, that there was no viable alternative to working through the bureaucracy already in place. The great difference, however, between the Korean and Japanese scenes was the unpalatable reality that Imperial Japanese rule for the past half-century had intentionally left few Koreans with much experience of higher administrative or competence in the English language. Yet the Japanese empire through its educational, economic and bureaucratic structures was to provide an uncomfortably long-lasting postwar legacy for both Korean states. The ex-colonialists were either shipped home or transported to the camps and mines of Siberia, but their handiwork did not dissolve so quickly.

The United States at first had little time to consider any such comparable long-term ambitions for South Korea. It was inevitably a novice in the confusing maelstrom of Korean politics and all too frequently found itself having to react to unforeseen events. Under these circumstances it is difficult to endorse the claims of those who see clear-cut American objectives for the peninsula or calibrated plans for linking South Korea into either a regional security or economic scheme under the patronage of Washington. From September 1945 until the outbreak of the Korean War in June 1950, the picture is rather one of shifting policies and priorities. The cynic might argue with some justification that these changes not only confused American audiences but might almost have been designed to ensure that opponents of the United States in the region would face a succession of sleepless nights. It is doubtful if American actions during this half decade have sufficient coherence to warrant the confident descriptions of South Korea being recruited as an American client state for front line service within any American regional order, linked to a still broader international rivalry with Communist forces. There was no pattern book and Seoul could hardly be tailored in this manner.

The United States' stance in South Korea rested in considerable part on domestic developments on the peninsula. Here right-wing Korean figures gradually strengthened their position and gained American backing by presenting themselves to both the people of South Korea and the Truman administration as strongly anti-Communist. Events appeared now to be confirming the fears of the State Department planners, who had cautioned in October 1943 that 'Korea may appear to offer a tempting opportunity' for the Soviet Union. The concern was that Soviet 'occupation of Korea would create an entirely new strategic situation in the Far East, and its repercussions within China and Japan might be far reaching'. Washington watched as Hodge failed to control a near chaotic political situation inside South Korea, where Secretary Marshall was informed that an estimated 30 per cent of the population in September 1947 backed 'Communist leaders who support the Soviets behind United States lines'. After the breakdown in an attempt to organize pan-Korean elections, under the supervision of the UN Temporary Commission on Korea, the scene was set for firmer American policies. General Hodge was replaced and South Korean politicians who opposed Communism gained greater favour. Such figures played a similar message to two different audiences simultaneously, which resulted in their opponents within South Korea and their sponsors to the north being seen as unpatriotic and potentially subversive.

The rise of the long-exiled, elderly nationalist Syngman Rhee was based on clear identification with this fervent anti-Communism. Rhee had been far from popular with General Hodge, who rowed frequently with him, while the British consul-general in Seoul in February 1947 regarded the aspiring Korean leader as no more than 'a megalomaniac' who was quite prepared to spill the blood of opponents and supporters alike to gain his ends. Yet Rhee, who had a Princeton doctorate, a non-Korean wife and decades of experience of political intrigue, managed to gain power in 1948 through somewhat dubious elections in South Korea. He would then lead an unpleasant conservative regime that remained in place until he was finally overthrown in 1960. Not surprisingly, Rhee immediately reckoned he was not only the President of the Republic of Korea (ROK) but maintained that he represented the entire peninsula. The United Nations, which in its infancy was largely dominated by the United States, equivocated on this point, while leaving affairs largely in the hands of its unfortunate UN Commission for Korea. What was clear, however, was that the Truman administration, after withdrawing its ground troops because they were held to be too weak, had allied itself to President Rhee. In the summer of 1948, South Korean politics was transformed. The country gained a new leader, a new constitution, a new assembly and a new ally in the shape of the United States. General MacArthur's visit to Seoul in August 1948 symbolized the beginnings of this crucial US–South Korea relationship, which was to be followed only days later by similar developments in Pyongyang.

The Soviet Position in Northeast Asia

North Korea was equally beholden to its protector. The Soviet Union appears initially to have been content to dominate only half of the peninsula, possibly out of a wish to be seen to be in cooperation with the United States. This may have been part of the Kremlin's strategy for gaining a share in the supposedly Allied control of occupied Japan, but also perhaps because of Stalin's relatively limited concern with Korean developments. Speculation aside, the role of the Soviet Union in North Korea was considerable. It largely refrained, for example, from following standard operating procedure and deliberately avoided carting off looted industrial plant from its newly acquired occupation zone. It also granted Pyongyang credits and provided technological assistance for the creation of a new Communist state that was virtually a Soviet satellite. The culmination of close Soviet–North Korean ties was seen in August and September 1948, when the Soviet Union quickly emulated its version of constitutional developments taking place simultaneously in Seoul. Stalin encouraged North Korea to elect its own people's assembly and formally establish the Democratic People's Republic of North Korea under Kim Il Sung as the designated prime minister.

The Democratic People's Republic of Korea shared only one transcendent belief with that of its detested ROK opponent. Each rival regime was equally insistent from 1948 onwards that the keys to control of all Korea rightfully belonged in its hands. Kim Il Sung and Syngman Rhee both claimed to be the only legitimate leader of their nation. Outside observers tended to regard North Korea in this period as stronger militarily and more stable politically than South Korea, but information was clearly fragmentary and domestic uncertainties compounded all judgements. Rhee's forces had little of the recent battle experience of Kim Il Sung's returning volunteers, who had fought in the Chinese civil war, and it was far from apparent what the attitude of the US government might be in any border clash between the two Koreas. Washington was probably as concerned about South Korean provocations along the 38th parallel (an anxiety that would reappear later) as it was about the possibility of a major North Korean incursion. Secretary of State Dean Acheson, for example, in his important speech of 12 January 1950, explained the position of the Truman administration with regard to South Korea in equivocal terms. Acheson excluded it from the US government's defence perimeter, suggesting instead that self-help and then United Nations assistance should be the way forward for Seoul. Such ambiguity over what the United States might or might not do in a crisis in Northeast Asia can be assumed to have had a considerable impact on North Korean thinking.

Elsewhere in the region the Soviet Union consolidated its power. Since continental Northeast Asia was recognized as its sphere of influence, it had a free hand to adopt whatever policies it deemed immediately appropriate for Manchuria, over the strategically important Kurile Islands, and within its own Maritime Provinces. It now had significant military strength on the ground, transportation advantages through control of the South Manchurian Railway, and the bonus of warm-water naval facilities at Port Arthur and Dairen. Plainly there was no deterring Moscow if it decided to clear the Kurile island chain of its Japanese population or deal as harshly as it wished with Japanese POWs and civilian internees caught up in the panic exodus from former Manchukuo at the fag end of the Pacific War. Yet when it came to longer-term considerations over the future of Manchuria, the position became less clear cut. The Yalta agreements certainly spoke of temporary Soviet domination of what had become in the 1930s, thanks to massive Japanese state and private capital investment, a highly important and newly industrializing region. At the same time it was also increasingly apparent that the Chinese Communists were being encouraged to spread out through Manchuria, officially in order to take the surrender of defeated Japanese forces but also, of course, to secure the region as a valuable pawn for the inevitable intensification of the Chinese civil war. What could not be clarified initially was how the Soviet Union would respond to these accretions of Chinese Communist power. A strengthened CCP in Northeast Asia was hardly likely to be viewed with overmuch sympathy by the Kremlin, since it added to Soviet border insecurity and might be the prelude to revanchist demands for the huge chunks of once Chinese territory annexed by Tsarist Russia in the nineteenth century. Imperialism in Asia was not an exclusively European and American sin, though Communist propaganda had long found it highly convenient to pretend that it was.

Soviet military control of Manchuria lasted until April 1946. It was still unclear, though, during this period, how to interpret the imprecisions of Moscow's behaviour towards the two contending sides in the Chinese civil war. The Soviet Union had signed a friendship treaty with the Nationalists, presumably in order to consolidate its gains in Northeast Asia and through doubts over the possibility of eventual success for the CCP in the struggles ahead with the Nationalists. Yet it had also encouraged the People's Liberation Army (PLA) to strengthen its position in Manchuria. What is clear, however, is that as the Soviet forces withdrew in 1946, fierce fighting erupted throughout the region.

The Emergence of Communist China

Within China proper, the end of the war against Imperial Japan had already proved to be merely the prelude to yet more warfare and misery. Foreign governments might well have their own views on the possible outcomes of this new round in the long-lasting Chinese civil war, but only the United States had the potential to influence events. Yet the Truman administration adopted a generally cautious approach and was to disappoint its many critics who advocated a greater involvement in Chinese affairs. Faced with the dilemma of whether to commit military force to aid the Nationalist government or stand by and watch the emergence of a second major Communist regime in East Asia, the United States behaved with circumspection. President Truman and his advisers were wary of ordering in US troops for a host of sensible reasons. American caution began with an awareness of the near impossibility of being able to alter the military situation on the ground, given the immense size of the subcontinent and the successes to date of the Communists in what their leaders termed the War of Resistance. At the end of the Pacific War the United States had sent US marines to assist in the disarmament of Japanese divisions in northern China and to hand over equipment to the KMT for future use. This action had enraged the CCP and aroused Mao's worst suspicions of American objectives in China. American intervention, moreover, had failed to do much more than temporarily slow the ineluctable success of the Communists.

Yet Mao's generals had themselves broken the rules over the Allied surrender arrangements. Chu Teh stated emphatically that since it had been his armies that had defeated Japanese forces and liberated much of northern China, it was the CCP that was more than entitled to secure the peace on the ground. In turn, President Truman ordered US transport planes and amphibious craft to be deployed immediately to enable Chiang Kai-shek's officers to enforce the surrender. Everyone was jockeying for position in a chaotic period of rival negotiations; local armistices were broken and private deals were made among war lords, Japanese commanders and Chinese in differing uniforms. It was soon apparent, however, that Chiang's men and their American patrons were the overall losers in this confusion. General Lin Piao, a future member of the Chinese politburo, captured vast quantities of munitions and organized entire new divisions out of a multitude of surrendering forces in Manchuria. Nationalist troops deserted en masse and Manchurian irregulars changed sides, while in turn sizeable numbers of Japanese soldiers found themselves staying on in Northeast Asia with their officers committed to protecting Nationalist China.

There was little that the Truman administration could do to assist the government of China unless it was prepared to undertake major military intervention on the Asian continent at the end of the most exhausting and costly overseas war in US history. Consuls in the remotest Chinese regions might testify to the popular expectation that 'America will come and fix everything up' but the belief in eternal friendship between the United States and Nationalist China hardly accorded with the more unpleasant realities of a central government barely able to administer or exercise power. The United States would certainly wish to give moral and political support to Chiang but beyond this it would only consider some form of economic and financial assistance. The onus was on Chiang to demonstrate that he was in control and that his regime might undertake immediate reform of its own structures and work to improve the lot of those under its sway. It was a foregone conclusion, however, that the KMT could hardly risk change. Truman's economic adviser for Chinese affairs warned the President in December 1945 that the principles of 'Chinese political and economic democracy' could be quickly agreed to by the KMT leadership but that it would take external effort to translate such impressive phrases into any substantial reality. Chinese inexperience and inertia, Edward Locke told Truman, made it imperative that Washington step in to initiate substantial reforms and propose reconciliation to avert the impending civil war. Such suggestions had been made frequently in the past and had fallen each time at the hurdle of Chiang Kai-shek's resistance to any change that might threaten his system of government.

The despatch of the Marshall mission to China in December 1945 was intended to explore how far the administration was prepared to go along this interventionist path. It reflected both the deteriorating situation within China and the increasing rifts within domestic opinion in the United States over appropriate courses of action. General Marshall was sent to China in the wake of serious charges from Ambassador Hurley, who claimed there had been disloyalty among US foreign service officers in East Asia. Hurley bitterly attacked the administration by alleging that his policies had been undermined by the Communist sympathizers in his ranks. Undoubtedly this echoed the frustrations of some Republicans that China was likely to turn Communist in the near future. Any abandonment of Generalissimo Chiang was seen by such vocal and well-organized elements in the United States as the betrayal of the wartime leader who, it was held, had gallantly fought Imperial Japan to a standstill and deserved greater American assistance in his hour of need.

Policy papers hurriedly prepared for General Marshall indicate clearly that the Truman administration was wary of persuading Chiang to agree to a future broad-based government. Marshall himself recorded at a meeting with President Truman that if, 'the US abandoned continued support of the Generalissimo, there would be the tragic consequence of a divided China and of a probable Russian reassumption of power in Manchuria, the combined effect of this resulting in the defeat or loss of the major purpose of our war in the Pacific'. Yet it was always hard to envisage the goal of persuading all parties within China to work towards 'a broadly representative government' where 'autonomous armies', such as those of the Communists, would thereby be eliminated and 'integrated effectively into the Chinese National Army'. British Foreign Office minutes noted that the United States had long supported Chiang Kai-shek's regime and therefore could hardly claim much neutrality in its efforts to gain a ceasefire and a multi-party government of national unity.

It was also pointed out that the extent of Soviet support for the CCP was less apparent; even Chiang, when reviewing the situation with Marshall, had to admit that Moscow 'did not want to appear to be unfriendly to the outside world'.

General Marshall made some initial progress. He was able to engineer approximate agreements that saw the KMT and Communists both committed to short truces, but these intervals failed to lead to any satisfactory political deal. Chiang rightly said that his Communist opponents would be influenced by Moscow and he doubted whether there was much willingness on the CCP's part to work with any other political party. For their part, the Communists sensed that the KMT would be most unlikely to give up substantial powers to rival coalition partners. By October 1946 General Marshall had failed. Chiang then tried to divert attention from himself by convening a National Assembly instructed to work towards a new constitution and broad-based government, but Mao was in no mood to cooperate. The Communist leadership now felt that nothing could be gained from an American-backed coalition for China when power was seen ultimately to rest with the KMT. It was a case, as Marshall had predicted immediately after his arrival in Nanking, of the CCP using 'delaying procedure' to exploit the fact that its own military position would continue to strengthen in the months ahead.

The seemingly interminable Chinese civil war now resumed in earnest. The initiative passed from the Nationalists to the Communists as their forces gained still more Manchurian territory and the failures of the KMT's economic and financial policies made even the barest of existences a struggle for most of the Chinese population. War, hyperinflation and near starvation were hardly the best of advertisements for the continuation of American military, economic and political support to a beleaguered Chiang Kai-shek. By 1948 the writing was on the wall. The British ambassador could report to the Foreign Office that the KMT represented the lesser of two evils, but almost simultaneously he noted that since British commercial interests in northern China had to be protected, there ought not to be any 'squeamishness about reddening our hands'.

The end came swiftly. Chiang's armies melted away, while his supposed supporters blamed their leader for failing to assert himself above the rival groupings that had long comprised the KMT. The result was an ignominious, pellmell retreat that only stopped when Chiang reached the comparative safety of the island of Taiwan. On 1 October 1949, Mao Tse-tung proclaimed to the world from Beijing's Tiananmen Square that China was now reunited and gave notice that it intended to regain its past glories under the banner of Communism. The nation was about to stand up and demonstrate its commitment to modernization at home and assertion abroad. Whatever the future outcomes to these huge challenges, China had at the very least the satisfaction of knowing that a generation of civil war was over.

The consequences for international relations in the region were equally enormous. The United States had to accept the humiliation of being seen to have lost its major ally in East Asia. Instead of an anti-Communist regime in China, there was now a new government in Beijing whose centralized political and economic system closely paralleled that of the USSR. Furthermore, to add to its embarrassments, the world would shortly witness the signing of a Sino-Soviet treaty of friendship that could only present fresh difficulties to a Washington already bitterly divided on party lines over where responsibility should be placed for the China débâcle. Under these circumstances there was no question of the Truman administration instantly recognizing the People's Republic of China. Yet the issue of how to respond to what many in the United States regarded as a godless, brutal regime could not be ducked by refusing to establish diplomatic relations. The practical realities still had to be faced and policy options needed to be formulated to cope with this new China.

As was only to be expected, given their highly vocal attacks on China policy since 1945, a sizeable portion of the Republican Party with links to the so-called China Lobby eagerly joined in the general condemnation of the Truman administration. The opposition was well financed, partisan and astute. It argued that far greater attention deserved to be placed on Asian affairs and that the government's European priorities should be reviewed instantly. It was hardly coincidental that such views echoed the long-held stance of Douglas MacArthur, who insisted that the United States needed to reckon with a future international system where the Asia-Pacific region might dominate the globe. MacArthur, not surprisingly given his illustrious career, claimed that the Pacific would serve as America's manifest destiny for the next hundred years. He saw the era of 'the white man' as being far from over in an Asia where demography and economic potential pointed to 'stupendous opportunity' for his own nation. There was, MacArthur had reported from his Manila head-quarters in 1935, a 'renaissance' under way affecting 'every person and every mile of territory' in the Asia-Pacific region which would permit huge benefits for the industrialized world. In MacArthur's view the emerging 'industrial and economic revolution in East Asia, with its grow-ing demand for credits and manufactured goods' could become the United States' new frontier on the Pacific Rim.

Geopolitical predictions aside, there were indeed faults with American policy that could be exploited for political ends in an electric atmos-phere where the convention of bipartisanship in foreign affairs had been scrapped. Dean Acheson, for example, made the administration's position even more difficult by virtually ruling out the prospect of aid to Taiwan in his speech to the National Press Club in January 1950. The fury of the China Lobby was palpable, while little was being done to gain better relations with Beijing. What slight prospects there may have been for improvement were made even more difficult by the manner in which the PRC mistreated American consular officials and by the political strength of Truman's domestic opponents.

The new Chinese regime saw that as long as Taiwan continued to win such strong support from within the American political and foreign policy establishment, it would be highly improbable that diplomatic relations could be established with Washington in the foreseeable future. Yet unless there was a swift reduction in official ties between the United States and Taiwan, there was virtually no prospect of an accommodation between Washington and Beijing. The fact that the US government promptly moved its embassy from Nanking to Taipei, cut off economic aid to continental China and worked hard to maintain Taiwan's seat in the UN Security Council all confirmed to the PRC that the Americans were incorrigible. The Taiwan factor certainly compounded the already considerable dilemmas for the President and his advisers, who received a huge correspondence from writers of all persuasions on the fate of China. Acheson may at first have entertained some slight hopes that a future reconciliation with Mao's regime might be possible, but the angry denouncements that the Democrats had 'lost' China soon eliminated this option. One later critic even went so far as to lengthen the charge sheet to incorporate the administration's alleged ineptitude over the entire region by titling his attack 'How the Far East was Lost'.

The Korean War Begins

Despite these seismic domestic upheavals in China and differences over the handling of Korean affairs, the Asia-Pacific region from the summer of 1945 to the summer of 1950 had shown at least a degree of stability based on informal spheres of influence among the major powers. This all changed within hours of the North Koreans' tank and infantry incursions across the 38th parallel into South Korea early in the morning of Sunday, 25 June 1950. The consequences of these sudden developments on the Korean Peninsula catapulted what until then had been a largely unknown local issue in Northeast Asia into the forefront of international affairs. Over the next three years the Korean War was to become the storm centre of the Cold War, with massive political, economic and human consequences that were to blight the region for the next fifty years. American foreign policy in the Asia-Pacific would be changed irrevocably by the decisions made by its leaders to resist the surprise invasion that had so effectively caught the administration off guard.

Korea's predicament, in the wake of Imperial Japan's surrender, can only be described as highly unenviable. It was, as we have seen, divided geographically and politically, with ultimate authority resting in the hands of the two rival superpowers. Efforts to broker an arrangement whereby Korea might at last be both united and independent came to nought. The US War Department had warned within weeks of Japan's surrender that the situation risked becoming impossible. By January 1947 it had defined the peninsula as its most serious problem, since there appeared to be little prospect of either cooperation with the Soviet Union or the rehabilitation of South Korea. These concerns, however, did not prevent the Pentagon, admittedly under intense political pressure to demobilize rapidly at the end of hostilities, from recommending that all American troops be withdrawn from South Korea. President Truman, acting on the advice of General Eisenhower (a fact that Paul Nitze as head of the Policy Planning Staff [PPS] would never forgive or forget), had unfortunately ordered the last GIs out of South Korea in December 1948.

By the spring of 1950, however, the Truman administration had begun to provide at least a modest degree of support to South Korea through military aid and foreign economic programmes. Yet this was a relatively minor contribution to a more general policy of strengthening American power around the globe in the light of a worsening relationship with the Soviet Union and its allies. In April 1950 the National Security Council (NSC) feared that the USSR had the initiative in what it defined as 'the conflict with the free world'. It held that Moscow's recent successes in the Asia-Pacific region 'have led to an increasing confidence on its part and to an increasing nervousness in Western Europe and the rest of the free world'. It was imperative, therefore, to bolster US support to nations on the margins of the Eurasian landmass in order to prevent local Soviet encroachment and to signal to the United States' allies that Washington was fully prepared to defend these nations in an emergency.

Commentators within the federal bureaucracy pointed out that the construction and then retention of a strong alliance system to rival that of the Soviet Union was in fact the central objective behind the proposed American military build-up. Yet, as John Foster Dulles noted in a memorandum to the State Department, there were limits to what the United States could do in the new circumstance of the loss of China. Dulles, who had been commissioned by Truman to assist in the gaining of a Japanese peace settlement, reckoned that it was imperative for the administration to make a political stand in order to demonstrate 'our confidence and resolution'. If such a calculated move were not attempted then, in Dulles' view, 'we can expect an accelerated deterioration of our influence in the Mediterranean, Near East, Asia and the Pacific.' He warned that the

> situation in Japan may become untenable and possibly that in the Philippines. Indonesia, with its vast natural resources may be lost and the oil of the Middle East will be in jeopardy. None of these places provide good 'holding' grounds once the people feel that Communism is the wave of the future and that even we are retreating before it.

Dulles' forceful suggestion, which echoed the opinions of others within the State Department, was that a firm stance be made over Taiwan. He encouraged the administration to announce the neutralization of the island, in order to deter the 'joint Chinese–Russian expedition in form- ation'. Since the 'eyes of the world are focused upon it', Dulles and his friends felt that the despatch of American warships to the Taiwan straits would both deter Mao and convey the correct international message. It would also, though Dulles did not refer to the point, ensure that Chiang's hawks would be prevented from making senseless and provocative incursions onto the China coast. He hoped that this would signal to allies and opponents alike that the United States had the backbone to defend Taiwan even at the risk of war. It would also dispel the perception that only a direct act of aggression on 'our own citadel of the North Atlantic and America areas' would lead to military retaliation. While Dulles readily acknowledged the dangers of conflict, he argued that prompt action was vital 'in order to preserve peace in the world and to keep the national prestige required if we are to play our indispensable part in sustaining a free world'. His generally cautious measures, however, stand in contrast to the grand rhetoric of global preponderance expounded by the State Department's Policy Planning Staff and the strategists who spoke so confidently of frustrating the Kremlin and its lackeys.

It remains the case also that President Truman had yet to endorse either the lengthy findings of his National Security Council or the related foreign policy proposals before the summer of 1950. NSC 68, as the lengthy recommendations were to be officially termed, would require very substantial funding and his administration had still to be invited to come to any conclusions. Planners warned Truman that the unwelcome domestic consequences of the proposed large-scale military build-up might well be both a decline in the general standard of living and an increase in taxation. The press, however, was able to point out the con- siderable disparity in size, if not necessarily of equipment, of Soviet and American armed forces. The public mood in the light of the announce- ment of Russia's acquisition of the atomic bomb and the hysterical charges of Senator McCarthy on the infiltration of Communists within the federal government was decidedly critical. Influential correspondents writing to General Omar Bradley, chairman of the Joint Chiefs of Staff, welcomed indications of preliminary shifts taking place in US commitments. Vannevar Bush, for example, noted that the 'Marshall Plan has prevented the conquest of Western Europe by subversion. The Truman doctrine has ended advance by military catspaws in Europe, if not in the Far East'. Bush warned, however, that the military readiness of US forces was far from ideal and that 'while we recognize the position of the front line, neither we nor our Allies are in a position to defend it. While we recognize that we must support our Allies we are not in a position successfully to do so'. Two months later events on the extreme periphery confirmed the accuracy of this diagnosis.

The origins of the Korean War remain controversial. What can be confidently established, however, is that the Truman administration saw the North Korean attack in June 1950 as tantamount to a challenge to the United States' position as supreme defender of the West. It is less clear whether North Korea had in fact been provoked into making its initial move in order to respond to South Korean border infiltration. Yet regardless of possible South Korean incursions, it now appears that Kim, after repeated requests, had indeed eventually gained Stalin's reluctant approval for what was felt to be an easy victory over Seoul. Kim's persistence paid off.

The explanation of why President Kim could obtain Moscow's backing continues to be debated. Important considerations may well have been Kim's impatience over Korean reunification and the fact that any movement across the 38th parallel would distract the United States from European business. A key component of the decision was certainly the reality that the Truman administration had dithered over maintaining any resounding US commitment to South Korea. It should also be noted that Ambassador Dulles immediately sensed that the attacks on South Korea were linked to the United States' preparation of a Japanese peace treaty to shore up its strategic posture in the Pacific. The extraordinary unpreparedness of the United States, where parallels with the surprise Japanese aerial attack on Pearl Harbor in December 1941 come immediately to mind, suggests at the very least a lack of coordination with its client state in Seoul. Although President Truman responded to the incursions from North Korea in characteristically robust style, his administration was badly let down in the first weeks of the fighting by the poor performance of US troops. Units drawn from the Eighth Army, who had previously been enjoying nothing more strenuous than the diversions of occupied Japan, were hardly fit for combat. Once hurriedly despatched to defend the border area, these GIs quickly found themselves in a badly officered, poorly fought and chaotic retreat down the Korean Peninsula.

Suddenly there was much talk in Washington of another Dunkirk in the making. Fortunately for the West, the line held as US morale improved and Kim's men exhausted themselves in attempting to capture what became known as the Pusan perimeter. It had been a near thing, though, and events had quickly underlined the glaring results of the Truman administration's comprehensive reductions of American military units in the late 1940s. The United States, in the first urgent months of the Korean War, had possessed no strategic reserves. By the dreadful autumn of 1950 the consequences of the popular wish to balance the federal budget were only too visible on the bare hills and in the paddy fields of South Korea.

After a brief pause to regroup and consolidate, US forces and small attached allied units began to counter-attack. Initial success was rewarded with further gains as confidence grew; the retaking of all South Korean territory was quickly realized following MacArthur's inspired amphibious landing at Inchon in mid-September. The next issue was whether to march north in the face of fears in some quarters that this might result in direct Chinese military intervention to shore up North Korea's fragile defences. Despite veiled warnings of this eventuality from Chinese sources to sympathetic diplomats, the United States and its more reluctant allies took their fateful decision to advance across the 38th parallel into North Korea. The history of both the peninsula and indeed the entire region was about to alter. General MacArthur might confidently predict in early October that his forthcoming victory would shortly lead to the establishment of 'a united, independent and democratic government of Korea'. But it was not to be.

China Intervenes

As the US, South Korean and allied troops threatened to approach the North Korean–Manchurian border, the military situation changed. MacArthur had assured Truman at their Wake Island meeting of 15 October that his intelligence staff reckoned there was 'very little' chance of Sino-Soviet intervention. By the end of October, however, the presence of substantial numbers of Chinese 'volunteers' was readily apparent. Statements from Chinese leaders on the eternal friendship enjoyed by North Korea and the PRC and the fact that divisions of PLA forces were already stationed on the peninsula threatened to reveal the simple truth that China meant what it said. Beijing, it appeared, felt imperilled by the proximity of UN forces to its borders and was certainly encouraged to do so by Stalin, who held firm to his promise to provide vital air support for poorly equipped Chinese ground troops. Announcements were received that further invasion of North Korean soil would lead to active resistance by Beijing's troops, but the US government was not about to order its men southwards. The risk of action by China would have to be taken, if the allied goal of Korean reunification were to be achieved. The sudden scale and ferocity of Chinese counter-attacks against MacArthur's forces, however, instantly invalidated all the earlier boasts from GHQ in Tokyo. Gaunt, frost-bitten GIs were once again to be seen straggling south as they found their uncertain progress impeded by lengthy columns of refugees, who were subject to the bitter, endless cold and instant hostility from all sides. By the end of November the full extent of the potential disaster that now threatened the United States was reported by MacArthur to the Joint Chiefs of Staff in the blunt sentence, 'We face an entirely new war'.

What the United States also faced was a divided domestic arena and major disagreements with its allies on how best to respond to China's intervention. It was a certain recipe for chaos. US forces were split across inhospitable terrain, 200 000 PLA troops were known to be opposing them, MacArthur was insisting on nothing less than total victory, and the President was under daily attack from his Republican opponents for what they held to be his bungling policies in Northeast Asia. There was also loose talk from the White House of the possible use of tactical atomic weapons, which had Prime Minister Clement Attlee scurrying across the Atlantic to counsel restraint on President Truman. Public opinion in the Commonwealth and what would shortly be termed the Non-Aligned Movement (NAM) was alarmed at the threat of a global confrontation. This view was also shared by some Americans, such as the diplomat George Kennan, who would write later in his memoirs that he 'saw in the North Korean attack adequate reason for us to undertake military operations for this limited purpose; I did not see in it justification for involving ourselves in another world war'. Unfortunately, the domestic hysteria of late 1950 made the formulation of a clear regional policy for Northeast Asia virtually impossible. It left Kennan noting that Congressional differences ruled out both open diplomacy with the Soviet Union and full discussion 'intelligently with our allies'.

In addition to fresh setbacks on the battlefield, there were increasing disputes on both the home and international fronts. General MacArthur used interviews with sympathetic newspapers to advocate an extension of the war beyond the Yalu River which divided North Korea from Manchuria, claiming that as commanding officer he should have the right to take virtually any military action he deemed necessary to defeat the enemy. MacArthur and his many supporters wished to take the war to China proper in order to obtain victory, even if his proposed bombing raids on Chinese communications in Manchuria and beyond ran the risk of precipitating a still wider and potentially global confrontation between the Communist powers and the United States. Many in the Republican

Party repeatedly argued that it was nonsense to stand firm against the Soviet Union and its satellites in Europe and yet appear timid in Northeast Asia when American lives were being lost in the meat-grinder of an inconclusive and confused war. The general's domestic opponents, however, saw this as a bid by MacArthur to run the war as he judged fit, in disregard of the limitations which had been placed on action that risked leading to a yet more dangerous conflict. The implications for the United States and its allies of further escalation, followed by probable counter-attacks by Sino-Soviet forces, were serious in the extreme. The uneasy postwar international system appeared to be in jeopardy.

President Truman and his advisers then began an exhaustive review of their options. Under the changed circumstances of December 1950, it was necessary to determine the appropriate politico-military strategy to be deployed in the wake of China's robust intervention, recent American military failings, the divisive domestic environment, and much allied concern. It was, as Truman had admitted to his staff on first hearing of the news of China's intervention, the worst moment of his presidency. On 28 November 1950 he acknowledged plainly that 'we've got a terrific situation on our hands'. Truman's most recent biographer has rightly seen the period immediately after the beginning of these vast Chinese attacks as critical both in terms of the conduct of the Korean War and in the much wider arena of world politics. Decisions taken then were to have far-reaching effects on relations between the superpowers and the conduct of the entire international system.

The administration agreed to continue to conduct a limited war. There was to be no unleashing of Chiang Kai-shek's forces and no bombing of Manchuria. Truman's opponents, who contended that an extension of the geographical boundaries and a relaxation on types of weapons to be permitted in the desperate fighting were essential for victory, complained that the outcome under the President's ruling could be no better than stalemate. Yet Truman and his advisers held that this was more satisfactory than risking an all-out war with the People's Republic of China. The administration, while certainly shocked by China's action, determined that Korea was not the place for getting embroiled in a general war. The Soviet Union's strengths in Central and Eastern Europe and the threats this posed to the Western alliance were deemed to be of paramount national importance. Truman insisted that there was to be neither retreat from Korea nor an overt attack on the PRC. The atomic bomb was not to be used against Chinese cities or on its military and civilian installations close to the North Korean border. Omar Bradley answered Truman's many critics by memorably stating that to launch an all-out attack on the PRC would be 'the wrong war in the wrong place at the wrong time against the wrong enemy'.

What did change, however, were the army commanders. Shortly after Christmas 1950, General Matthew Ridgway took over the Eighth Army as the replacement for General Walker, who had died in a road accident in Korea. This led to an improvement in morale, and within a month to a halt in the long retreat down the peninsula. Then, finally, in April 1951 President Truman dismissed General MacArthur. It was, as some commentators said with hindsight immediately after the event, a long overdue act. Yet it was a decision that carried with it such significant domestic political costs that no amount of evidence of MacArthur's insubordination made it any easier for Truman to take. The President's critics attacked at every point. They claimed that the general was entitled to express his views on the conduct of the war and that he was correct to insist that Communism had to be defeated in Asia with whatever weapons were available or soon it would win in Europe. Eventually the firestorm ignited by MacArthur's dismissal did burn itself out, but Truman had thereafter to face massive unpopularity. European governments might be delighted that MacArthur had been relieved, yet it remained hard to convince fellow Americans that a limited war in Korea was the only war worth fighting. The British Chiefs of Staff would no longer have to reckon with the precipitation of a general war in the Far East, but it was much more difficult to justify an inconclusive war in Korea to the very many bereaved parents of American marines and airmen. President Truman never regained the popularity he had earned so defiantly by winning the 1948 general election, though he stuck doggedly to the policies he had initiated when the Korean War had erupted. Speaking almost exactly a year after the fighting had begun, Truman insisted to an audience in Tennessee that he had been right all along. Lambasting his critics, he argued that a limited war was the only way to counter aggression in Korea and yet avoid 'tying up all our resources in a vast war in Asia' with the Soviet Union and the People's Republic of China.

The Impact of the War on the Asia-Pacific

The consequences for the United States and its allies in the region were also profound. In the light of the casualties suffered and the international commitments made by Washington in fighting the Korean War, it became an axiom of American foreign policy thereafter to prevent any possible repetition of the events of June 1950. While there remains no categorical answer to the tangled question of where responsibility should be apportioned over the origins of the Korean War, it was readily apparent from 1953 onwards what would be the US and South Korean response in any future emergency. Secretary Dulles, in the course of explaining to President Rhee in July 1953 where the US administration stood over the sensitive question of an armistice, emphasized the steadfastness of his nation. Dulles underlined that American cooperation was near total and stressed that 'Never in all its history has the US offered to any other country as much as is offered to you'. He concluded his letter by declaring that 'You did not find us lacking in the past and you can I believe trust us for the future'.

Substantial American support for South Korea coincided with a series of political and defence agreements that were concluded with the United States' allies in the region. Indeed, it appears highly probable that the fact that the United States was in the process of terminating its occupation of Japan and considering both a peace treaty and a security pact with Tokyo influenced events on the Korean border in June 1950. It was certainly Dulles' immediate view that the beginning of the fighting in Korea was linked in the minds of his Communist adversaries with crucial diplomatic negotiations over Japan's future. The fate of Japan could hardly be divorced from the situation of its near neighbour; there was concern that a moderately pro-Western Japan that was endangered by a formidable adversary across the straits was most unlikely to remain for long in the American camp. Diplomats and commentators alike appreciated at once that serious instability on the Korean Peninsula would inevitably alter the balance of power in the entire region. It was widely reckoned to make it considerably harder for the United States to gain the degree of support it sought from a nervous Japanese government in order to conclude an effective post-occupation military pact. Yet the Korean War paradoxically led to greatly enhanced American economic and financial involvement in Japan and contributed to Tokyo's ongoing reconstruction. Massive war-related orders from the US government helped boost the recovery of the Japanese economy and in doing so made it easier for the Yoshida cabinet to gain approval for the very defence arrangements that North Korea and its Sino-Soviet allies had intended to prevent in the first place.

The vital importance of the US–Japan security pact to Washington did not, however, lead to any enthusiastic endorsement of these arrangements from within the region. Other states were disturbed by the successful termination of the American occupation through the San Francisco peace treaty and the defence agreements that ensured the continuing stationing of US forces in a newly sovereign Japan. Even the staunchest of America's allies noted disappointedly that these new American-designed schemes granted preferential treatment to Japan, while vocal Congressional members of the China lobby complained that the United States' wartime friends had been abandoned. Tokyo might indeed be the prize of the region, given its recent wartime endeavours and the addition of its formidable industrial potential to the balance of power, but the very closeness of US–Japan ties left others out in the cold.

To ensure that America's Pacific allies would support the Japanese peace treaty and to allay their fears of any future Japanese aggression, a series of other security pacts were quickly concocted. The dual-purpose chain of treaties that stretched from Hokkaido to Hobart was intended both to protect others from Communism and to assure everyone that Japan would be constrained from ever returning to menace Asia. The United States portrayed itself both as the region's self-appointed police-man against global Socialism and the alert watchdog over Japan. In its efforts the Truman administration was reminded through its interdepart-mental National Intelligence Estimate of September 1952 that the Sino-Soviet alliance was founded on 'common hostility to a resurgent and non-Communist Japan and to US power in the western Pacific'. It was held to be in the mutual interest of both Communist signatories to gain 'the elimination of Western influence from the Far East'.

The United States made fresh commitments to the region as the Korean War continued. The desperation of the fighting underlined for the first time the importance of relations with nations about which few Americans could claim even the most rudimentary knowledge or readily identify on the map. Suddenly the US government began presenting itself as the shield of new-found allies and the promoter of values that were intended to distinguish its friends from the rival Sino-Soviet grouping. Yet the caesura that Washington was keen to draw was much less absolute than it purported to be. The internal political realities of most of the Asia-Pacific region hardly matched the rhetoric of statements from American officials; the distinctions the Cold War appeared to demand were frequently false. The Bureau of the Budget's commentary on NSC 68 strongly challenged this prevailing official stance that the 'free world' stood united and innocent against the 'slave' world. It noted that it was 'not true that the US and its friends constitute a free world. Are the Indo-Chinese free? Can the people of the Philippines be said to be free under the corrupt Quirino government?' It also underlined the danger of assuming that many, in what would shortly be termed the Third World by French geographers, would automatically look to the United States for leader-ship simply because of Washington's military might. Instead, the Bureau of the Budget argued, 'their friendship is to be had at the price of sup-port of moves which will improve or, failing that, replace their present governments'. The fault with NSC 68, in this opinion, was that the unfortunate Chinese experience was not being carefully analysed in order to prevent any possible repetition in the future. The Bureau warned that a 'revolutionary movement taking advantage, however cynically, of real elements of dissatisfaction cannot be stopped by the threat of force alone'. Yet in the tense atmosphere of American domestic politics, fol-lowing the 'loss' of China and anger over the Soviet Union's new atomic status, ideologically correct audiences welcomed the idea of pro-Western divisions enlisting in battle order under the banners of representative democracy, free enterprise and Christianity. Such shock troops would apparently have little difficulty in confounding the combined forces of one-party Marxist orthodoxy, state-controlled economies and atheism.

The nation that the United States saw as its most important and successful Asian protégé was postwar Japan. Yet the American transformation of occupied Japan, while certainly a surprise to the more sceptical members of the British Foreign Office, who held that Japanese society was incapable of reforming itself, was considerably less complete than the self-congratulatory MacArthurian press releases would have American audiences believe. Indeed, substantial portions of Douglas MacArthur's later lavish praise of postwar Japan had been used almost verbatim by the general in very different circumstances a decade earlier. He had boasted from Manila in 1936 that with 'adequate protection this country will flourish as a brilliant product of democracy, contribute to stability and peace in the Far East, and advance the living standards of its people to the full extent attainable under efficient use of its own resources'. Then, however, his full-blooded rhetoric had been reserved expressly for the Philippines and its political and security partnership with the United States.

Ten years on and it was tempting for the American proconsul and his loyal staff from the old prewar Manila days merely to delete all references to the Philippines and substitute instead the name of their new ward. In both cases there was a strong element of make-believe. MacArthur's approval, for example, of a modified imperial institution, assiduously supported by the highly conservative and ever vigilant Imperial Household Agency, hardly suggested that the United States had swept the stables clean. No doubt the harsher critics of the American occupation underestimated the considerable achievements of the New Deal in occupied Japan. It required, however, a gigantic leap of faith to imagine that the signing of the San Francisco peace settlements had left the Japanese establishment and the bulk of the conservative electorate as automatic followers of the American designs on the Asia-Pacific region. In some instances the extent of the incomprehension could be deep indeed. The British mission in Tokyo, for example, wrote to the Foreign Office in September 1950 noting that Prime Minister Yoshida had relayed the details of his recent audience with the Emperor. Yoshida told the acting head of the mission that

> once again he emphasized to His Majesty the generous nature of the Treaty. The Emperor agreed that it was indeed a generous Treaty and to him unexpectedly generous. He then added, however, that it was for him a bitter

blow that Japan should in the reign of the grandson of the Great Emperor Meiji have lost all her overseas possessions. Yoshida says that he told the Emperor that this was no time for murmurs of that sort.

The harsh truth was that no Japanese government in the 1950s could risk antagonizing a largely pacifist electorate by taking any active measures to bolster the regional policies of the United States; reluctant acceptance of the necessity of the security treaty was as far as Tokyo was prepared to go. Former Prime Minister Ashida Hitoshi noted ruefully in July 1953 that 'when Japan is attacked from the outside the Japanese people will be playing "pachinko" because the United States armed forces will be taking care of defense'. This was hardly a ringing endorsement of shared US–Japan objectives, yet it was sufficient to retain a formidable series of American military bases on Japanese soil. At least Washington's minimum goal of the initial months of the occupation can be said to have been realized by 1952.

From the early 1950s onwards, the United States could boast of its ability to project military power and thereby political influence throughout the vast Asia-Pacific region from its safe havens within Japan. This foundation was then buttressed by additional security pacts that completed a semi-circle of defence treaties that stretched from Tokyo to Wellington. As with the case of Japan, it was rarely apparent what precise contributions would be made by these partners to the American arsenal, but as a crude psychological message to potential adversaries of the United States it served a useful political purpose. The fact that journalists attending the San Francisco peace conference immediately saw these events as confirming the division of the international system into two halves is a reminder of the intensity of the Cold War in Asia by 1951. The era of American globalism can be said to have begun with the initialling of security pacts with not only Japan but also with South Korea, the Philippines, Taiwan, Australia and New Zealand.

Each treaty had its individual characteristics but all shared a common foundation of reliance on the military might of the United States to deter Communist external aggression and domestic disorder. The most pressing regional issue was that of assisting South Korea. Given the situation that faced the Republic of Korea during and after the Korean War, it was clear that protecting the security of Syngman Rhee's nation was a primary international concern of Washington. This was the case both in order to demonstrate continuing American resolve in the Asia-Pacific region and to ensure that the already large casualties suffered by US forces should not be seen at home as having been borne in vain. The conclusion of the Korean War was marked by a formidable increase in public statements and subsequent action that underlined the resolve of the United States to stand ready to repulse a second invasion of South Korean territory. While senior US military figures expressed disappointment at having been ordered to fight only a limited war (and thereby obliged to reckon with the prospect of an unsatisfactory and inconclusive outcome), the foreign policy establishment saw the necessity after 1953 of explicitly spelling out the resolve of the United States in any future Korean crisis. American national interest now dictated that the Korean Peninsula should be transformed into an area of major geopolitical importance where challenges to South Korean security would be met head-on.

South Korea received categorical assurances from the United States. In a near total reversal of policies that had applied in the late 1940s, Washington was now prepared to station substantial numbers of troops on the peninsula and to provide the necessary funds for military and economic support to the ROK government. The South Korean military, through its training, weaponry and battle order, became very largely an appendage of its American counterpart, while serious efforts were made to encourage the reconstruction of the weak, war-damaged Korean economy. American officials unfortunately had far less success when it came to transforming the domestic political situation. Limited attention was placed on the unpleasant nature of the autocratic South Korean government, though it was hoped that any amelioration of the security situation and the beginnings of economic growth might contribute eventually to a lessening of the domestic repression.

Other nations in the region also benefited from this recent concentration of the American official mind on the Asia-Pacific region. The Korean War undoubtedly acted as a catalyst for far greater and more detailed involvement in the fate of what by the mid-1950s had become the United States' new alliance partners. Containment and largesse went hand in hand. Indeed, several nations saw this as their opportunity to capitalize on the United States' determination to resist Communism by exerting considerable pressure on Washington. Chiang Kai-shek, for example, pleaded with Washington in June 1953 for an immediate mutual security treaty between the United States and South Korea, to assist Seoul and doubtless to prepare the ground next for enhanced ties between the United States and Taiwan. Chiang's argument that a pact with South Korea would 'contribute impressively to the unity of the free nations' prompted Eisenhower to reply that 'we would stand ready to lend encouragement' to any Asian moves towards new mutual security coordination efforts.

Australia too gained a most welcome security arrangement which was, in effect, the quid pro quo for accepting the San Francisco peace treaty. By agreeing to jettison much of its antipathy towards postwar Japan,

Canberra won the United States over to the consideration of regional security arrangements. In the end these hopes of multilateralism were dashed by dissension over membership of a possible Pacific pact, but the final welcome result was a tripartite pact comprising Australia, New Zealand and the United States (ANZUS). The ANZUS treaty provided necessary safeguards for Australasia and also held out the possibility of incorporating Tokyo at some future date into a wider regional security framework. Less attention, however, was paid to the fact that Australia, at least as far as the understanding of the United States was concerned, acknowledged that any attack on American bases in Japan, Okinawa and the Philippines would be required to be met by all its allies in the Asia-Pacific region. The ANZUS pact may indeed have been slightly less one-sided than it appeared at the time but the general public's impression of its terms was clear. It was recognized moreover that the United States had finally replaced Britain as the only Great Power able and willing to offer protection to both Australia and New Zealand. Certainly this can rightly be seen as the continuation of wartime shifts, but it was never-theless a diplomatic revolution for Canberra and Wellington. The creation of ANZUS angered British Foreign Secretary Sir Anthony Eden, who correctly saw the pact's deliberate exclusion of his own nation as both a personal affront and body blow to British prestige and influence. ANZUS provided incontrovertible evidence that the United States alone had the vision and resources to shape pro-Western regional developments to its overall design.

New Alliance Structures

Broader security pacts also emerged in the wake of the Korean War. The most important and the most inclusive arrangement of this period was the South East Asia Treaty Organization (SEATO). Yet for all the hopes and hoopla that accompanied its birth, the seemingly blessed infant was a sickly child whose very survival was soon to be questioned. SEATO depended on the leadership and might of the United States in a region that had moved during the Truman era from being an area of little concern to being one of considerable importance. In part, of course, the same point could be made of other regions where the United States found itself taking on the mantle of British traditions and power, yet the new attention was little short of a sea change.

The first public indication of a more comprehensive American approach was seen with the signing of the Manila pact with the Philippines and Thailand in September 1954. This led shortly afterwards to the formal organization of SEATO with its headquarters in Bangkok. Through SEATO the United States drew up its first multilateral collective security organization for portions of the Asia-Pacific region. On paper, at least, it appeared formidable. In addition to American leadership, SEATO gained pledges of support from Britain, France, Australia and New Zealand as well as Thailand, Pakistan and the Philippines. Yet the understandings behind SEATO spoke only of consultation in the face of armed attack and included the proviso that there would have to be the requirement of unanimity before action could take place. It was also obvious from the outset that SEATO lacked any sizeable number of Asian members, and the absence of major regional powers such as India and Indonesia clearly weakened the hopes of the Eisenhower administration to be seen to be buttressing Southeast Asia from Communist insurrection. The position of South Vietnam, Laos and Cambodia, the three countries that had particular relevance for SEATO, was also confusing. The SEATO strategy had been intended for their protection, yet first Cambodia and then Laos soon opted out of the embryonic scheme, leaving the United States with little more than a fig leaf of collective support by the early 1960s when it decided to intervene in strength in South Vietnam.

Indo-China was at the centre of American concerns for the future of Southeast Asia. Strategic planning in Washington was based on the assumption that whoever controlled the former French territories would be able to dominate all neighbouring states. The National Security Council warned that 'the loss of any single country would probably lead to relatively swift submission to or an alignment with communism by remaining countries of this group'. The same body stated in a lengthy policy paper of November 1953 that the primary objective of the United States in its attempts to 'reduce the relative power position of Communist China in Asia' should be by developing the political, economic and military strength of non-Communist Asian countries'. Time and again American planners and policy-makers made note of the diminution of Western power in the Asia-Pacific region. It was necessary for the United States 'to cope with the altered structure of power which arises from the existence of a strong and hostile Communist China, and from the military alliance of Communist China with the USSR'. How this could be best achieved, however, was less clear. It was one thing to recognize that there had been 'a radical alteration of the power structure in the Far East' and to note that the West had been excluded 'from the whole vast area between the Amur, the Himalayas and the Gulf of Tonkin', but solutions were thin on the ground. The unpleasant power realities were apparent; whether it might be practical to alter the situation to the advantage of the United States proved much more difficult to envisage.

American planners found themselves repeating the concepts and phrases first adopted during and immediately before the Korean War. It was regarded as imperative to secure 'the preservation of the territorial and political integrity of the non-Communist countries in the area against further Communist expansion or subversion'. This defence of vital national interests might incur the risk of war, but as the spread of Communism in Asia by November 1954 had led to the annexation of 'all of Mainland China, North Korea and, more recently ... the northern part of Viet Nam', there appeared few alternatives to active resistance. By the mid-1950s a series of coordinated regional measures had been effected that were intended to contain the People's Republic of China. The shock of China's 'human wave' tactics during the Korean War, following on from Mao's commitment to assist his North Korean brothers and cooperate with Moscow, ensured that Beijing was now a major power at the centre of American regional calculations.

The American commitment to bilateral and multilateral alliance structures was a direct consequence of the Korean War. Once Beijing had demonstrated its formidable military strength through large-scale intervention on the Korean Peninsula, the United States adopted a very different stance towards the PRC. The battlefield taught the United States to respect Chinese prowess and to try to ensure that in any future conflict the results of the next emergency might be different. China had stood up, and in doing so it had spurred American policy-makers to rethink their approach to Asia. The potential setbacks that the United States faced in the region were stated bluntly in the light of the close Sino-Soviet relationship and the considerable friction between the supposed allies of the Americans. The NSC's Planning Board warned of the need to recognize the 'vulnerability of the non-Communist countries in the area militarily, and in varying degrees, politically, economically, and psychologically, to further Communist expansionist efforts'. The divisions between rival Asian states and their reluctance to forget their differences compounded these difficulties. This was hampering attempts to 'combine their collective resources for their own defense and welfare' and delaying progress towards 'a Western Pacific collective defense arrangement including the Philippines, Japan, the Republic of China and the Republic of Korea, eventually linked with the Manila pact and ANZUS'. The problems of working even incrementally towards a modified system of political and economic pan-Asianism were long to remain a huge handicap to American aspirations for closer and more responsible regionalism.

By November 1954 it was apparent that senior American planners had substantially increased their objectives for the region and yet they were still less than sanguine over how the perceived dangers to United States security could best be met. There were distinct risks that the United States might find itself taking on massive new burdens without the support of reliable and effective friends in the region. These new American responsibilities might not, it is true, be as extensive as those already accepted for the defence of Western Europe in the Cold War, but there can be little doubt that very few states indeed in the vast Asia-Pacific region greeted the United States' new roles with enthusiasm. Countries that were grateful to accept US security guarantees were generally hesitant over contributing much to these newly initialled pacts. The much heralded offshore defence chain relied almost solely on American might and resolve. Equally, the plans to create a strong regional economic link-age, with the cooperation of newly reconstructed Japan, came to little in the years immediately after the Korean War. Asia's doubts over Japan, expressed by Carlos Romulo of the Philippines in his remark to Yoshida at San Francisco, that 'We shall want some clear sign from you of spiritual contrition and renewal', underscored the vast and understandable im-balance of memory against hope. Instead the rival, developing economies of non-Communist Asia looked overwhelmingly across the Pacific to the American market and rarely considered that salvation might lie in closer integration within the region. The Achesonian rhetoric of a great crescent of vibrant new Asian economies had hardly begun to materialize in this era.

Washington's problems in Asia were worsened by continuing differ-ences with its European allies. There were, it was admitted, 'divergences on Far Eastern policy with our European allies, principally with respect to our posture toward China, which limit the extent of political and economic pressures which can be maintained against the Asian Com-munist regimes without divisive effects on the basic United States-led coalition'. The United States felt justified, however, in going it alone if attempts to bring Britain and France round to American policies for the region failed. It was necessary, in the opinion of the NSC, to persuade others that the United States' approaches were correct and to stress that 'in its Pacific role, the United States should be less influenced by its European allies than in respect to Atlantic affairs'.

The China Problem

The question of how to deal with the People's Republic of China remained the great conundrum. Beijing had not been recognized diplomatically by the United States in the months following the coming to power of Mao Tse-tung's Communist regime, and the subsequent intervention of the PLA in the Korean War had made it increasingly unlikely that this policy was about to change. However, other states, including Britain, had been quick to establish diplomatic relations with Beijing, and many of these governments were only constrained from more actively voicing their reservations over American policies towards the PRC out of fear of weakening Washington's involvement in NATO. The United States preferred instead to organize a coalition of non-Communist states that would by their collective strength force the PRC to negotiate a general settlement in the region that would be to the advantage of Washington and its allies. Central to any such arrangements would be agreement that the Nationalist government of China on Taiwan was entitled to continue in existence. It would require recognition by Beijing that there were two Chinas and that each should function as the government of the area under its control. The idea was anathema to the PRC. It was as adamant in its refusal to deal diplomatically with the United States as the Americans were in their determination not to recognize the 'Red' Chinese. The failure on both sides to work towards the establishment of diplomatic relations continued to fester. Yet by 1954 the United States hoped to be able to persuade Beijing in the future that it should accept 'the existence of two Chinas, neither of which can be wiped out without a new world war'. To illustrate its seriousness, the Eisenhower administration worked to build a defence arrangement with Taiwan and its offshore islands, making it apparent that any aggression would be met with force. 'The military forces of the Nationalists', American planners noted in November 1953, 'constitute the only readily available strategic reserve in the Far East and as such assist in discouraging the Chinese Communists from further military adventures'. It was undeniable that the Nationalist troops might be ageing and beset by factionalism but they were still 'a valuable deterrent force'.

From 1949 onwards the United States had also instituted severe trade restrictions on the new Chinese government which were intended to dent its overseas commercial relations. They served additionally to remind the PRC yet again that Washington would only be prepared to reduce such restrictions if Beijing were to modify its stance in Asia. The embargo on American trade with the PRC and the much-resented controls placed on its allies were designed to deter Beijing from further expansion, weaken its economic position and damage the Sino-Soviet relationship. The British cabinet, concerned over the fate of the isolated redoubt of Hong Kong and still hopeful that its China trade and investments might not disappear entirely, gave only grudging support to these anti-Chinese measures. London preferred what it termed a 'selective embargo' and feared in February 1951 that overt action would increase 'China's intransigence and the risk of Chinese retaliation, particularly against Hong Kong'. Yet there remained doubts about whether such Western pressures on China would effectively undermine its existing ties to the Soviet Union, while conversely few expected that any belated reversal of this policy by offering concessions to Beijing might in its turn destroy the Communist alliance.

Consequences

The ending of the Korean War prompted a major re-evaluation of US policies for the entire Asia-Pacific region. Even before the ceasefire had been signed at Panmunjom, America's allies had been quick to encourage Washington to avoid giving the slightest hint of any possible retreat from Asia. As the Korean War ended in an unsatisfactory armistice, President Chiang Kai-shek, for example, was reported as recommending to a sympathetic Admiral Arthur Radford that 'there was great psychological need for a restatement by President Eisenhower of the determination of the United States not to abandon Asia to Communism'. Chiang's views soon proved to be a remarkably accurate survey of what transpired in the wake of the Communist Chinese intervention on the side of North Korea. The United States did indeed rush to repair and strengthen its links to the region. In a series of very public events that had commenced with the signing of the Japanese peace settlements at San Francisco in September 1951, the Asia-Pacific area was subjected to a series of bilateral military and intelligence pacts. It was hoped that a more comprehensive multilateral quilting might eventually be sewn together from these beginnings. Enhanced financial and commercial arrangements were also prepared to better integrate non-Communist Asia with its American counterpart.

Yet these American-sponsored alliances were achieved at a price. The NSC noted in the autumn of 1953 that 'the capabilities of the non-Communist Asian countries vis-à-vis the Chinese Communists are for the moment almost purely defensive'. It warned that 'the central immediate problem is the capacity of the non-Communist countries to hold against or to be assisted to hold against the political, economic, and military thrust of the Chinese Communists'. The near total reliance of American allies on the United States for military protection and economic improvement was rarely balanced by any corresponding acceptance of mutual cooperation. It was all very well for the United States to be seen to be the self-proclaimed leader of the Free World in much of Asia, but there was considerable uncertainty over whether the Americans had reason to expect genuine support from the region. Japan, for example, on whom the United States was obliged to place so many of its hopes, was simply not prepared to consider rearmament in depth during the 1950s. Even if the conservative-led Japanese cabinets had been more willing to face the domestic outcry against any substantial military build-up, there remained fierce external anger surrounding Imperial Japan's behaviour in the recent past. Prime Minister Winston Churchill personified these anxieties when he instructed his Chiefs of Staff in April 1953 that he was only 'in principle in favour of the rearmament of Japan within carefully considered limits and under United States guidance'. He fully appreciated that this policy 'might well be the only effective manner of balancing the growing power of Communist China in the next decade', but other American allies in the region were even more cautious. Chiang Kai-shek, for example, was understandably loath to see any increase in Japanese influence over American leaders and complained in June 1953 that the centrality of Taiwan's strategic and political role in the fight against Communism in East Asia was being undermined by 'placing relatively undue influence on Japan'. Among both victors and vanquished alike, memories of the Pacific War frequently complicated domestic stances on how to respond to the Cold War and made it well nigh impossible for Washington to craft a new liberal order among its highly disparate allies. Each non-Communist nation in the region looked eagerly to the United States for military and material gain, while avoiding wherever possible overmuch debate with its neighbours. The only sterling silver link that bound together the myriad offshore defence pacts and the supposed great crescent of developing economies was the power of the United States.

Since it was the United States that had acted almost unilaterally as the region's security underwriter in the years after the Korean War had erupted, it followed that the responsibility to respond in any subsequent emergency would rest very largely on that nation's shoulders. Only then would it have to make good on its hugely spreading political commitments or risk undermining the credibility of its by now global alliance systems. It was one thing for the Truman and Eisenhower administrations to devise novel programmes that criss-crossed the region and underlined their common purposes, but all too soon unpleasant and potentially costly demands began to be heard from their friends in need in Asia. The testing of the United States was set to continue.

3 Postwar: Asia-Pacific, 1953–1960

I think the Japanese were extremely fortunate to have the
Americans as their conquerors. I've always told them that, too.
Oh, they were lucky.

Sir George Sansom, 1957

In the struggle between the socialist and capitalist camps, it was no
longer the West wind that prevailed over the East wind, but the East
wind that prevailed over the West wind ... they are also divided
internally. Earthquakes are likely to occur over there.

Mao Tse-tung to Chinese students in Moscow, 17 November 1957

Vietnam is not a gift of nature.

Introduction by Tran Van Dinh to Le Duan,
This Nation and Socialism are One (Chicago, 1976)

'In terms of power, and especially of military power, China already
overshadows the area.' So began the Foreign Office's pessimistic statement on the political background to the Asia-Pacific region in the summer of 1960. In an exercise that reviewed developments since the Korean
War, British officials noted that the PRC's

> own strength is supplemented by that of the two Communist bloc satellites,
> North Korea and North Vietnam. But for the presence of Western forces, and
> especially of the strategic nuclear deterrent, the rest of the area, with the
> exceptions of Korea, Vietnam, Formosa and the Indian subcontinent (in all of
> which the indigenous forces depend largely on Western logistic support and
> Western arms and equipment), would be a military power vacuum.

In opposition to what the Foreign Office termed in the prevailing Cold
War jargon 'the free countries', there stood a formidable Communist
grouping. The Sino-Soviet bloc was assisted both by divergences of policy
between London and Washington over how best to proceed with regard
to China and by general doubts over the stability of most of the nations
that professed to be on the side of the West.

The 1950s were the high noon of Cold War international politics in the region. It was a decade marred by open conflict, brinkmanship, subversion and counter-insurgency. At the end of the decade the British view assumed that the United States would remain as it had since the end of the Pacific War as the champion of the West and its allies against what was seen as the rapid rise of China. The Foreign Office's report to the cabinet stated that the 'most nearly certain major development during the next ten years will be the continued growth of Chinese power'. London reckoned that China's burgeoning economic modernization would in all probability lead to the production of nuclear weaponry by the mid-1960s and 'the extension of their own sphere of influence' in the region.

The one consolation for British planners was the position of the United States. It was expected to remain as 'by far the most important Western provider of aid and source of influence throughout the area'. Washington, however, was judged also to be holding firm to its view that the PRC could not be trusted, though the Foreign Office made the point that the grounds for this had shifted from the original moral disapproval to blunt opposition to Chinese expansionism. This left little prospect for negotiation as the United States' policy 'has been and remains one of containment plus isolation'. The British, in turn, were ambivalent. The appreciation of American military might was evident, but the unlikelihood of the United States displaying much flexibility in policies towards the PRC remained a disappointment. Yet the consequences for the West of any faltering by the United States in its containment policies with regard to Beijing were also regarded as highly serious. In much of the Asia-Pacific region, it was underlined, there might well be defections to the Communist bloc if 'any sign of Western weakness' were in evidence.

The key to international rivalries in the region was Southeast Asia. It was here that the contest between the United States and China was to be at its most bitter in the 1950s and indeed beyond. The Foreign Office saw this rivalry as being two-faced. There was both an obvious political fight and a less transparent 'East–West struggle … reflected in prolonged economic competition'. The battle lines throughout the decade stood as they had since the Korean War, with the United States and its assortment of willing and unwilling allies continuing to be arrayed against a Sino-Soviet grouping over the future of weak and unstable regimes in Southeast Asia. It was hardly coincidental that this intensification of Great Power rivalries in Asia also reflected the gradual working out of an informal but relatively stable international system for the division of Europe. Once this had been achieved through the construction of bipolar political, military and economic structures, best exemplified in the emergence of NATO and its Warsaw pact counterpart, there was less room for confrontation on the European subcontinent. Prime Minister Harold Macmillan noted to John Foster Dulles in June 1958 that

> so long as the West did not do foolish things, the balance of military power was such as to prevent any formal, global war because of the enormous destruction that would result. Therefore the struggle between the two contending points of view represented by the Communists and ourselves would probably move from one field to another, and specifically it would move into the fields of economics and of propaganda.

Greater clarity and more frequent meetings among both the leaders and the officials of the United States and Soviet Union produced a growing recognition that the postwar borders of Europe had become fixed and that any attempt at forced change would have frightening consequences for the entire international system. As this process evolved, the Cold War intensified in Asia.

At the heart of these regional differences, following the armistice that ended the Korean War, stood the divided quasi-states of Indo-China and the small offshore islands close to China's Fujian province that had been occupied by Nationalist China as Chiang Kai-shek fled to Taiwan in 1949. The 1950s clearly saw a migration in the geographical focus of the Cold War in Asia. Once an approximately equal division of the Korean Peninsula had been reluctantly agreed on at the end of the three years of bitter fighting in 1953, the political boundaries of Northeast Asia were set. Since then the region has witnessed singularly few instances of transfer of territory and no changes over national reunification on the Korean Peninsula or Taiwan. The position with regard to Southeast Asia could hardly be more different. Here the emergence of new nation-states, massive military interventions by the Great Powers, guerrilla movements and internal political changes stand in contrast to the unchanging boundaries and regime continuities of its neighbours to the north.

Great Power Intervention and Indo-China

Indo-China's future dominated international relations in the region throughout the 1950s. It was an issue that had begun, as we have seen, with the determination of France to regain its Asian territories after the Second World War and by 1950 it had developed into an intrinsic part of the increasingly global nature of the Cold War. Yet the contestants changed during this decade. France finally quit the region it had dominated since the establishment of its rule in Cochin i.e. China in the 1860s and was promptly replaced by the United States as the upholder of Western interests. After the humiliation of French defeat in the siege of Dien Bien

Phu in 1954 and the international settlement at Geneva that partitioned Vietnam along the 17th parallel, it was the United States that moved to centre stage. Its long apprenticeship as the prompter and paymaster to Paris was now over. France could not have lingered so long without substantial support from the United States. However much successive governments in the French Fourth Republic might have wished to use Indo-China to underline their nation's claims to being a postwar Great Power, little would have been possible without foreign financial, military and logistical aid. The United States was first the treasurer and then the outright successor to French colonialism in the region.

The seeds of American involvement were sown in the mid-1940s when the Truman administration encouraged the return of the French to Indo-China. Much that was to follow in American policy most certainly predates the popular notion that the United States only found itself entrapped in the Vietnam quagmire in the early 1960s. There was, in truth, considerable continuity in thinking from the Truman years through to the Johnson era. The wish to deter Asian Communism provides a clear trail through the state papers from 1945 onwards.

The débâcle of Dien Bien Phu in 1954 clarified the public position of the United States. The end to nearly a century of French rule in Indo-China allowed the Eisenhower administration to identify more readily what it intended for the area once it was free of its awkward links to the French. The fact that for almost a decade successive presidents had been shoring up a European colonial regime could now be conveniently ignored and the justification for American support to a nominally independent government in South Vietnam made more palatable. The message of anti-Communism was now far easier to trumpet. By February 1955, for example, coherent general policies for the entire Asia-Pacific region were being prepared that were both hugely ambitious and quite free of any specific thought of the views of other powers within the area and beyond. Indeed, the context was not simply that of Asia itself but now proved even broader. Joseph Dodge, the chairman of the Council on Foreign Economic Policy, reported in January 1955 that future economic assistance for Asia 'should be regarded as only one part of the development of an over-all world program to strengthen the forces of freedom against Communist advances. This program consists of five basic elements – political, economic, military, psychological and counter-subversive, all of which are interrelated'. Dodge, who had won his spurs as the author of a major report that had successfully tackled inflation in the last years of the American occupation of Japan, adopted a long-term strategy to defeat what he described as 'the magnitude and effectiveness of Communist Bloc economic programs in Asia'. It was a case of a revitalized United States being prepared to unilaterally 'minimize the danger of increased Communist influence or domination of the free countries of Asia'.

By the early 1950s Indo-China had become central to American policies in Southeast Asia. Support for the French had been greatly increased at the time of the Korean War, both to shore up France's position and to head off fierce domestic criticism of President Truman from his opponents within the Congress and the country. It was as if the United States had suddenly discovered Indo-China in 1949–50 and simultaneously reckoned that it knew how the region might win its salvation. The panacea was to be money. It quickly became, as we have seen, the accepted view that Indo-China required generous financial and economic support. This funding could then be converted where necessary into military materiel, with which the French might hold the line in Southeast Asia. What had altered within Washington was not so much the government's perception of Indo-China but a new willingness to commit itself to a far more active role. Acting Secretary of State Dean Acheson had noted in December 1946 that a 'Communist-dominated, Moscow-oriented Indochina' ought to be opposed by the United States; four years on and Acheson could now, as Secretary of State, substantiate those earlier comments and support 'the non-Communist elements in Vietnam'.

Yet the policy soon collapsed. For France and its friends in Vietnam, substantial American aid to Indo-China coincided with the unhappy period known simply as the attempted 'Bao Dai solution'. This granting of pseudo-independence to Vietnam through the use of the former Emperor Bao Dai failed as it never began to satisfy nationalist sentiment. What these postwar years did demonstrate, however, was a mounting American involvement in Indo-China and a wish to encourage the succession of French cabinets of the Fourth Republic to work towards some form of serious accommodation with Vietnamese opinion.

This goal was difficult at best and probably little short of impossible. France feared that any concessions to the Viet Minh would undermine Paris' colonial policies in north and equatorial Africa, which in turn risked leading to the collapse of the nation's resolve to be seen as a restored Great Power. The Truman administration wished to shore up the French position in Indo-China, while hoping to avoid the direct criticism from outsiders that inevitably accrued to France as it became entangled in a dirty colonial war. The United States hoped against hope that a solution might be found that could accommodate both its European ally and those Vietnamese who stubbornly pressed on for full, unqualified independence. There was optimistic American talk of letting Indo-China join the French Union on the understanding that it would be permissible for Vietnamese nationalists to withdraw from the scheme at a later date, but this could never begin to gain French governmental approval. For

France, its union with Indo-China and, of course, its wider empire was intended to provide bonds that could not be severed. The French state and its territories overseas were viewed as component parts of the same republic, with shared policies and representation in Paris.

The United States became increasingly involved in these debates from 1949 onwards, not least because the fall of the Kuomintang in China and the domestic political furore associated with Senator McCarthy had made it highly dangerous to be seen to be offering concessions to Communist regimes overseas. Washington welcomed the Bao Dai experiment as a means of draining off the expansion of China and its Communist poison from within the Asia-Pacific region. France could consider itself fortunate that the United States came to its rescue in Indo-China, since there was simply no prospect of Paris funding further large-scale war unilaterally in the early 1950s. France's casualties were growing, its army badly needed new equipment, and public unease was evident. The buckling on of Cold War armour throughout Asia by the United States was to sustain the French in Indo-China for the next half-decade.

Yet in the end the result was the same. France was given time and money but eventually had to accept a defeat that was merely postponed by American support and largesse. Initially French officials were defiant. Jean Letourneau, minister responsible for Indo-China, told *Le Monde* in April 1950 that

> France does not intend to let her sons be killed in Indochina like mercenaries without any recognition of the task she is accomplishing. France has the right to speak out clearly in the knowledge of the justice of her cause. If this is not understood, France will have no alternative but to leave to others the defence of positions which are of vital importance to the whole free world.

But it was far from easy for the United States and France to reach an approximate agreement on policy for the subregion. Even the 'Bao Dai solution' was widely seen as more of an American than a French programme, since French officials were intent on restricting the autonomy of the nominal leader of Vietnam. If Bao Dai had really expected that the French would grant his country full independence he was soon to be disappointed. He reportedly told the American chargé at Saigon in June 1950 that he had no budgetary powers and was seen to be thoroughly demoralized. It would appear unlikely, however, that the US government was taken in by the French and it is surely sensible to assume that the State Department was prepared to overlook the unkept promises of full independence for Indo-China. The United States preferred to place Vietnam within the wider context of deterring Communist aggression in Southeast Asia and the unprecedented measures being taken by France towards greater economic and political integration in Western Europe.

The Truman administration was fully aware of the strains on France and its national resources caused by the inconclusive and prolonged war in Indo-China. Statements made to the NSC in August 1952 stressed that Asian nationalism would continue to contest the claims of all remaining colonial powers. The NSC identified Indo-China as the critical area where, it bluntly warned, 'an increase of strength has enabled the French Union to stand off the communists but has not brought them within sight of success'. Yet neither the United States nor Britain could envisage a way forward that might assist the French and sway at least some of the Vietnamese nationalists. Bao Dai's return from the Riviera to his homeland made little difference, since neither side in Indo-China took him seriously or reckoned that he was in a position to greatly influence policy. The idea that Bao Dai might siphon off Vietnamese elements from Ho Chi Minh was thought improbable in London. The Foreign Office reported in November 1950 that 'the French have taken great military risks since the war, without comparable political risks, and when real political concessions are made, it may again be the old story of too little and too late'. In other Asian capitals the response was even less flattering to the French. Prime Minister Nehru, for example, in New Delhi refused even to recognize the Bao Dai regime, seeing it as merely a puppet government. Senior British officials on the ground were more optimistic than diplomats in London, but time and again the message from Western sources was similar. The long-term future of the West's interests in Southeast Asia, it was maintained, rested on defeating the opposition in Indo-China. Malcolm MacDonald, the British Special Commissioner for the region, stressed, in language identical to that found in countless State Department files, that Chinese Communism was a formidable threat not only to Indo-China but also to Malaya, Thailand, Indonesia and Burma. Under the circumstances there appeared few options but to support the French and their policies.

Since the British had major difficulties in suppressing Communism in Malaya and faced the possibility of either a Chinese invasion of Hong Kong or of internal subversion in the territory, it was left to the United States to provide concrete measures to bolster the French position in Indo-China. From 1950 onwards Washington moved closer to involvement in Indo-China out of recognition that France could no longer fight on without massive assistance. The Policy Planning Staff in Washington judged that neither Paris nor London possessed the 'political and economic capacity to maintain' their commitments to NATO or to territories overseas. Thus Paul Nitze, the director of the PPS, reckoned in July 1952 that a serious reassessment of American policies was called for to better match the new balance of global forces. Yet the United States could hardly escape the dilemma of how to strengthen its ties to France without alienating Vietnamese opinion or being able to persuade the American public to take on fresh burdens. President Truman tellingly reminded the National Security Council in September 1952 that 'it was extremely difficult to get the American people to realize the increased size of our responsibility' in areas where Britain and France were no longer able to sustain their power.

Much, however, was done. Members of the PPS could point out in the autumn of 1952 that Indo-China had deservedly gained American priority in the region, though it acknowledged that the situation was felt unlikely to progress beyond what it predicted would be 'political and military stalemate' by the mid-1950s. The advent of the new Eisenhower administration, following the loss of the White House by the Democrats after two decades in power, did not greatly alter the Asia-Pacific policies adopted in the last years of the Truman presidency. Secretary of State John Foster Dulles, who had finally obtained the post he had long coveted, was quick to inform the NSC in March 1953 that there would be no relaxation over maintaining 'the vital outpost positions around the periphery of the Soviet bloc'. Dulles, clearly speaking after consultation with Eisenhower, insisted that there must be no repetition of 'the fuzzy situation', which he felt had been an open invitation for Soviet-led aggression towards South Korea in 1950. For Dulles it was a case of defending both America's Asian redoubts and NATO, since 'the loss of any one of such positions would produce a chain reaction which would cost us the remainder'. Clearly the now fashionable Asian domino thesis was being extended globally and the objective was 'to avoid losses of key positions to the Communists, who won't themselves invite a global war, but who will stand ready to pick off all the choice positions offered to them locally by "civil wars"'.

On the ground, however, the French were weakening and the prospects for the continuation of French rule appeared bleak. If the Indo-Chinese situation were not to deteriorate further, more would now have to be forthcoming from outsiders. Yet divisions appeared between allies and among the military and civilian heads of the American establishment over what might constitute an effective policy. The talk of providing 'major assistance to France and Indochina to effect a favourable solution to the Indochinese war' had now to move from the easy generalities of staff reports to the more difficult and potentially dangerous stage of concrete action. American lives could be at risk. By the summer of 1953 the tone of NSC assessments had altered and a new urgency and pessimism is apparent. There was now 'a great danger that France, contemplating the eventual loss of her present position in Indochina, will lose the will to continue that costly war'. The onus was on the United States to strengthen French resolve and to gain its cooperation 'at the highest political level'. The issue was seen to be as much between France and the United States as the fight against Communism in Southeast Asia. What was proposed was greater military and economic aid from Washington in exchange for specific French agreements on the direction of the war. The United States' involvement in Vietnam was growing as it shuffled out of the distant stands onto the edge of the field. The spectator was about to become a player.

Greater attention was now placed on precise political objectives. The NSC staff began with the statement 'insist on full independence for Indochinese states by February 1954' and then added the rider that this should lead next to 'affiliation with French Union, as the best safeguard against Communist encroachment after independence'. Instead of waiting patiently for France to move beyond the Union to independence for Indo-China, the process was to be reversed. It was also hoped that economic support and a military alliance in conjunction with 'a regional pact involving other states of Southeast Asia and the Southwest Pacific' could be devised, after 'outright victory in Indochina' had been gained.

All this was premised, of course, on success on the battlefield. Yet the Eisenhower administration's concern that the French never appeared to be quite ready to start the final offensive continued to scupper the long-term political arrangements. Indo-China could hardly be expected to join the interlocking chain of other American outposts in the region, if the military situation failed to improve. This in turn hinged on success in Vietnam, which would have required the training of more pro-French Vietnamese forces and substantial American aid to engage secure Viet Minh positions along the Red River delta of northern Vietnam. France had certainly committed tens of thousands of troops, though, as in its interventions of the 1860s, it was again noticeable that the bulk were Africans officered by French regulars; Churchill pointed out from London that the French people themselves were not prepared to do the dying. Indo-China appeared to be important for the free world but it was largely French colonial troops and graduates from St Cyr and the Sorbonne who had the misfortune to be called upon to defend the West's interests.

Under these circumstances, it was never likely to envisage direct American or British military intervention in support of France in Indo-China. The opportunity to do so was rejected once the US government refused at the critical moment to despatch paratroops or consider bombing with a lethal combination of napalm and tactical nuclear weapons, unless the British would also agree to join in. The result was the failure to lift the siege of Dien Bien Phu, the obscure and badly sited air strip near the Laotian border. This was to prove the greatest defeat in French colonial history since the loss of Quebec, and to signal the end to French rule in Indo-China. Yet from the autumn of 1953 the United States had been forced to reckon with either outright French defeat or the only slightly more palatable thought of the Indo-Chinese Associated States staggering on with some outside help. The NSC meeting of 13 October had been warned that General Navarre's plan 'may be the last French effort in Indochina. Should it fail to achieve its objectives we believe that, unless the US proves willing to contribute forces, the French will in time seek to negotiate directly with the Communists for the best possible terms'.

These predictions came true the following year. The French finally lost their war and the Americans watched with disappointment as the diplomatic endgame unfolded in Geneva. The two events were connected, since the Viet Minh had launched their offensive against General Navarre's men in order to gain leverage at the international conference called in response to peace feelers that had originated through an enterprising Swedish journalist. French opinion had been divided over whether this was an appropriate action, since it clearly implied the abandonment of Bao Dai's government, but once the military situation soured there was little domestic will left for continuing against Ho Chi Minh and his generals.

The Geneva conference is often described as one of Foreign Secretary Anthony Eden's triumphs. Certainly he worked astutely to convene and then negotiate at length between all parties, but it took more than one man to produce an agreement. The Soviet Union also played a useful role and the eventual arrangement to divide Vietnam was the work of many hands. What is more certain than the authorship of these arrangements is the defiance displayed by the United States towards all attempts to provide for a radically changed situation in Indo-China. Dulles disliked the whole concept and refused to attend in person, though, in fairness, there were similar attitudes within the French delegation. Georges Bidault, the Prime Minister of a badly divided nation that could not agree on whether to quit Indo-China or stay and defiantly fight on, felt that the Vietnamese representative at Geneva should not even be spoken to. Bidault stated that to do so would have been a waste of time, since Pham Van Dong 'had only one aim: to kick us out of the door'. To complicate matters further, the French government itself fell and Bidault was replaced by Mendes-France as premier in mid-June – though it may well be that portions of what would eventually form the final accord had been discussed unofficially at least before the defeat of the seemingly intransigent Bidault.

The Geneva settlements were a compromise that evolved out of French military defeat in Indo-China and the refusal of the United States to provide the last-minute military aid that might have saved Dien Bien

Phu. In essence both the United States and the Soviet Union wished to avoid a Great Power confrontation in Southeast Asia and were prepared to make concessions to this end. Much of what followed had been made possible by the Eisenhower administration's refusal to order aerial bombing from carrier-based planes against the Viet Minh as they rallied to capture Diem Bien Phu; this was later described graphically as 'the day we did not go to war'. Dulles certainly sulked in his tent over the outcome, but the protracted agreement to partition Vietnam at the 17th parallel was assumed to be final. It was heartily disliked by both of the new Vietnamese regimes, yet pressure from the Sino-Soviet bloc had ensured that Ho Chi Minh sign up to the ceasefire agreements for Vietnam, Laos and Cambodia. After a decade of bloodshed, it appeared that Indo-China at last had the opportunity to enjoy a period of peace. Intervention by outside parties had seemingly manufactured arrangements that ought to hold. Commentators drew comparisons with the similar divisions of Germany and Korea, suggesting that this compromise solution to Indo-China's problems had left the world one less international issue with which to concern itself.

Yet despite the cautious welcome given to the Geneva documents, it was not to be. The considerable pressure that had been applied by Britain, France and the Soviet Union during the negotiations had brought a comprehensive ceasefire and redrawn the political map of what until the mid-1950s could be termed Indo-China – but at a price. President Eisenhower was quoted as saying in July 1954 that since the United States had not been a party to the Geneva agreements it was 'not bound by them'. The 'loss' of the northern half of Vietnam could be seen by critics in Washington as yet another humiliation at the hands of global Marxist-Leninist forces and a dangerous precedent for an already unstable Southeast Asia. The fact that Eden had achieved a diplomatic success at Geneva was also a personal nightmare for Secretary Dulles, who had expected before the final event that the British 'would be able to pass as the peacemakers and go-between for east and west'. The idea of the British foreign secretary returning from Geneva waving a piece of paper and declaiming 'peace in our time' was a major setback for Dulles. The two men did not get on and Eden for his part never forgave Dulles for apparently double-crossing him over the Japanese peace treaty negotiations.

The American administration feared for the future and attempted to support the new regime in South Vietnam. The Joint Chiefs of Staff had warned Secretary of Defense Charlie Wilson in April of the consequences for the military of 'Chinese overt intervention in Indochina' and noted that the 'indigenous forces' of the Asia-Pacific region stood in obvious inferiority to their Communist counterparts. In a sober assessment,

Admiral Radford wrote of the ominous prospects for the West under such circumstances. The goals of the United States ought therefore to include the encouragement of collective self-help among its friends in the region to engender 'a local counterbalance' to the growing power of the PRC. Yet it remained unclear how the United States would respond to Chinese action in Southeast Asia, particularly if it were of a subversive nature that would necessarily preclude the mounting of an open show of coalition force.

The question of how best to strengthen the United States' ties to the region remained to be solved. The fact that Eisenhower and Dulles had refused to send US marines or paratroopers to support their friends in Vietnam obviously underlined the immediate limits to American policy, but the call for tougher measures was heeded. The United States was not prepared to abandon South Vietnam, nor would it wish to be seen to be cowering in its bunker. To demonstrate political resolve, the administration went on the offensive. Eisenhower saw the improvement of regional collective security arrangements with its Asia-Pacific partners as a means of both demonstrating resolve and, equally importantly from the President's domestic perspective, the only tactic that would win Congressional approval in an emergency. Eisenhower wanted 'to be sure that someone was ready to go along with the United States in the event of open unprovoked Chinese communist aggression'. Allied assistance could then help disguise what would inevitably be very largely an American show. The objective, Eisenhower said bluntly to his advisers on 2 June 1954, was 'to keep the Pacific as an American lake'.

The formation of an alliance structure in the region followed from American objectives. It was, however, difficult to corral friends together and to demonstrate to opponents that a pro-Western grouping might have substantial strength in the making. The United States saw that Communist elements had not only won power in North Vietnam but were intent on control of the supposedly independent new states of Laos and Cambodia, as well as working through liberation movements elsewhere. Much that US planners had been forecasting for nearly a decade was apparent by the mid-1950s, yet the American response was still relatively muted. President Eisenhower hoped for allies but knew from State Department papers in November 1954 that the situation in Southeast Asia was 'extremely precarious'. The creation of the Manila pact, signed by the United States, Britain, France, Australia, New Zealand, the Philippines, Thailand and Pakistan in September 1954, did little to disguise the recent disappointments over Indo-China. SEATO was overwhelmingly Western in membership and could not attract such important Asian states as Indonesia and Burma to its ranks. While it might at least show outsiders that the United States was to remain committed to the region, it was clearly structured as a reaction to recent disappointments. Over such events, the post-mortems differed. While some felt that the success of Ho Chi Minh was due to 'the lack of courage of our allies', acrimonious debate in the National Security Council, invariably chaired by a forceful Eisenhower, could hardly alter the political realities. What had been clearly dented, however, was American prestige, and the administration appeared divided over what should be done to repair the position. Secretary Dulles cited Vietnam and Finland as instances where the United States might warn the Soviet Union unequivocally that any attempt at annexation would result in war. Moments later, however, the Secretary of State would tell the NSC that the Indo-Chinese states were 'not really of great significance to us'.

For the remainder of the 1950s relatively little was done by the United States to create a substantial collective structure. It elected instead to strengthen individual countries on the assumption that the prospects for true regionalism were slim. Attention was concentrated on the now familiar type of assorted political, military and economic policies that might shore up and sustain vulnerable states. For South Vietnam, defined somewhat improbably as Free Vietnam in initial documents, this meant an endorsement of the regime headed by Ngo Dinh Diem that had come to power at the end of the first Indo-China War. Diem had an uncomfortable inheritance. His country – it would be absurd to speak confidently of any such entity as the nation of South Vietnam in 1954 – was poor, uncertain of its relations with outside powers and faced with a huge influx of refugees from the north, who had scrambled across the border to avoid Ho's home-made brand of nationalism and Communism.

Diem needed the United States and it soon became apparent that the United States would have little choice but to support him. His ruthlessness against rivals and his long-established reputation for being vehemently both anti-Communist and anti-French were held to be good signs. Diem began by making certain that Bao Dai was quickly removed and the monarchy abolished through a rigged referendum, while simultaneously Ho Chi Minh came at last into his inheritance in Hanoi. Both the new leaders who had replaced the departing French now had to wrestle with attempting to create viable societies and adequate economic systems for countries wracked by a decade of war and uncertain of foreign assistance. Reconstruction was inevitably the shared primary goal of Ho and Diem, though their political means and policy achievements were to prove highly disparate.

During his exile in the United States in the early 1950s, Diem had attempted to persuade American Congressional and Catholic leaders that he was the man best equipped to revitalize Vietnam. American sources now began to talk of the 'Diem Solution' to the hurdles facing the nominally independent state of South Vietnam. The phrase, of course, conveyed echoes of the unlamented Bao Dai era, but the Eisenhower administration reckoned that Diem had some prospect of success. Yet there was immediate disagreement from members of the National Security Council over the wisdom of appearing to be granting protection to the new South Vietnamese government. Secretary of the Treasury Humphrey, for example, flayed Dulles for even suggesting that the United States might fight to safeguard either South Vietnam or the offshore islands between Taiwan and the PRC. American resources were not infinite, Humphrey maintained, and as he put it, 'we can't do everything for everybody at the same time'. Humphrey fiercely disagreed with Eisenhower over the need to defend allies around the globe. Arguing that it made better sense to limit commitments, he was reported as saying that 'since we will eventually get pushed out of certain areas, would we not be better off if we withdrew from places like Indochina before we were actually pushed out?'

Unlike some of his successors, President Eisenhower listened to his cabinet. He concluded, as might have been expected, by finding a middle ground between those who would pull back and those who wished to stand firm. In the case of Southeast Asia the administration chose to honour existing alliance promises but to act cautiously with regard to instituting new ones. Eisenhower was not about to retreat from Taiwan's offshore islands or announce ringing new support for South Vietnam. Chiang Kai-shek had earned his credentials; Diem had yet to do so. Eisenhower agreed with Humphrey's view that 'we should not make binding treaties with the nations of South[east] Asia', but he was certainly not about to refuse assistance to anti-Communist regimes in the region. Eisenhower did not wish for his country to be 'an Atlas, bearing the weight of the world', yet he was prepared to offer judicious amounts of aid.

The recent unhappy experience of the United States in Indo-China, however, was not immediately forgotten, and the scale of American assistance to South Vietnam during the remainder of the 1950s was relatively limited. This was partly because of the need for Diem to demonstrate his worth and partly through the eclipse of attention on South Vietnam by more pressing issues in the region. The future appeared to be contingent on American–South Vietnamese cooperation, which in turn rested on the efforts of Saigon to prove its worth as a country that might find some salvation through good works and a degree of national unity. The State Department reported to Dulles at the start of the Bangkok meeting of SEATO in February 1955: 'Doubts that existed with respect to Diem have been resolved in his favour. If he were to collapse it is too late to think of any successor. There is good hope however that free Vietnam can be saved from Communist domination'. Yet this prognosis remained severely qualified by both domestic and external realities. The United States had to yet to assist in the building of 'an effective army loyal to the independent government of Vietnam', the position of Chinese minorities in the country was unclear, and the larger issue of American security stances for the entire region had also to be thrashed out. For the present, though, Washington put consideration of long-term commitments to South Vietnam on hold as it faced more pressing issues in East Asia.

The Taiwan Crises, 1954–58

From its intervention in the Korean War onwards, the People's Republic of China was seen by the United States as the greatest danger to the Asia-Pacific region. Throughout the 1950s American leaders spoke out repeatedly against what Dulles defined in 1955 as the 'expansionist ambitions' of Beijing. Dulles told the Manila pact members that the Sino-Communist bloc was on the move and that the combination of Russia and China represents 'enormous power' deployed through gaining 'control of governments and then [assuring] planned coordinated action'. To safeguard the more vulnerable pro-Western states, Dulles offered two assurances. The first, not surprisingly, was the active support of the United States and the second was the consolation that the PRC faced the risk of having to fight on more than one front in any regional emergency. Dulles invariably reckoned that subversion was more likely to be the Chinese way of warfare, but he could underline to his audiences that if it were to come to outright conflict in Southeast Asia, Beijing would be at a huge disadvantage. The PRC, Dulles suggested, would then have to throw its forces against the 'anti-Communist potential' in the region and beyond, citing both the might of Chiang Kai-shek and the availability of massive American forces that exceeded those deployed in the Pacific War.

Taiwan was regarded by the Eisenhower administration as a vital, if difficult, ally. It was important militarily because of its estimated 300 000 troops in the field and important politically as a symbol of anti-Beijing resistance. The fact that it had strong, loyal and vocal friends in the US Congress only added to its status as a pro-American bastion worthy of succour, though not even Dulles wished in reality to 'unleash' the KMT forces against its continental opponents. Taiwan might appear to others as little more than a vulnerable island outpost which, in addition, claimed possession of a number of small contested islets less than a dozen miles from the Chinese mainland. While critics might question whether this was worth the scale of commitment afforded by the Eisenhower cabinet, these doubts did little to prevent the continuation of massive US support.

The two regional crises of the mid and late 1950s over the offshore islands in the Taiwan Straits held defiantly by the Nationalist government illustrate the degree of sustenance on offer. When in December 1954 George Humphrey spoke up strongly against the continuation of American support to Taiwan's vulnerable Quemoy and Matsu islands, Eisenhower simply smiled at his advisers and, as the official transcript laconically notes, 'the President invited Secretary Humphrey to "take on"

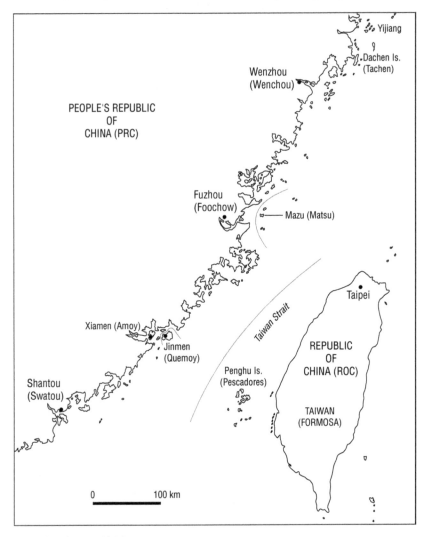

The Taiwan Straits crisis, 1954-55
Based on Gordon H. Chang, 'Nuclear Brink: Eisenhower, Dulles and the Quemoy-Matsu Crisis', International Security, *12(4): 23.*

Chang Kai-shek'. Taipei felt that it could count on the United States. What it could not know, of course, was the extent to which the administration would back up its frequent professions of commitment and its high level of anti-Communist rhetoric. The President's refusal to send bombers and then marines into Indo-China in April 1954, when France came literally begging for immediate and massive support, might have served to remind some among Chiang's entourage of Eisenhower's possible hesitancy to act. The President, when it suddenly became Taiwan's turn to experience a major Cold War crisis, responded in much the same manner as he had over Dien Bien Phu.

The first Taiwan Straits affair has close parallels with the United States' handling of the last phase of the first Indo-China War. The offshore islands claimed and therefore garrisoned by Taiwan were perilously close to the South China coast. It followed that the PLA could shell Quemoy and Matsu at will, as and when it wished to draw attention to Beijing's trumpeting of sovereignty over the entire Chinese subcontinent – and indeed its dissatisfaction with Taiwan's very existence. Any attacks might also be the prelude to the much more serious prospect of a possible invasion of Taiwan, though the amphibian capabilities of the Chinese military were usually dismissed as amateurish. (The offshore islands could also, as a sympathetic Admiral Radford informed the NSC in September 1954, be used 'as a jumping-off post for a Nationalist invasion of the mainland'.) Chinese scholars now tell us that the objective was to move 'from small to large, one island at a time, from north to south, and from weak to strong'. This reflected a growing Chinese confidence after considerable, though terribly bloody, military success in Korea; it was a calculated ploy to probe at the weakest points held by Taiwan and thereby test the resolve of the United States and attempt to discourage a proposed US–Taiwan defence treaty. The issue, as so often in this decade, hinged on how Washington would respond to what, by the mid-1950s, appeared to be a regular crop of Asian troubles. President Eisenhower's advisers were divided on the question.

The diplomatic moves made by the United States also had parallels with its recent attempts to gain allied support in Indo-China. Once again it hoped that Britain would be willing to assist and that the United Nations could assume responsibility for finding an amicable solution, though Eisenhower was far from clear on which of the raft of political and military options he personally preferred. Events quickly limited his predilection for ambiguity. In January 1955 the northernmost Dazhen islands came under heavy fire and had to be evacuated. The United States quietly withdrew Taiwanese military and civilian personnel but began to reckon with the use of atomic weapons if the PLA were to advance further and next attack Quemoy. It was a confusing period of mixed indecision and resoluteness that ended fortunately in April 1955 when the PRC called for a peaceful solution. The Eisenhower administration was relieved, since it disliked the prospect of defending Chiang Kai-shek's outermost islands when it knew it would be impossible to gain effective domestic or overseas support.

The crisis worked to the advantage of the Nationalists on Taiwan. It won increased backing from the United States in the shape of a prized Mutual Defense Treaty with Washington and was seen, at least by its friends abroad, as being entitled to enhanced protection from PLA bullying. Indeed, Chiang used the second Straits crisis of 1958 to proclaim Taiwan's willingness to fight on alone and stated his public refusal to withdraw from Quemoy and Matsu. Chiang's behaviour could only remind observers of similar bombastic statements from South Korea's Syngman Rhee when he too risked being left isolated by Washington. Eisenhower, for his part, spoke of the psychological damage of retreat. He had lectured his advisers earlier on wishing to avoid drawing lines in the sand around the globe, since this would then permit all of the United States' opponents to know in advance where the administration would stand firm and where it might withdraw under the threat of force. Yet it can hardly be claimed that the administration appeared either strong or coherent over its handling of the Taiwan Straits crises. Eisenhower had no wish to go to war over the defence of the offshore islands and left Chiang in no doubt that the US–Taiwan treaty did not cover any such contingencies. The PRC was able to provoke the American eagle and then retire with impunity from its menacing claws. Mao Tse-tung had apparently wished to caution the United States that China's role in the recent solution of major issues in the Asia-Pacific, such as the Korean armistice arrangements and the Geneva conference over Indo-China, did not imply Beijing's acceptance of an evolving American order in the region. The Taiwan Straits crises may well have been initiated by Mao to signal his impatience with American backing for Taiwan and the system of pan-Asian alliances then being constructed to secure US interests. Mao had told Chou En-lai in July 1954 that it was more than time to 'announce to our country and to the world the slogan of the liberation of Taiwan' in order to disrupt 'the collaboration between the United States and Chiang, and to keep them from joining military and political forces'. It has been suggested by Chinese scholars that Mao hoped in the first instance to draw international attention to the iniquities of Taiwan's status, but having achieved this initial goal he made some serious miscalculations. The United States did indeed immediately assist the Taiwanese military and, since Mao was neither prepared nor willing to risk a second major Sino-American confrontation so soon after Korea, he had little option but to halt operations.

The People's Republic of China also discovered in 1955 that the Eisenhower administration was seriously considering the use of nuclear weapons to deter any prospective invasion of Quemoy and Matsu, though this, in its turn, further spurred Beijing forward in its drive to acquire a nuclear capability. The NSC minutes indicate that the President, clearly buoyed up by his success in gaining a settlement on the Korean Peninsula through the threat of atomic bombings, was almost gung-ho at the prospect of a similar *démarche* over the offshore islands. Yet the administration was also left in no doubt that other nations did not share its concern for defending the Taiwan Straits positions. Britain, for example, held that a distinction needed to be drawn between standing firm over Taiwan and going to the brink for some obscure outposts that were militarily and politically unimportant. The United States was once again almost friendless but once again remained adamant that no concessions were to be offered to Beijing over any relaxation of existing policies. Taiwan was still the government of China in American eyes, and neither the United States nor the PRC was capable of shifting the views of the other during the Geneva ambassadorial talks that were held from 1955 to 1957 to promote the opening of Sino-American dialogue. The bombardment of Quemoy and Matsu in 1958 by China demonstrated only too clearly that there had been little movement between the adversaries and that confrontation rather than negotiation would again be attempted to secure Beijing's objectives.

The second Taiwan Straits crisis was designed to gain what the PLA had failed to acquire in the earlier engagement. This time the aim was to conquer Quemoy and Matsu themselves, and as in 1954–55, the hope was that differences between Taipei and Washington would work to China's advantage. This proved to be a miscalculation. While most certainly aware of the potential dangers of possible overreaction or misunderstandings in its dealings with Chiang Kai-shek, the Eisenhower administration ordered a massive show of naval force in the area. It was clear to all that these nuclear reinforcements were designed for use, if there were to be an escalation of the crisis. Eisenhower, as we have seen from earlier NSC debates, held that possession and deployment of nuclear weaponry was invariably regarded by all parties to be to the United States' great advantage, if the administration judged that crucial national interests were at risk. Certainly this view stands confirmed in the light of the intense diplomatic activity adopted by the Soviet Union in its efforts to defuse the situation. While not wishing to be seen to have defaulted over the Sino-Soviet security pact of 1950, the Russian leadership worked behind the scenes to persuade Mao Tse-tung to desist.

Employing a major shift in his readings of the contemporary international situation, Mao suddenly discovered in September 1958 that the former perils of possible attack and encirclement by the United States and its Asia-Pacific allies on China's borders were now at an end. This highly convenient ideological change implied that Sino-American confrontation was a thing of the past and that future world events would hinge on the intensifying competition between the major powers for political and economic supremacy in the Third World. Linked to this assessment was the PRC's decision to talk to the United States in the slight hope that Eisenhower might be able to persuade Chiang to withdraw from Quemoy and Matsu. Beijing insisted on its homely metaphor that 'nobody likes to lie down next to someone who snores', but eventually Mao decided that there would be no invasion of the offshore islands. The PRC could claim with some justification to have severely embarrassed the United States by showing up the dilemmas it faced in dealing with its Taiwanese ally, yet the weaknesses of China's military hand were also plain to see.

Sino-American relations form the uncomfortable backbone to much of the international power rivalry within the Asia-Pacific region during the 1950s. Throughout this decade, planners in Washington continued to voice their concerns over both the strengths of the PLA and the additional weight of the Sino-Soviet military and ideological alliance of 1950. This led some US officials to argue that a fracturing of the relationship through friendlier ties with Beijing deserved to be considered. Chinese Communist activities from intervention in the Korean War onwards led to the United States engineering a series of bilateral mutual security pacts on the edges of the region. Each side felt that its alliance arrangements were defensive structures designed to deter the other camp. In November 1953 the NSC argued that while the potential for 'Non-Communist Asia' might be considerable in the future, it remained the case in the 1950s and beyond that it would 'continue to require Western protection against Communist military attack'. Yet the strengths of the American-led coalition have to be questioned. On paper the American and allied power projections appear impressive, yet it is possible to exaggerate the US commitment to the region. When it came to deciding, for example, whether to grant emergency military support to France in their moment of desperation at Dien Bien Phu, Eisenhower and his advisers refused support. This confirmed the prediction contained in the message sent by Churchill to Eisenhower in June 1954, where the Prime Minister had bluntly ruled out British intervention in Indo-China. He added that 'if we were asked our opinion we would advise against United States local intervention except for rescue [of American citizens]'.

American allies within the Asia-Pacific region shared similar anxieties over the correlation between troop deployments and the exercise of power. In particular, the two key pro-American leaders in the area continued to harbour doubts over the extent of the United States' readiness to risk combat in the shared defence of proclaimed goals. Indeed, the cynic can hardly avoid recognizing that the Eisenhower administration was often more concerned to restrain Chiang Kai-shek and Syngman Rhee from sabre-rattling than to assist in their pipedreams of national reunification. Given these concerns over the trigger-happy tendencies of the two most formidable of America's allies, it is not surprising that Eisenhower found it difficult to calibrate his responses to regional crises. The results were politically unsatisfactory when measured against the Cold War rhetoric of the era and yet adequate in that the United States had avoided direct military confrontation with the PRC and could still claim to have stood its ground. In the process it was clear to all parties that there was relatively little allied unity. There was a pronounced tendency for Washington to determine policy by itself and to ignore views of others that might diverge from its own. This uni-lateralism, while understandable given the relative weakness of each one of its regional partners, would shortly afterwards lead to a series of extra-ordinary decisions in Southeast Asia and to eventual hubris.

The British and the Region

The 1950s mark the final decade of Britain's lengthy involvement as a Great Power in the Asia-Pacific region. It proved to be a period of hasty retreat from past colonial responsibilities and it saw a drastic weakening of British influence over the many political issues that beset the new states of Southeast Asia and the re-emerging old nations beyond Indo-China. The granting of independence to Malaya in the summer of 1957 and the refusal to remain involved in Indo-China after 1954, as the terms of its co-chairmanship of the Geneva Conference implied, serve as key markers to this irrevocable decline. Prime Minister Harold Macmillan had readily acknowledged in July 1957 that nationalism represented 'a tidal wave surging from Asia across the ocean to the shores of Africa'. The British transfer of power to the newly independent state of Malaya in the following month confirmed this international reality.

The British had hoped to avoid the fate of their fellow Europeans in Southeast Asia. Initially, as we have seen, Britain's intention had been to return in 1945 and postpone measures to introduce anything beyond circumscribed local autonomy for its territories. Since all plans, however, were contingent on events on the ground, the returning British adminis-trators quickly discovered the strengths of both Asian nationalism and the might of local Communism. This combination, as the French had finally to acknowledge by mid-decade, could prove lethal. To combat the spread of Communism on the Malay Peninsula, the British conducted a lengthy, expensive and ultimately successful counter-insurgency campaign. Yet these considerable accomplishments in the Emergency depended on active cooperation with the Malays, who clearly held that supporting the British forces would be the prelude to their own independence. The Communist campaign ultimately failed, but it was only after the appointment of the energetic General Sir Gerald Templer that morale improved in Kuala Lumpur and in turn generated relief in Whitehall. The winning of the Emergency required not only military effort but also political and economic reforms which gradually drained away much of the local Chinese support that had made possible the survival of the small number of Communist groups for so long. Once these counter-insurgency campaigns were shown to be successful, it was inevitable that Malaya would gain its freedom. The British hoped, not surprisingly, that this could be on terms favourable to their long-established commercial and economic interests and that the completion of a watertight defence agreement with London would further cement future Anglo-Malay ties.

Once Malaya had gained its independence, it became difficult to envisage a major regional role for Britain. Certainly it retained important military installations in Singapore, whose own position as part of the Federation of Malaya was problematic from the start, but it was difficult to see how London could assert itself much longer as a power of more than local importance. It was indeed a member of SEATO and had residual colonial responsibilities for Brunei and Hong Kong, yet the momentum was lost. Evidence contained within the Foreign Office's lengthy assessment of the political realities of the region in June 1960 spoke in the most cautious language of what might be expected of Britain in the future. The planners noted that 'United Kingdom influence on the course of events in the independent countries of the area is likely to be marginal except in the Commonwealth countries and in Nepal'. The Cabinet Office memorandum admittedly spoke of the present position, where

> we are deeply involved in this area, especially while we retain the base in Singapore, and responsibility for the defence and external relations, and as members of SEATO and Anzam, Co-chairman of the Geneva Conference, ally of Malaya, traditional adviser and recruiter of Gurkhas in Nepal, architect of the Colombo Plan, and friend of most of the governments of the area.

Yet these components hardly added up to real strength over events.

What was lacking was a more general framework and a greater influence on the policies of the United States. The continual carping between London and Washington in the Asia-Pacific region from the birth of the PRC onwards quickly marginalized hopes of a larger British performance. The consequences were spelt out frankly in the Foreign Office's assessment of June 1960. Its planners could only note that Britain can expect to retain some influence on the development of US policy towards China, on Dutch and French policies in the area (which are especially important in Indonesia and Cambodia respectively) and on Australia and New Zealand, who may come to take an increasing share of responsibility in the fields of defence and economic and technical aid.

Since little or nothing was claimed by way of British counsels towards a reviving Japan or a stronger China, the picture was clearly bleak.

Anglo-American differences were serious and continuous throughout the 1950s. President Eisenhower wrote to a revealing letter to Churchill in March 1955 that suggests how deep and apparently irreconcilable these divisions had become. He stated, in views that mirrored those of his predecessor at the time of the Korean War, that there was 'an apparent difference between our two governments that puzzles us sorely and constantly. Although we seem always to see eye to eye with you when we contemplate any European problem our respective attitudes towards similar problems in the Orient are frequently so dissimilar as to be almost mutually antagonistic'. The President continued in a rousing vein that contrasted American determination to oust Communism in Southeast Asia before it destroyed its opponents with the perception that Churchill's 'own government seems to regard Communist aggression in Asia as of little significance to the free world future'. The supine British were letting the West down and the American administration intended to remind London that it had to buck up.

Yet the problems grew. The most difficult and perennial remained the issue of China. No resolution was forthcoming over the question of recognition of the PRC, its admittance to the United Nations, or the parallel case of what to do with Taiwan. Since, as the Foreign Office stressed, 'the United States is by far the most important provider of aid and source of information throughout the area and can be expected to maintain this position', there was little that other powers might suggest to shift opinion. Britain and the United States continued to agree to disagree in a debate that left the Eisenhower administration unprepared to give ground. Any concessions to Beijing could only weaken Taipei, and that, in turn, was seen to have most damaging consequences for the maintenance of pro-Western regimes in the Asia-Pacific region. London might insist that the PRC could not simply be wished away and that it was better 'to recognize China as a fact' than to cold-shoulder a power of increasing importance for good and ill, but this was not the American stance. The only crumb of comfort for British ministers was the eventual ending of the differential trade embargo against the Chinese Communists. This had long left most of the United States' allies complaining that the economic arrangements imposed on Beijing were stricter than those on other Communist states, and Eisenhower was persuaded that it deserved to be scrapped.

The British were ambivalent over SEATO. The Churchill cabinet hoped that its membership would lead to an extension of its influence but knew that the driving force was the United States. The Committee on Future Developments in South East Asia was reminded by the Foreign Office in July 1960 that 'S.E.A.T.O. represents the first and only American commitment to the defence of the mainland of South and South East Asia. The United States of America has obligations both specific and moral, which we do not share, towards South Korea, Japan and For-mosa'. Yet given the view that both China and the Soviet Union were in agreement on expelling the West from Asia, it made sense for Britain and the United States to have an informal division of labour. For London, it was repeatedly emphasized that Malaya had priority. It was here that London was tempted to claim both success on the ground and point the way to other powers in the region. The parallels were far from exact, however, and the circumstances in Kuala Lumpur were hardly to be equated with those of Jakarta or Saigon. Certainly the Malayan counter-insurgency campaign was a political and military achievement, but the acute divisions between Malays and Chinese were not replicated else-where in postwar Southeast Asia. The numerical strength and external support of the Malay Communist Party were always small and the resources that the British were obliged to pour into winning their jungle war were huge. It also took trial and error to gain the adherence of those many Chinese who watched developments from the sidelines. Eventually an approximate cross-communal political structure incorporating Malays, Chinese and Indian elements was formalized that set the peninsula on an anti-Communist path to independence.

Malaya proved to be the exception. Elsewhere in the region social patterns were different and so too was the indigenous leadership. The British ended up with better results, but they were helped by cooperative Malays, notably the avuncular and skilful Tunku Abdul Rahman, and the almost total inability of the Communists, under the persistent former wartime guerrilla Chin Peng, to gain Malay support in the villages. In contrast to the situation that faced Ho Chi Minh, there was no rural lake in which the insurgents could swim at will. The independence of Malaya in 1957, then the combining of that state with Singapore, North Borneo and Sarawak in 1963 to form the federal structure of Malaysia, left only Brunei and Hong Kong inside the British fold in the region. The advent of Malaysia gave London some military responsibilities, but its economic strength in Southeast Asia had been deteriorating throughout the postwar period. It therefore looked to Japan to play an increasingly important role in the reconstruction and then development of an area of great potential to the Western economies. The old adversary from the Pacific War was soon seen to be winning the peace. The expansion of Japanese trade and inward investment throughout Southeast Asia would be a trend that Washington, in its turn as regional overlord, would continue to encourage.

The United States and Northeast Asia

If Malaya proved to be the country where Britain played its hand best, the record of the United States in postwar Japan warrants decidedly broader praise. From the outset the stakes over Japan were higher, the risks greater, and the eventual results were to have not merely local but global consequences. Malaya, in contrast, while an important sideshow, had little of the centrality that Japan presented to international rivalries, initially within the Asia-Pacific region and eventually far beyond. In both instances, it is noteworthy that the power claiming overall responsibility was able to get on with its policies with relatively little outside interference. MacArthur ran occupied Japan as his private fiefdom, while the British could attempt to do likewise in their Malay possessions because, unlike the Dutch and French, they were not beholden at all times to Washington for arms and aid.

Yet nothing that the British were tentatively proposing to adopt in Southeast Asia can compare with the bloodless revolution imposed on post-surrender Japan. The scale, energy and speed with which the United States attempted to transform an alien society through non-violent means has few historical precedents. Implicit in this wave after wave of constitutional, agrarian, educational and labour reform was the expectation that after the termination of the occupation Japan would continue to subscribe, albeit approximately, to the values inculcated by SCAP GHQ and remain a friend of the United States. The first decade after the signing of the Japanese peace settlements certainly tested these assumptions to the hilt.

For the Japanese electorate the two issues of economic reconstruction and the security treaty with the United States predominated. The first inevitably reflected the national determination to go beyond mere economic survival to envisaging at least the future prospect of a decent job and adequate housing. Japan's trade union leaders and opposition political parties, however, hoped to widen their members' perspectives to consider broader issues than the price of rice and the chances of better housing in the hastily rebuilt cities. In the 1950s, though, it was far from clear whether the national economy, beset by perennial balance of payments problems and acute suspicion from overseas competitors in third markets, would be able to sustain its encouraging growth efforts. It was equally difficult to foretell the direction of Japanese foreign policy.

Questions of economic betterment and the United States–Japan security relationship were intertwined. Washington reckoned that it could best ensure a continuation of its influence over Japan (and thereby retain vital tenure of a host of military bases throughout the archipelago) by providing a lifeline to the Japanese economy. American policy-makers reasoned that the all-important political goal of an increasingly prosperous Japan might be attainable through the granting of easy access to US markets and the provision of relatively free and secure trading arrangements elsewhere. Such approaches, when combined with considerable financial and technological assistance either through American or international institutions, underwrote what would shortly be heralded as the Japanese economic 'miracle'.

The extent of American sustenance for a Japan that had by 1955 exceeded its peak prewar economic performances might have been a reminder to the nation that unsuccessful imperialism does not pay. Most Japanese, however, had no wish to look backwards to their own misdeeds and many preferred to concentrate on the dangers that the present close association with the United States appeared to foretell. The opposition to the conservatives, who had brought Japan through the last years of the occupation and the San Francisco negotiations, warned that Tokyo risked losing its sovereignty through the highly visible and highly dangerous linkage to Washington. Central to Japan's return to international society had been its lukewarm acknowledgement that it intended to remain an ally of the United States. After a lengthy period of hard bargaining, Dulles and the Pentagon had obtained assurances from Prime Minister Yoshida that his nation would permit American forces to be stationed in Japan after the Japanese peace treaty came into effect. This was decidedly unpopular with an electorate that hoped somewhat unrealistically that it could have its independence without any further American garrisoning. The issue was to colour US–Japan relations throughout the 1950s. At the heart of the difficulties was the very obvious American military presence; it was impossible not to imagine at times that the already lengthy occupation era was set to continue indefinitely. Japanese sensitivities were such that no cabinet in Tokyo would have found it easy to explain or justify a US–Japan security pact that recalled for many citizens the humiliations of the Western-imposed 'unequal treaties' that followed from Commodore Perry's 'opening' of Japan. After the euphoria of the San Francisco peace treaty quickly dissolved, it began to appear that Japan in the 1950s was in fact little more than a semi-sovereign state.

Given the groundswell of public disapproval, it was clearly necessary for these problems to be addressed. The two governments began to consult on how best to safeguard what were seen as essential components of the United States' commitment to the defence of the entire Asia-Pacific region against the prospect of domestic protest that might jeopardise the future of pro-American governments in Tokyo. Some progress was made but neither party was eager to be seen to be giving ground. President Eisenhower, however, reminded his cabinet on 6 August 1954 that a degree of sympathy for Japan's political and economic plights was essential. He noted: 'Don't let us let Japan reach a point where they want to invite the Kremlin into their country. Everything else fades into insignificance in the light of such a threat'.

Japan for its part took the view that as an almost unarmed state in a region of tension among the Great Powers, it could expect to be protected by the Pentagon. At the same time many felt that all such security must be both invisible and designed to avoid giving offence to the Communist regimes that largely surrounded Japan. Not surprisingly, the United States reacted with irritation at the naïve commentaries from Japanese ministers and the increasingly strident opposition camp. It seemed that the Japanese nation felt entitled to carp at the American military, while refusing to commence any substantial rearmament of its own that might thereby reduce the US presence. When pressed by American officials to act with a greater sense of responsibility for the security of his nation, Yoshida was quick to plead the twin excuses of continuing poverty and inbred pacifism. Although Yoshida undoubtedly prevaricated, it is to his credit that before he left office in late 1954 he did gain parliamentary approval for a Japan–United States Mutual Defense Agreement and the beginnings of a Self Defense establishment.

Thereafter the question of the revision of the US–Japan Security Treaty became embroiled in the complex and carnivorous world of Japanese domestic politics. Since it had been agreed by both governments that the original treaty would be subject to later alteration, there was no way that public debate on revision of the security pact could be avoided. Domestic opinion, however, was bitterly divided and the situation exacerbated by the emergence of Kishi Nobusuke as prime minister in 1957. Although the US administration quickly regarded the new premier as giving 'every indication of being the strongest Government leader to emerge in postwar Japan', Kishi was a controversial figure both because of his wartime ministerial record and his unpopularity within his own party. Yet it is hardly coincidental that Secretary of State Dulles, the architect of the Japanese peace settlements in the final months of the Truman presidency, could recommend to Eisenhower in June 1957 that revision of the US–Japan security pact be undertaken. 'I feel that the time has come', wrote Dulles, 'to take the initiative in proposing a readjustment of our relations with Japan and to suggest to Mr Kishi that we work toward a mutual security arrangement which could, we would hope, replace the present Security Treaty'.

The following three years proved to be both more violent and vexatious than Dulles could have imagined. The efforts to gain parliamentary approval for the revised security treaty led to huge street demonstrations, the trampling to death of a University of Tokyo female student, and well-publicised fisticuffs in the Diet. The result was a rather Japanese outcome that partly satisfied the conservatives and yet gave a series of consolation prizes to the opposition camp. The Leftist opposition had mounted a virulent twin campaign against the Americans and Kishi, the individual they held to be Washington's poodle. After the security crisis had ended, the United States and Japan were rewarded with a modified defence pact. Kishi, however, found himself deserted by many within his own Liberal Democratic Party (LDP) and was obliged to resign, while President Eisenhower had felt it politic to cancel his planned state visit to Tokyo. Both sides had won something, though in terms of the regional scene there can be little doubt that the ratification of the new security treaty was the glittering prize.

The feeling shared by many observers in Western Europe and Asia that Japan served as a Pacific satellite of the United States was hard to refute during the 1950s. The British Labour Party figure Aneurin Bevan warned that Japan risked being seen as a partner in 'White Imperialism in the Far East'. Tokyo's own foreign minister bluntly told Dulles in August 1955 that 'he wanted to be sure that the United States did not intend to keep Japan in a semi-independent position'. What neither the LDP nor the wider public were prepared to accept, however, was the frequently rehearsed American governmental argument that Japan could voluntarily alter its misgivings by contributing more to its own defence. This, as Dulles maintained when meeting Foreign Minister Fujiyama in September 1957, ought to be based on close cooperation with Washington, which would thereby enhance its status in the wider world. It was, however, simpler and cheaper for successive Japanese leaders to call for rice before guns and to invoke its so-called nuclear allergy as a prohibition against serious thought on regional security. Even the State Department had to acknowledge that the prospects for any substantial shift in Japan's strategic thinking was slight. There was, wrote the Office of Northeast Asian Affairs in June 1957, little likelihood that Tokyo would grant US or UN forces the use of its territory as a 'staging and base area' in a regional conflict or permit the deployment of nuclear weapons.

The 1950s were clearly a decade of uncertainty and polarization for Japanese society and its antagonistic politicians. Dulles' hope that 'Japan would develop into a truly great country in the Far East and the Western Pacific; great in the sense of contributing to the welfare, peace and stability of the area' remained unrealized. Yet for all the sound and fury behind the security crisis, considerable progress had been made in at least laying the foundations for later herculean economic growth. While the more general acceptance of the necessity of a closer US–Japan strategic relationship remained in question, some lessons had been learned. It was now recognized by the political establishments in both nations that it was imperative to avoid any future repetition of the exhausting and dangerous months of 1960. The entire alliance should not be put at risk a second time.

After the typhoon, both sides worked to smooth over differences by adopting a quietist approach. This reduction in tension was conveniently aided by substantial evidence of economic expansion within Japan, which in turn was greatly assisted by cooperation from the United States. Ambassador MacArthur, the nephew of the occupation's overlord, had earlier written from Tokyo to emphasize what many saw as the United States' best card in the debate over how to redesign US–Japan relations. Japan's 'basic foreign policy and alignments', maintained MacArthur in a passage that he underlined for his State Department superiors, 'will ultimately and inevitably be dictated by her over-all economic needs, particularly access to foreign markets'. There was therefore no alternative to staying close to Washington. However, this emphasis on a liberal trading system was hardly at the forefront of the minds of Japanese unionists, students and housewives as they protested at the regional dangers that they felt accrued from any endorsement of the revised security pact.

The political solution the conservatives deployed after the June days of 1960 was simple and highly effective. To distance the entire nation from concentrating again on what the Left termed subservient imperialism in the wake of American global hegemony, the LDP stressed the emerging strengths of the Japanese economy. The evidence of first recovery and then sustainable expansion acted to distract the electorate from concern over US bases on Japanese soil. Instead, government officials in Tokyo were able to proudly announce the end of the so-called 'catch-up' era and the first use of the self-congratulatory statement that Japan was now 'an economic superpower'. During the 1960s the nation's GDP quickly exceeded that of its Western European rivals and the public began to anticipate the day when even the United States might be within Japan's sights. A decade that had begun so ignominiously for the Japanese establishment ended on a highly celebratory note with Expo '70. Instead of looking back to the political intensity of mass street demonstrations in Tokyo, the country paid homage to its more recent industrial and technological achievements at the Osaka world fair. Few could have predicted that Japan would prove itself so successful in the 1960s; fewer still had any inkling that these hyper-growth years and the restored relationship with the United States would barely survive into the first years of the next decade.

The China Question and the Asia-Pacific States

All the United States' allies had to reckon with the inflexibility of American policy towards Beijing. Japan, however, was particularly concerned with each stance taken by Washington, since its past history, geographical position and current ideological differences with the PRC combined to leave Tokyo nervous in the years following the San Francisco peace settlements. Sino-Japanese relations after 1949 were a product of the Cold War, yet Japanese cabinets of the 1950s nevertheless hoped to be able to gain at least some opportunities to talk and trade with Beijing. Certainly Japan's freedom to manoeuvre was highly constrained and it would be bad history to maintain that politicians such as Yoshida and his immediate successors achieved significant results, but the attempt was made on repeated occasions.

Japan's options were severely limited by American action taken before San Francisco. The US Senate was determined to make it apparent to Japan that recognition of the Nationalist government on Taiwan was a sine qua non for subsequent approval of the peace treaty. The so-called 'Yoshida Letter', by which the Prime Minister had to agree to curtail his hopes of gaining some links to Beijing, was a disappointment to many across the political spectrum in Japan. The whole episode was a salutary lesson for the Japanese establishment, since it demonstrated in a seemingly abrupt and cold manner that Tokyo's once and future overlord was not about to permit any backsliding over Taiwan.

Over the possibility of re-establishing commercial links with continental China, however, the picture was brighter. Although the negotiations took time and the trade volume was initially small, there remained always the expectation that more could be accomplished in the future and that useful political dividends might accrue in the process. Yet the Japanese were constantly aware of American disapproval and the monitoring of all such activities at a time when the CIA in Washington was advising the Eisenhower cabinet that the PRC was 'wooing its fellow Asian states. While steadily reinforcing its military threat in the Taiwan Strait area and firmly reiterating its claims to Taiwan, Peiping [Beijing] also apparently believes that for the present it is necessary to move toward its objectives by political action'. The same National Intelligence Estimate of November 1955 reported that the PRC 'remains determined to eliminate the Nationalist government as unfinished business of the revolution'.

Ambiguities remained over probable Japanese approaches to Beijing. There was concern by 1955 that Japan 'will assert progressively greater independence of the US, while normalizing relations with the [Sino-Soviet] Bloc', though analysts reckoned that Japan's 'security and economic needs' would prevent any rupture with the United States. Tokyo's differences with the United States had similarities with the difficulties Britain faced in the 1950s when it too tried repeatedly to persuade the Eisenhower administration to change tack. In both instances it proved impossible to alter more than peripheral issues. Japan was obliged to recognize Taiwan, its trade with the PRC was limited, and the establishment of semi-official links with Beijing was hard going. China wished to extract every possible advantage it might gain from talking to Japan, while successive Japanese cabinets had constantly to reckon with the reactions of Washington to potential developments. The United States kept a tight rein on Japan, much as it refused to change its China policies to accommodate what successive British conservative governments held to be the political realities of the Asia-Pacific region. American officials did so both because of the scope of their commitments to Taiwan and out of fear that to concede even an iota might lead to the opening of the floodgates to much more substantial change. The result was that the United States generally won the day but received little in the way of genuine support from its principal allies in Western Europe and Northeast Asia. Misgivings remained.

Tokyo could take some consolation, however, in its attempts to approach Beijing via semi-official channels, which provided a second track to its orthodox pro-American diplomacy. This could be justified by the conservative cabinets of the 1950s on domestic political grounds, by pointing out the degree of public sympathy for the PRC on the Left and by the widely shared view in business circles that trade should be able to circumvent ideological barriers. From Shigeru Yoshida onwards, Japanese politicians paid the closest attention to events within China and calculated how best to respond to their powerful and ambitious neighbour.

Behind much of the activity was a general wish to separate trade and politics. This became almost a principle in Japan's post-1949 approaches to Beijing as it allowed all but the staunchest of pro-Taiwan groups within conservative ranks to argue that this bought some form of insurance for the uncertainties of the future. It also won support from realists who felt it simplistic and demeaning for their nation to be beholden to Washington and to continue to ignore the PRC. Yoshida stated in 1951 that 'the Japanese government desires ultimately to have a full measure of political peace and commercial intercourse with China, which is Japan's close neighbour'. It quickly became evident also that differences over how to treat Beijing cut across party lines and that strange bedfellows emerged, whereby, for example, leaders of the idiosyncratic Japan Communist Party wished to ignore the persistent trumpeting of Beijing's 'people's diplomacy'. Public opinion, while far from well informed on Asian international relations, was divided. Some groups recognized Japan's guilt for the miseries inflicted on the Chinese subcontinent during the era of

Japanese imperialism, while others recalled that Chiang Kai-shek had been quick to put a stop to demands for apologies and reparations for past barbarism.

To the relief of Washington, Sino-Japanese links in the 1950s were slight and tentative. The PRC remained most suspicious of the Japanese government and of the symbolic fact that its peace treaty was signed with Taipei at the very moment that the San Francisco peace settlements were ratified in April 1952. Beijing, however, wished to weaken Japan's military and political relationships with Washington and had some successes in the mid-1950s when Prime Minister Hatoyama appeared to favour closer and more normal ties with the PRC. Domestic political changes, noticeably the emergence of Kishi as Premier in 1957, curtailed what would have been a striking success for Chou En-lai had he been able to disrupt the Tokyo–Washington partnership. Where events proved more successful was over the establishment of a series of quasi-official trading arrangements. These reminded both sides of the potential for closer and more profitable exchanges, though they were hardly comparable to the vast and largely unexpected growth in Japanese trade with the open American market. The United States, for its part, made every possible effort to welcome Japanese exports and ensure that American technology and finance were available to expanding Japanese industries. It was largely successful in diverting Tokyo from any close contacts with Beijing. Yoshida might assert in the Diet that ideological differences could be transcended and that 'we are willing to do business with her', but his claim that it did not matter whether 'China is red, white or green' was proved to be false. From its inception, although Sino-Japanese trade served both economic and political goals, the sums involved were relatively small and of far greater importance to a poor, under-developed China than a bustling, aspiring Japan. Tokyo in the 1950s never strayed too far from the America connection.

Asia and the Non-Aligned Movement

The United States buttressed its case for cold-shouldering the PRC by pointing to its behaviour in Southeast Asia. It was not lost on the State Department that China had been a leading sponsor of the Non-Aligned Movement, which professed to offer a third alternative to the bipolar divisions of the Cold War, and that Chou En-lai had played a major role at the Afro-Asia conference at Bandung in April 1955. In the autumn of 1955 the United States feared that 'the shadow of Communist power' had grown to the extent that the situation in Southeast Asia was 'extremely precarious'. It held that any failure to 'deal effectively with the problems of less developed areas will weaken the free world and benefit international communism, even in countries where actual Communist take-over is not imminent'.

Washington intended that greater economic assistance, organized on a regional basis, would contribute to weaning away some of the poorer, newly independent states from the dual attractions of Communism and the NAM. By 1950 British officials had already hoped to 'build up a united front against Communism through the medium of our estimate of China'. The results may have been mixed but a consortium of Asian and Western powers did agree to meet and discuss how best to formulate economic and financial programmes that were wider than the piecemeal approaches of individual donor nations in the past. Certainly Prime Minister Nehru of India held reservations, not least because he had seized the initiative in an effort to solve the Indonesian situation at the New Delhi conference of January 1949, but the subsequent meeting of Commonwealth leaders at Colombo twelve months later marked a new beginning. What started as an experiment in intra-Commonwealth economic and technological cooperation would soon be widened to incorporate the United States and its Filipino and Japanese friends. This was vital for the expansion of the original Indian and Australian initiatives for the Colombo Plan, since, as the Foreign Office admitted in 1960, British funds have been 'almost entirely limited hitherto to members of the Commonwealth'. The inclusion of Washington in the Colombo Plan made larger funds available, though the divisions within the Western camp also grew alarmingly after 1950 when, as we have seen, issues of recognition of the PRC and support to Indo-China left Washington and London poles apart.

By the early 1950s the virulence of the Cold War had encouraged Asian states to attempt to articulate a viable alternative to the bloodshed and military alliances that criss-crossed the entire region. Nehru, in particular, insisted that other avenues had to be explored and hoped that some form of Asian unity might be discovered that could scrap the bitter divisions and intolerances of current regional relations. The Indian Prime Minister acknowledged that, with the possible exception of ties between New Delhi and Rangoon, any sense of 'some common understanding and common objectives' was generally lacking, though he was ever optimistic in his quest for 'some common approach'. Nehru could point to the five principles of peaceful coexistence agreed with Chou En-lai during the recess of the Geneva conference in June 1954 as at least a sign of a more positive approach to international politics. However innocuous and however titled, the Nehru–Chou discussions in New Delhi were held to give hope to others. They could then form 'a solid foundation for peace and security [in which] the fears and apprehensions that exist today would give place to a feeling of confidence'.

The Bandung Conference of non-aligned nations marked the flowering of Nehru's aspirations. Spurious or not, the 'spirit of Bandung' had an immediate impact on the Asia-Pacific region. It was, not surprisingly, a political development that disturbed the United States. While spokesmen at the Indonesian conference made great play on the prospects for a set of neutralist foreign policies that offered a viable alternative to the two global power blocs, the US government reckoned otherwise. Yet the political realities were different. China's Chou En-lai, for example, spoke softly at Bandung to win the support of small states wavering between the pro-Western camp and the alternative attractions of the Sino-Soviet grouping. Beijing had hopes of influencing Burma, Indonesia, Laos and Cambodia, while not entirely giving up on swaying Pakistan and Thailand. Each nation, of course, had its own objectives, and in terms of international stature in the mid-1950s it was Nehru who could claim a greater impact than Chou En-lai. Not only had Nehru worked the hardest to persuade leaders from the Indian subcontinent to attend but he also had the imagination to appeal to African figures as well. The coldness of the US reaction to this extraordinary meeting of Third World states was widely seen as evidence that the mere holding of the Bandung conference represented something of a success for India and the Indonesian hosts. By way of contrast, Moscow sent enthusiastic greetings to the delegates on the correct assumption that the movement was likely to veer strongly to the Left from the much-publicized moment of its inception.

There were pro-American nations in attendance at Bandung. None, however, had representatives with the presence of Nehru, Soekarno or Chou En-lai. The United States reckoned that in numerical terms at least it could count on a majority of non-Communist governments for voting purposes at the conference and that these 'good friends of the free world' would resist the Chinese line on anti-colonialism and anti-Americanism. This proved wide of the mark, though in his assessment of Bandung Secretary Dulles insisted to the cabinet that the final communiqué was very largely 'consistent with our own foreign policy'. Yet even Dulles had been obliged to acknowledge that Chou En-lai had 'very astutely' adapted to the mood of the conference and had returned from Bandung with 'a certain personal success'. Information from the Lebanese ambassador Dr Malik, however, who had held extensive discussions with Chou at the conference, went some considerable way to tempering Dulles' initial commentary and left Malik claiming that 'the emergence of Communist China was a distinct defeat for the West'. The behaviour of Chou En-lai was, in the opinion of the anti-Communist Malik, a 'setback' for the United States and its friends. The Bandung conference marked greater receptivity within the Afro-Asian world towards the ideals of Communism and the rise of the People's Republic of China in particular.

Beijing gained sizeable political dividends from the conference. One Indian commentator, who interviewed Nehru later on his recollections of Bandung, held that 'the spreading of the Bandung Myth' created 'the impression that a large part of mankind was seized by one of those mass hysterias that swept over Europe in the Dark Ages'. China may not have believed all that it said on these virtues of the promotion of world peace and cooperation but it was now seen by some in the Afro-Asian world to be on the side of the angels. Beijing began to win others to its cause, which was that the PRC deserved to be recognized as the legitimate government of China and thereby entitled to representation at the United Nations. It also gained the friendship of newly independent states, who welcomed the attention given to them by the PRC.

Sino-Soviet Quarrels

Yet it was not only the United States that was disturbed by the attention that the new China had gained by the mid-1950s. The Soviet Union was also concerned that its predominant position within the Communist bloc might be undermined in the emerging world. It was hardly coincidental that Moscow now displayed greater attention towards the Afro-Asian states and at the same time showed greater rivalry towards the PRC. The Soviet Union also reversed its earlier general policy of dismissing the newly independent nations as being little more than quasi-bourgeois satellites of their former colonial masters. Instead of the arming and funding of Asian Communist parties loyal to Moscow, the USSR now worked to prove its credentials as a supporter of the new governments it had previously worked to destabilize. If Washington by the time of the Geneva and Bandung conferences had been obliged to take the PRC seriously, the same too can be said of the Soviet Union in its dealings with Beijing from these triumphs for Chou En-lai onwards.

Soviet foreign policy under Stalin had been based on the assertion of Moscow's right to be regarded as a Great Power in Europe and the Asia-Pacific region. Stalin's actions in the immediate postwar period had aimed at making gains without taking major risks in his relations with the West. The USSR, as we have seen, wished to lead any pro-Communist governments that might emerge from the process of decolonization and to work with limited resources to undermine the return of the prewar metropolitan powers. In reality, it could claim few successes before the outbreak of the Korean War. For example, its efforts achieved relatively little at the Calcutta Conference of 1948, which had been designed to foment subversion and encourage local Communist parties in the

Indian subcontinent, in Malaya, throughout what would shortly be titled Indonesia, and in the Philippines. Only by his considerable assistance to North Korea from the outbreak of the Korean War onwards did Stalin commit himself to the region. This new awareness was seen through the granting of Soviet materiel and the valour of the Soviet air force in the war above the peninsula. Its Mig-15s often had the edge on American fighter planes and all aircrew were under orders not to use Russian when communicating during combat.

The position changed dramatically with the death of Stalin in March 1953. Slight evidence that the Soviet Union might be reconsidering its advocacy of armed struggle in the region and could temper its criticism of the new states, such as India, had emerged before 1953, but the entire character of Soviet foreign policy was now reassessed. For the first time kind words were addressed to the emerging Afro-Asian bloc, and the principles of non-aggression and peaceful coexistence espoused by Nehru became part of Moscow's official rhetoric in 1955. The Asia-Pacific region was now to be regarded as a zone of opportunity where Soviet efforts to help solve the two international scars of Korea and Indo-China demonstrated that Moscow could indeed play a constructive role that was appreciated by its friends and rivals alike. Neither the Korean armistice agreements nor the Geneva conference could have been concluded successfully without the efforts of the Soviet Union. The Eisenhower administration might dislike these realities but the manner in which the 'Big Four' foreign ministers of the United States, the Soviet Union, Britain and France met in public at Geneva was clearly to Moscow's advantage. Moscow also enjoyed watching the constant Anglo-American discord over the PRC and appropriate policies for Taiwan and the offshore islands.

While issues involving Cold War dealings with the United States and Europe were at the centre of postwar Soviet policies, regardless of who was at the helm, the new attention displayed towards Asia reflected a belated recognition of the Third World. Once he had gained power in the post-Stalin period, Nikita Khrushchev intended to swim in these waters to gain advantage for his nation at the expense of the West. The Soviet Union pressed its friendship with the new Asian states in the expectation that its actions would stand in contrast to the Eisenhower administration's cooler behaviour. The Non-Aligned Movement shifted rather quickly into a vehicle for anti-capitalist statements and the concept of an emerging Afro-Asian bloc existing equidistantly between the two major nuclear powers disappeared. Neutrality was replaced by alignment.

Regional stability, however, rested more on Moscow's dealings with other powers in Northeast Asia. Relations with the PRC and Japan had greater significance than the offering of limited financial and technological assistance to the new states of Southeast Asia. Since Beijing had quickly shown its military prowess in the Korean War and shared a common and disputed border with the Soviet Union, neither Stalin nor his successors could simply relax their guard. Rival political and ideological claims to the leadership of Communism also emerged in the 1950s to add a further ingredient to a tense relationship. Initially, Mao Tse-tung had deferred to Stalin and been eager to put his name to the Sino-Soviet pact of 1950, but there were half-hidden strains from the outset. Both governments had their own concept of the path to Socialism and both worked to collect potential allies, who would subscribe to their version of how the future was to be realized.

Third parties found the task of assessing Sino-Soviet ties difficult. The tendency was to suggest that the two nations might continue to need each other but to hint at a possible breakdown in the years ahead. Secretary Dulles, for example, liked to employ the 'wedge' analogy and suggest that the United States ought to maintain maximum pressure on the PRC in the expectation that this would lead to an eventual split between Beijing and Moscow. Dulles reckoned that any weakening of the material position of the PRC would lead to its resentment at having to go cap in hand to the Soviet Union. The British approach, as we have seen, was the reverse of the American strategy. The Foreign Office felt it would be more useful to treat China with politeness and offer it economic inducements that might bring it closer to the West and thereby effect a divorce from the Russian camp.

The 1950s proved to be uncomfortable years for Moscow and Beijing. Mao Tse-tung simultaneously recognized that the Soviet Union was the chief architect of the global Communist movement and resented the manner in which he felt the PRC was treated by first Stalin and then Khrushchev. Chinese pride and Soviet arrogance were almost certain to create difficulties as a weak Beijing was obliged to seek massive assistance for economic and technological reconstruction in highly inauspicious circumstances. China also disliked the Soviet Union's military leasing of Port Arthur and the joint ownership of what had in pre-revolutionary days been termed the Chinese Eastern Railway, yet even after these issues had been resolved the relationship stubbornly failed to bloom. Khrushchev may have brought well-intentioned policies to the discussions but Beijing remained unhappy.

In the realm of international politics, Sino-Soviet differences worsened as Khrushchev attempted to moderate Chinese anger at the manner in which the two superpowers worked to mediate their differences under the shadow of the bomb. Mao disliked the recognition by the Eisenhower administration and Khrushchev's politburo that an approximate US–Soviet balance of terror, in an era that US officials repeatedly termed 'nuclear plenty', left both sides with greater opportunities for cooperation. China was the odd man out in what it saw as a bipolar world where Washington and Moscow looked to their own allies for loyal support rather than angry denunciation. China wished to go its own way in the world. It was contemptuous of the Soviet Union's seemingly supine behaviour with regard to the United States and of Moscow's gentle handling of dissident Communist regimes in Europe and Asia.

The fracturing of Soviet–Chinese relations was apparent by the end of the decade. Thousands of Soviet advisers and engineers working on projects within China were ordered home, while promised Soviet assistance for the development of China's nuclear programme was cancelled. The strains were telling and it was the Soviet Union that appeared to be the principal loser, since it could no longer count on Beijing's friendship. Mao Tse-tung feared that the Soviet Union would rather divide the globe with the United States than join forces with fellow Communist states to oppose imperialism. The Russians, however, did not trust Mao; his bizarre economic experimentation of the Great Leap Forward period and his military challenges to the United States over the offshore islands crises made him unpredictable in their eyes. These anxieties mirrored the events of the Korean War, where Stalin had wished at all costs to avoid a direct Soviet-American confrontation and therefore worked to ensure that Washington understood that the conflict should remain limited and that diplomacy be given its chance to gain an early ceasefire and armistice. Issues of personality, ideology and national rivalry had rapidly dissolved what a mere decade earlier had been heralded as the new dawn of international socialism. The aspirations of 'equality, mutual benefit, and mutual respect for territory and sovereignty' that Chou En-lai had listed on 1 October 1949 as the basis for establishing diplomatic ties with the PRC were now in jeopardy.

The Soviet Union and the Region

Moscow received other setbacks in Asia as it wrestled with managing its vital relationship with the PRC. Its record in dealing with North Korea was also less than successful, though its disagreements here obviously had less impact on the region than the public split with Beijing. Over North Korea, the Soviet Union found itself unable to continue to exert the type of leverage that undoubtedly existed when the North Korean regime was founded. Kim Il Sung gained large loans from the PRC as his regime attempted to improve its industrial base and strengthen its military forces after the destruction of the Korean War, but his political and ideological dependence on Moscow gradually decreased. Kim, whose respect for Stalin appears to have been steadfast, was unprepared to accept the Soviet Union's de-Stalinization campaigns of the mid-1950s.

Despite frequent visits to Moscow and the presence of very large numbers of foreign troops, the Korean leader reckoned he could devise his
own road to Socialism. The result was the *jun'che* scheme, which stressed
the need for North Korean self-reliance based on a slavish respect for the
great leader himself. Even Pyongyang, it seemed, was able to escape from
the status of obedient vassal to the position of a small, semi-independent
state able to play off Moscow and Beijing to its own advantage.

Soviet–Japanese relations proved an additional disappointment during
this decade. Although some progress was undoubtedly made in 1955–56
to solve the issues of the Pacific War and its territorial consequences, the
position thereafter deteriorated. Opportunities for rapprochement, once
lost in the mid-1950s, would not be regained in the rest of the twentieth
century. The initial negotiations between Moscow and Tokyo were the
consequence of changes within the factional political balances of the
conservatives in Japan. In an attempt to reduce the nation's subservience
to the United States, Prime Minister Hatoyama Ichiro responded posi-
tively to Foreign Minister Molotov's announcement that his nation
wished to normalize relations with Tokyo. The new Japanese cabinet,
intending to put some distance between itself and the pro-American
stance of Yoshida's supporters, declared, through Foreign Minister
Shigemitsu, that Japan wished 'without prejudice to its co-operation with
the "Free World" to normalize relations with the Soviet Union and China
on terms mutually aceptable'.

Talks were held in London from January 1955 to August 1956 and
were followed up by further meetings in Moscow. Even after making due
allowance for interruptions, this was an extraordinarily protracted business where the length of the negotiations could only be regarded as
evidence of major difficulties. Little came of this intense period of Soviet–
Japanese activity beyond agreements to disagree. Differences centred on
the Russian wish to reduce Japan's links to the United States, epitomized
by the security pact, and Japan's frustration over the politically sensitive
Soviet occupation of what Tokyo held to be its northern territories. The
term describes a small group of strategically important islands lying
between Hokkaido and the Kuriles which were occupied by the Soviet
Union in August 1945. In the end all that was accomplished was the
restoration of diplomatic relations without, however, the signing of a
peace treaty that would have resolved the territorial dispute and ushered
in a more relaxed era.

Commenting shortly after the event, Dulles claimed, perhaps with a
touch of false bravado, that US–Japan relations remained unimpaired.
He reckoned that neutralism was not even a remote possibility, since he
questioned whether even the Japan Socialist Party would adopt that
course. 'Any government coming into power would want to collaborate

with the United States', maintained Dulles, but he may have deliberately ignored the strains of the Hatoyama interlude. American officials in Tokyo were obliged to take the ailing Japanese Premier much more seriously, and Hatoyama's attempts to break free of the US–Japan strait-jacket contributed to the upsurge of national feeling in favour of the forthcoming revision to the security treaty. After Hatoyama's negotiations with Moscow and Beijing, the era of automatic American dominance that had lasted since the initial days of the occupation was at an end. The Prime Minister had done both his nation and US–Japan relations an indirect favour by reminding the bureaucratic elites on both sides of the Pacific that the alliance required greater attention and deserved to be subject to periodic alteration. Moscow, however, gained relatively little from this outcome. It had worked hard to move Japan away from its American moorings but had largely failed to gain the anticipated political dividends that this process was intended to engineer. Ironically, the Soviet leadership had next to witness a strengthening of US–Japan ties in the years after 1960 as Washington and Tokyo jointly appreciated the necessity of avoiding any repetition of the recent security crisis. Khrushchev, unfortunately for the USSR, hardly helped his cause by nursing an unwise European sense of superiority over a Japan that his country had crushed in August 1945 in what he boasted was Moscow's revenge for the humiliations of the Russo-Japanese war. Such attitudes also surfaced in his handling of Chinese affairs and contributed to a series of unsatisfactory outcomes. The Soviet Union's push to the East largely failed.

The Eisenhower administration must also take its share of any credit for rebuffing the Soviet diplomatic offensive in the Asia-Pacific region. Since Dulles had regained his political career and would indeed win his greatest international success by working to devise the San Francisco settlements, he did not need to be reminded of the political and strategic value of Japan to the United States' position in Northeast Asia. He was therefore quick to draw Tokyo's attention to the fact that under the terms of the San Francisco peace treaty, Japan was prohibited from transferring 'the sovereignty of the territories without the consent of the signatories'. The State Department also stressed to Tokyo that any arrangements over the northern territories, where the USSR had proposed handing back a portion of the area claimed by Japan, could well jeopardize future discussion on the even more sensitive issue of the possible reversion of Okinawa. Failure in the Soviet–Japanese negotiations in London and Moscow was obviously welcome, and, indeed, assisted, by the US government. The result for the Sino-Soviet bloc was noted by the *People's Daily* in October 1956 when it wrote that Washington intended 'to perpetuate its occupation of Japan, turn Japan into its colony and war base for aggression and try by this means to keep up tension in the Far East'. Whatever their own differences, this statement represented a rare occasion when both major Communist states could find themselves in total agreement. Yet the imperatives of the Cold War had continued to link Japan firmly to the United States and had thereby prevented the working out of solutions to vexing territorial questions and the normalization of relations between the most important neighbouring states of the region. Such international rigidities ensured that little would change in the next decade.

4   War: Vietnam, 1960–1975

For most Americans the word 'Vietnam' spells confusion and
complexity. It had never been an area of significant interest to them
before, and they awoke rather suddenly to its very existence only
after their government had made what they were told were
irrevocable commitments there.

> George M. Kahin and John W. Lewis, *The United States in Vietnam*
> (London, 1969)

... they all share the blame; this is not a unique error of Lyndon
Johnson. He was the man that was holding the bag at the time
when the birds came home to roost, if that is not too mixed a
metaphor.

> Edwin O. Reischauer, LBJ Library Oral History Collection.

War
Hunh! Yeah
What is it good for?
Absolutely nothing.

> Edwin Starr, 'War', 1970

The Kennedy Years and Vietnam

The 1960s form a period of consolidation for the United States in its
dealings with the Asia-Pacific region. Much of the policy formulation
of the previous decade remained in place during these years and led
ineluctably to an ever-expanding American involvement in South
Vietnam in an attempt to prevent the emergence of a Communist regime
in Saigon. By the end of the 1960s this incremental process had produced
the most disastrous and the most divisive episode in postwar American
foreign policy. The original Cold War regional premises of the Truman
and Eisenhower administrations were continued by Presidents Kennedy
and Johnson. Each in turn enlarged existing commitments in their determination to defend South Vietnam and to protect its allies throughout
the wider Southeast Asian region from the contagion of Communism.

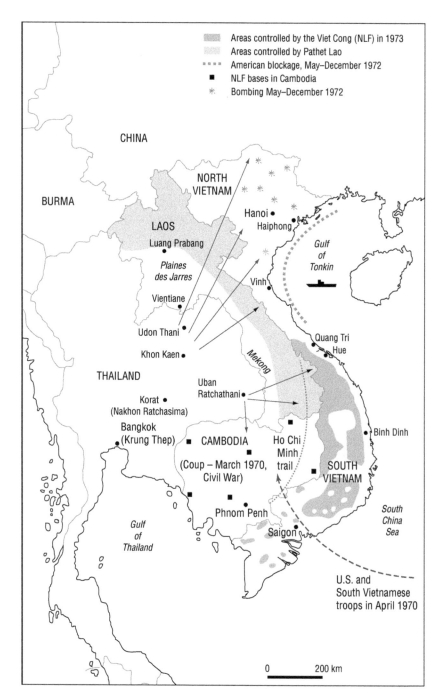

The Vietnam War, 1969–73
Based on Geir Lundestad, East, West, North, South: Major Developments in
International Politics 1945–1996 *(Oslo, 1997).*

Responsibility for decisions taken in Vietnam spans the entire first post-war generation of American political, military and bureaucratic leadership.

What became the second Indo-China war had its roots within the often chaotic realities of South Vietnamese society in the years after the French had left in the mid-1950s. There was, as we have seen, a wish to stand firm in the face of what the National Security Council had defined in September 1956 as highly unpleasant consequences for the United States should its resolve weaken. In a sober assessment, the NSC stressed that the United States alone could 'counteract the Russian-Chinese thrust into Southeast Asia'. While 'the loss to Communist control of any single free country would encourage tendencies toward accommodation by the rest', the planners feared that the

> loss of the entire area would have a seriously adverse impact on the US position elsewhere in the Far East, have severe economic consequences for many nations in the free world, add significant resources to the Communist bloc in rice, rubber, tin and other minerals, and could result in severe economic and political pressures on Japan and India for accommodation to the Communist bloc. The loss of the Southeast Asia mainland could thus have far-reaching consequences seriously adverse to US security interests.

Similar reports would emerge in the next decade that stressed repeatedly the need for the United States to help 'Free Viet Nam to develop a strong, stable and constitutional government to enable Free Viet Nam to assert an increasingly attractive contrast to conditions in the present Communist zone'. It was therefore essential, in the opinion of the NSC, that Washington should 'prevent the Viet Minh from expanding their political influence and territorial control in Free Viet Nam and Southeast Asia'. To this end the United States should 'assist the Government of Viet Nam to undertake programs of political, economic and psychological warfare against Viet Minh Communists'. What changed during the 1960s was the extraordinary increase in the scale of the American commitment to further these ends.

The Kennedy administration began by assessing its options. It fully appreciated that South Vietnam was vulnerable to external and internal subversion and was warned that the Diem regime was unpopular for failing to institute comprehensive land reform. It was also briefed on the changes in Sino-Soviet strategy towards Vietnam, which had begun the previous year with Ho Chi Minh's determination to take the fight to the south. Communist elements in South Vietnam were then organized in a new entity entitled the National Liberation Front (NLF), which also employed tried and tested techniques for encouraging non-Communist groupings to shelter under its supposedly liberal wings. These changes on the political front were next matched by a military offensive where pro-Communist guerrillas and regular troops waged war on South Vietnamese officials and worked to destabilize an already fragile state.

The new administration wished to appear bold. It had won a very narrow general election in November 1960 with the help of some highly dubious practices and now intended to demonstrate that Kennedy's belief in a new frontier could be realized in Southeast Asia. The President's inaugural speech had concentrated on foreign policy issues at a time when it appeared that the United States was in danger of losing international prestige through its mishandling of relations with the Soviet Union and its allies, notably Castro's Cuba. The Cold War was being rekindled as Kennedy took office.

Evidence appeared of a determination to bind world Communism together in the face of the deterioration of Great Power relations. In November 1960 the Conference of 81 Communist and Workers' Parties met in Moscow to reaffirm solidarity and discuss global strategy. This represented an important gathering of the Communist clan. It produced agreement over both the handling of relations with the United States, where the Soviet Union's wish for détente would have a role, and the use of national liberation movements in the Third World, where China's preference for armed struggle was approved. Under the patent compromises embedded in the Sino-Soviet text, it followed that Western-backed stooges such as Ngo Dinh Diem could expect no mercy; reunification of Vietnam would follow once South Vietnam had seen the foolishness of its ways and its present leadership had been toppled.

The formation of the National Liberation Front was an important consequence of the Moscow meeting. Thereafter Ho Chi Minh scrapped what remaining hopes he may still have possessed of securing a diplomatic solution to the long-held aspirations of his government and party. Armed struggle was now the order of the day. This decision to ignore the Geneva accords over the partition of Vietnam was tantamount to an open challenge to the architects of the original settlement, which had been premised on the existence of two separate and independent states within Vietnam. Article 16 of the cessation of hostilities agreement signed at Geneva had ruled out all 'introduction into Viet Nam of any troop reinforcements and additional military personnel'. Communist spokesmen, however, would respond to this charge of violation by noting that the NLF was merely a domestic, peaceful force for change within South Vietnam, ignoring the backing that it received at various times from Hanoi, Moscow and Beijing. The NLF in its ten-point programme of December 1960 called Ngo Dinh Diem the 'lackey of the US' who 'has been carrying out the US imperialists' political line'. Once this 'disguised colonial regime of the US imperialists' had been eliminated, it would then be possible 'to advance toward peaceful reunification of the Fatherland'.

Yet the next years would see little peace in Vietnam. President Kennedy inherited a situation where the United States had assumed responsibility for counter-insurgency operations but remained decidedly unhappy with the conduct of the Diem government. By 1960 American officials would report to Washington their frustration at encouraging Diem to 'take the necessary political, social, psychological and economic actions to win over the population', while his opponents in the NLF simply called his entire family and its hold on government a 'fascist dictatorship'. Attempted coups, arbitrary violence and failures to institute land reform, despite the presence of the American authority whose handiwork had proved so successful in the Japanese countryside during the occupation, suggested that the weaknesses of the Diem regime would hardly be repaired through American aid and advice. Kennedy, however, had come to power with a reputation as a firm anti-Communist, who felt that Southeast Asia was of considerable importance in the need to show resolve in the Cold War across the entire global spectrum. He was not about to sound the retreat.

The President acted with speed. Within days of taking office, he approved plans to increase American financial and political assistance to the regime in Saigon. He did so in order to be seen as determined in the face of Moscow's very public support for wars of national liberation. Kennedy was also anxious to appear assertive because he was simultaneously making decisions over Laos that might give the impression of weakness in future summit meetings with the Soviet Union, where new challenges over Berlin, for example, could be expected. Vietnam was therefore regarded as important both for itself and because it would be seen as a test case for judging the nature of presidential resolve in foreign policy. In 1961 the administration was eager to bolster the Diem regime in the light of what Kennedy himself defined in an address to the United Nations as 'the smoldering coals of war in southeast Asia'. The State Department White Paper on the threat that North Vietnam posed to America's ally in the south warned of huge dangers. It claimed that 'there can be no doubt that the Government of the Republic of Viet-Nam is fighting for its life'. Kennedy's advisers proposed measures to help Diem. It is doubtful, however, if the attention to counter-insurgency schemes, the strategic hamlet programmes or the introduction of new weapons for the South Vietnamese forces gave more than a temporary boost to Saigon. The Diem regime continued its old ways and began to share some of the unattractive characteristics of Chiang Kai-shek's earlier rule on the Chinese mainland. The eventual result was the American-prompted coup of 1 November 1963 that overthrew Diem and let in a period of extraordinary instability in South Vietnam

President Kennedy was himself assassinated in Dallas shortly afterwards, leaving others to speculate on possible courses of action that he might have taken later to resolve the worsening situation. His friends and enemies remain fiercely divided on whether he might have used his second term in office to radically change policies and gain something comparable to the success he won over Laos. American policies towards Laos were intended to gain an international settlement that would neutralize the kingdom and avoid the loss of Laos to pro-Communist elements in the army. Some officials, such as Chief of Naval Operations Admiral Arleigh Burke, felt strongly that military intervention was a better option, arguing that the prospect of Laos going Communist would set off the domino effect and lead to the demise of a pro-Western Thailand and other Southeast Asian states. Burke was overruled and diplomacy became the road to a negotiated settlement at Geneva.

Kennedy wished to ensure that Laos did not go Communist. Given the Cold War straitjacket of American domestic politics, his administration feared the 'loss' of Laos to the left-wing military forces of the Pathet Lao. In a complicated situation, involving a relatively unimportant nation, Kennedy worked to prevent Communists loyal to neutralist groups from retaining power. The administration was concerned that the Soviet Union was supplying the government of Prince Souvanna Phouma with food and ammunition in order to forestall a series of American-backed rightists from overturning the regime in Vientiane. Fortunately for Kennedy, the Russians wished to avoid a confrontation with the United States and were prepared to use their influence in both Hanoi and Beijing to engineer a ceasefire and to initiate talks at Geneva in May 1961. After tortuous discussions that dragged on for months, a settlement of sorts was arrived at which allowed a neutralist Laotian government to assume power. Laos was a sideshow for the administration. While Kennedy's reputation was certainly enhanced by his involvement, it can hardly be said to have been anyone's finest hour. Considerable credit, as in the earlier Indo-China settlement at Geneva, deserves to go to the Soviet Union for being prepared to compromise with Washington and for using its influence on North Vietnam, the main backers of the Pathet Lao.

Laos had been defined by the National Intelligence Estimate's inter-departmental reports in July 1955 as 'a primitive, sparsely populated kingdom'. It was the authors maintained, poorly equipped 'to deal with the Communist threat because of popular apathy and rudimentary communications and transportation and because of long dependence on the French for most important administration and security functions'. The Pathet Lao, aided by North Vietnam and China, played on national-ist sentiment against the American economic and military programmes designed to help the Laotian government. Yet the more Washington interfered, the more that this was seen as leading inevitably to American domination in Vientiane. Kennedy endorsed the policies instituted by Eisenhower but then had to face the harder task of solving the civil war that had erupted in the summer of 1960 following the coup of Captain Kong Le. The result was contradictory. Kennedy intended to demon-strate resolve, yet in the end hesitated over approving recommendations from his National Security Council that would have led to a massive increase in American military assistance and the overt breaking of the Geneva agreements. The eventual agreement to neutralize Laos left the President both stronger and weaker. He had avoided intervention in a landlocked nation where his Communist opponents would have the advantage, but his many domestic critics felt that he lacked backbone and that Laos was almost comparable to a second Bay of Pigs fiasco. Failure to invade Castro's Cuba and failure to rid Laos of Communism were seen by some as tailored in a disturbingly similar pattern

Caution in Laos may also have engineered greater resolve in Vietnam. It has been suggested that unfavourable domestic reactions to the Laos settlement led to President Kennedy's determination not to leave himself open to such criticism ever again. One State Department authority on the region argued that if the Kennedy administration wished to make a stance in Southeast Asia, it would be far more sensible to select Vietnam. There, William Sullivan pointed out in the spring of 1961, 'we had military advantages. It was an articulated, functioning nation. Its troops were tigers and real fighters. And, therefore, the advantages would be on our side to have a confrontation and showdown in Vietnam and not get sucked into this Laos operation'. Yet it was never clear if Vietnam was in itself such an opportunity. Much would depend on the activities of other governments, who might not bend so easily to American wishes, and there was always a risk in imagining that the military power of the United States and its allies would necessarily prevail in a major contest. It needs to be stressed that the US Army had little experience in counter-guerrilla operations, preferring to continue to train its troops for its primary mission, the defence of Western Europe, rather than to consider coping with the different tactics required for operations on the periphery of the Asian continent. Reckoning with tank battles on the north German plain remained its central objective, even at the height of the Vietnam War.

The numerical extent of the United States' military engagement in Vietnam slowly increased under President Kennedy. He began with the institution of a special bureaucratic task force that recommended whole-hearted support for President Diem, though later accounts by partici-pants would acknowledge that the United States prepared these policy changes with less than total consideration of the probable Vietnamese reaction. Since any such discussions would be conducted through an American ambassador who was held to have made it a habit of being 'insulting, misinformed and unfriendly' towards Diem, there were clearly problems to be resolved on the American side. Yet it would take much more than a change of envoys to work a miracle in Saigon. Diem, who had survived a coup attempt in 1960, had his own agenda. He was widely felt to be surrounded by corrupt associates and quite prepared to deploy violence to smash opposition to his rule. However, as his secretary of state boasted to Secretary Dean Rusk in March 1961, 'President Diem and his entire government are 100 percent anti-Communists and have, during the last 7 years, co-operated fully with the free world and done all they could to prevent the Communists from taking over South Vietnam'.

Diem received fresh endorsements from the administration. Yet Kennedy rejected the recommendations of his senior officials when it came to the controversial decision on whether to send in US combat troops to Vietnam. Secretary of Defense Robert McNamara had concluded in November 1961 that the US objective remained that 'of preventing the fall of South Vietnam to Communism' by committing 'necessary immediate military actions and preparations for possible later actions', but Kennedy wished only to introduce a few specialist units. There was agreement, however, on the regional dangers. The American fear remained, as it had throughout the 1950s, that the loss of Saigon would lead 'to the fairly rapid extension of Communist control, or complete accommodation to Communism, in the rest of mainland Southeast Asia and in Indonesia. The strategic implications worldwide, particularly in the Orient, would be extremely serious'. Kennedy would, of course, agree that this had to be prevented, but he chose to use counter-insurgency means to do it.

US involvement in South Vietnam expanded. While certainly on a more modest scale than had been advocated by the State Department and the Pentagon, it was intended to 'put Diem in position to win his war against the communists'. Dean Rusk further informed the British ambassador that planned military involvement would exceed the Geneva accords but that any return to such earlier levels would depend in turn on Communist compliance. Rusk told Sir David Ormsby Gore, the UK Ambassador, that Diem was to receive

> increased airlift capacity, mostly helicopters, a 'Jungle Jim' unit, assistance with photo reconnaissance, some intelligence personnel and advice, additional military advisers so that we may be able to put US advisers down to lower combat echelons, [and] that we will back Diem on his own flood rehabilitation programs with heavy equipment trucks, technical advice, etc.

London was then informed by the US government that 'these moves did not involve sending organized US combat units, although it might become necessary to give serious consideration to putting in combat troops depending on the situation some weeks hence'. Escalation on both the political and military fronts was under way.

The despatch of American military reinforcements led to highly optimistic statements by senior US commanders. By the spring of 1962 voices were heard that heralded the imminent collapse of the Communist uprisings and the prospect of success for the West in South Vietnam.

Through a combination of President Kennedy's own preference for the novel use of counter-insurgency warfare, new air mobility and patient support for Diem, it was possible to believe that the United States could remain on the edge of the pitch and yet see its team through to victory. Ambassador Nolting, for example, cabled to the State Department in August 1962, in words that would be evoked throughout the decade, how by the end of the year it might be possible to claim that South Vietnam 'should begin to point to light at end of tunnel, which may be not far away'. Pentagon officials working with Secretary of Defense McNamara could also report in May 1962 that 'the mechanisms that are now in motion' would eventually succeed, though the important caveat was added that 'no alchemy or magic' could achieve 'a dramatic victory overnight'. Later McNamara would explain that he had been misled by his commanders and that the 'monitoring of progress – which I still consider a bedrock of good management – was very poorly handled in Vietnam'. He wrote in his memoirs, while openly acknowledging his responsibility for this error, that uncertainty over 'how to evaluate results in a war without battle lines' led to an obsession with 'quantitative measurements'.

Others, however, were reluctant to accept such optimism and felt that Diem had to go. Complaints, of course, had been voiced since the late 1950s. General Taylor noted in his report to Kennedy in November 1961 that 'Diem's instinctive administrative style is that of an old fashioned Asian ruler, seeking to maintain all the strings of power in his own hands'. Diem was criticized for his 'unwillingness to delegate military operations clearly to his generals' and for a refusal to mobilize the youth and intellectual elements of his nation as 'their country sinks towards a Communist take-over they do not want'. Defeat might not be inevitable but it was hard to see how South Vietnam under Diem could win its messy, small-scale war against the Viet Cong. American advice on the conduct of the war on the ground and the implementation of the strategic hamlet programme was frequently either rejected or reluctantly accepted. The air in Saigon was thick with rumours of coups long before the eventual dethronement of Diem.

President Kennedy stated on 2 September 1963, in what would prove to be his last comment on Vietnam:

> In the final analysis, it is their war. They are the ones who have to win it or lose it. We can help them, we can give them equipment, we can send our men out there as advisers; but they have to win it – the people of Viet-Nam – against the Communists.

Yet he added, 'All we can do is help, and we are making it very clear. But I don't agree with those who say we should withdraw. That would be a great mistake'. The ambiguities and escape routes that Kennedy carefully gave himself in these remarks suggest that he would have continued to press ahead, until a future crisis might have forced him to review his handiwork. His assassination makes it hard to estimate what would have followed next, but the evidence up to November 1963 indicates that still greater US involvement was on the cards.

The Johnson Presidency and Escalation

The coup that destroyed the Diem regime only days before the death of President Kennedy marks the end of the United States' limited involvement in South Vietnam. Once the Diem family had been overthrown, a wider commitment emerges that links the newly sworn-in Johnson administration to a more forceful conduct of the war. The process led to what quickly became known as the Americanization of the conflict, whereby the leadership of the fight and the forces under US command expanded proportionally. The transfer of responsibilities to the United States and the increase in its personnel were unmistakable. Within months of Lyndon Johnson inheriting the presidency (in addition to retaining most of the cabinet-level staff of his predecessor), the war in Vietnam had become a major issue for the American government. For the first time, Vietnam also emerged as a country of sustained domestic interest to the American public. Reportage increased as families began to follow events that many feared might well become of pressing personal concern with the deployment of more troops to Southeast Asia. Congressional attention also inevitably grew. In November 1963 there were 16 000 US personnel in South Vietnam; two years later the number had reached 180 000, while deployment would eventually peak at approximately half a million troops. It must be assumed that any open political system that can order and achieve with relative ease the despatch of such a vast number of conscripted soldiers is one where a majority of its people are in approximate agreement or at least acquiesce in decisions taken by their elected leadership.

Lyndon Johnson's administration undoubtedly found itself with a difficult and worsening situation, yet its efforts to devise a set of policies by which the United States could demonstrate its resolve and then prevail would end in disaster. The new president had visited Vietnam in May 1961 and was aware of the deterioration that had set in. Although certainly not privy to the innermost counsel of the Kennedy administration, Johnson had supported his president loyally on foreign policy issues. Over South Vietnam his thinking appears to have been the standard Cold War approach, seasoned with an appreciation of internal Vietnamese factors, particularly the wish to see economic improvement. He noted that if more attention were not placed on 'material security', all the considerable efforts of the past by both South Vietnam and the United States 'may go down the drain'. Johnson, who apparently dubbed Diem the Winston Churchill of Asia, also reported to Kennedy that increased American aid and military assistance 'plunges us very deeply into the Vietnamese internal situation' and that the attitudes of US personnel needed to reflect the jungle rather than the capital. The Vice-President hesitated, however, when he considered the likely consequences of more substantial American involvement in Vietnam. He stated, in what would shortly prove highly prophetic for his own administration, that

> if the Vietnamese government backed by a three-year liberal aid programme cannot do this job, then we had better remember the experience of the French who wound up with several hundred thousand men in Vietnam and were still unable to do it. And all this without engaging a single Chinese or Russian.

He cautioned that before the plunge, 'we had better be sure we are prepared to become bogged down chasing irregulars and guerrillas over the rice fields and jungles of Southeast Asia while our principal enemies China and the Soviet Union stand outside the fray and husband their strength'.

Yet President Johnson did take the plunge. He sensed that his ability to govern effectively would be destroyed if South Vietnam were lost to Communism. Johnson, who came to the presidency with hopes of creating a Great Society that might bind his nation together after the assassination of Kennedy and staunch the greater open wound of racism, wanted to avoid a weak compromise over Vietnam. In particular, he feared criticism of his foreign policy from the Right if his ambition to succeed domestically were to be realized. He may have reckoned that any greatly enhanced American role in Vietnam could lead to turmoil at home, yet he also knew that retreat would have major domestic and international consequences. No Texan, at least of Johnson's generation and background, wished to be branded a coward.

Johnson chose to expand the war. Policies that had been drawn up during the Kennedy presidency were approved: a series of covert naval operations began against North Vietnamese shore batteries. What may well have seemed a fairly innocuous episode was to have considerable repercussions for the new administration. The United States was now taking the war to the north in an expansion that was both geographical and political. The President's advisers wished to appear strong both to reassure South Vietnam and to spell out to Hanoi what it could expect unless it halted its large-scale incursions. They also calculated that the American public would prefer Johnson's shrewd mixture of pugnacity and apparent willingness to seem open to diplomatic overtures in contrast to the strident rhetoric of Barry Goldwater, the Republican candidate for the November 1964 general election.

The decision to attack positions in North Vietnam was an indication that the United States and the ever-changing governments in Saigon had failed to prevent pro-Communist forces from gaining ground in South Vietnam. Lack of military success led the Johnson administration to widen the war. The near unanimous passing of resolutions by both houses of Congress in Washington, coupled with warnings to Hanoi through third parties that it must desist in the south or 'suffer the consequences', indicates the seriousness of the American resolve. The passing of the Tonkin Resolution in August 1964, after the almost certain faking of evidence by the United States over alleged aggression by North Vietnam-ese ships against a US destroyer, immensely strengthened the adminis-tration's hand. While former members of the Johnson administration continue to defend their actions and maintain that their many critics have falsely attacked their integrity, the accusations have largely stuck. By obtaining a blank cheque from Congress, Johnson had secured legislative approval for future action, if and when he wished to take further measures against his enemies. Covert operations would be followed by overt air strikes against industrial and communication targets in North Vietnam once the President felt that greater military force was justified. At this juncture a senior adviser to Johnson noted that 'we are the greatest power in the world – if we behave like it'.

The American war in Vietnam now began. All branches of the United States armed forces were closely involved in what proved to be a remark-ably rapid escalation of the conflict. Troop levels increased and the conduct of the war risked becoming an all-American show. South Vietnam was to be saved by the United States. This would prevent what the Joint Chiefs of Staff had maintained in almost apocalyptic terms in 1961 to be the possible 'loss of Southeast Asia ... [which] would have an impact on all other areas of the world where the credibility of our guarantees to protect nations would be open to serious doubt'. Such opinions had long been part and parcel of US international policy and had led to officials arguing that in order to promote American goals in Latin America and the Middle East it was essential to draw the line in Vietnam. The Mekong stretched to Mexico. The assumed logic of this extreme version of globalism made it well nigh impossible for the Johnson administration to cut and run. Instead, it could only expand its efforts in the hope that at some time in the future the pain it intended to inflict on its opponents would persuade them to desist.

It is doubtful whether the Johnson cabinet understood events on the other side of the hill. Certainly foreign service officers reported regularly on the impact of Communist power on regional issues, but Presidents Eisenhower, Kennedy and Johnson were bombarded with virtually iden-tical memorandums warning that only intervention by Washington could shore up South Vietnam and thereby safeguard both neighbouring states and the reputation of the United States. The foreign policy rationale for expanding the war is hardly in doubt: Lyndon Johnson held that South Vietnam had to be saved from Communism, much as the West expected the United States to honour its commitments elsewhere. Weakness at any one point, the administration maintained, would automatically result in destabilization and foot-shuffling elsewhere. The American strategy of globalism assumed that all points on the periphery had to be defended in order to project US power and reassure its allies. By the mid-1960s the United States had created an informal empire against the Sino-Soviet bloc that was based on a formidable array of military alliances, advisory groupings and base agreements. This extraordinary structure was felt to be vulnerable to evidence of American irresolution. Johnson would explain in retirement what was clearly at the forefront of his mind during his presidency: if the United States 'ran out on Southeast Asia, I could see trouble ahead in every part of the globe – not just in Asia but in the Middle East and in Europe, in Africa and in Latin America'.

Yet the danger of being forced to increase US troops levels to prove that Washington would stand firm presented considerable risks at home. The Johnson administration reckoned that the pain it could undoubtedly inflict on North Vietnam through aerial bombing and on the Viet Cong through ground offensives in South Vietnam would achieve results, before domestic opposition made further reinforcements and resultant casualties increasingly difficult to justify. Since the US government would eventually have half a million personnel in the field, it was ever tempted to imagine that with yet another additional division the illusive victory might be tantalizingly close. From the summer of 1965 until March 1968, the expansion of US forces despatched to South Vietnam con- tinued relentlessly. The build-up was evidence indeed that the Johnson administration was committed to nothing short of the rooting out of Communism from South Vietnam, as it sought the end to infiltration both from the north and from the west down the Laotian border. The objective, as Johnson had put it in January 1965, while considering future policies, was a forthright commitment: 'I am determined to make it clear to all the world that the US will spare no effort and no sacrifice in doing its full part to turn back the Communists in Vietnam'.

Dissent

Alternative voices within the administration rarely made an impact on policy. The Departments of State and Defense may not have always been in agreement on details, but President Johnson and his loyal inner group of advisers prided themselves on their collaborative efforts. The adminis- tration opted for massive intervention. Among the small minority of those who urged caution in the mid-1960s were members of the CIA and Under Secretary of State George Ball. The CIA had often doubted the veracity of the domino theory and said so, but it was the long-serving Ball who had the opportunity to have more influence on decision-makers. He urged retreat. 'The alternative – no matter what we may wish it to be – is almost certainly a protracted war involving an open-ended commitment of US forces', Ball warned, 'mounting US casualties; no assurance of a satisfactory outcome, and a serious danger of escalation at the end of the road'. Yet the administration thought otherwise, preferring to ignore the criticism that was growing from Europe and elsewhere over the intensification of bombing raids on North Vietnam and the improbability of a negotiated settlement. While Secretary McNamara was receiving departmental advice on the need for more ruthless bombing, George Ball was arguing for 'a compromise solution' on President Johnson. There was little hope, in Ball's opinion, of military success and the alternatives needed to be explored before the United States was irrevocably committed to escalation. He warned of national humiliation as the probable outcome, unless 'we seek a compromise settlement which achieves less than our stated objectives and thus cut our losses while we still have the freedom of maneuver to do so'. Ball stated bluntly that there needed to be 'serious diplomatic feelers looking towards a solution based on some application of a self determination principle'. He thought approaches to North Vietnam's representative in Paris, rather than considering talks with Beijing, Moscow or the NLF, would make the most sense, since Hanoi was regarded as the most flexible of these parties. Ball had few grounds for knowing whether a diplomatic solution was possible but he had every reason to believe, as he told Johnson, that the 'South Vietnamese are losing the war to the Viet Cong'. He warned: 'No one can assure you that we can beat the Viet Cong or even force them to the conference table on our terms; no matter how many hundred thousand white, *foreign* (US) troops we deploy'. Yet since President Johnson had been assured only ten days earlier in May 1965 by Walt Rostow that victory in the guerrilla war was 'nearer our grasp than we (but not Hanoi) may think', it is hardly surprising that Ball's memorandum failed to persuade the White House. By the end of July 1965, Johnson had decided to commit significantly more US ground troops to South Vietnam. In his televised address to the American people on 28 July, the President announced that the number of American servicemen in Vietnam would be increased from 75 000 to 125 000; he also attached the important rider that additional troops would be sent 'as requested'. On the previous day, Senator Mike Mansfield had anxiously warned Johnson and his senior aides at a meeting of congressional leaders that a negotiated peace was infinitely preferable to 'an anti-Communist crusade'.

Mansfield cautioned that 'escalation begets escalation', but it was by now too late.

North Vietnam's War and its Allies

North Vietnam was, of course, severely weakened by the combined strength of US air strikes and the arrival of still more battalions of American and allied troops. This did not, however, break its resolve. Hanoi persisted, sensing that in terms of the wider, international public it was able to present a far better case than the United States. The obvious violations of any semblance of adherence to the Geneva agreements by the American bombing of the north were widely perceived to be in a different category from that of the actions of the Communists. The successes of the propaganda war gave North Vietnam a considerable advantage on which its leaders astutely capitalized. It also concluded that Washington did not wish for a diplomatic solution, until such time as the Viet Cong had surrendered, since the aerial offensives of 1965 and the wording of President Johnson's speech of April 1965 precluded the NLF from participation in any possible peace arrangements. Secretary Rusk confirmed the American position in January 1966 when he informed the House Foreign Affairs Committee that the administration would not recognize the NLF, while Ho Chi Minh at almost exactly the same moment declared that the NLF alone was 'the sole genuine representative of the people of South Vietnam'. Given such rival positions, any basis for even starting discussions through third parties would clearly be immensely difficult. At various times institutions as diverse as the United Nations, the International Commission charged with monitoring the Geneva accords, and the Vatican were put forward as suitable vehicles for starting informal debate, but little came of these attempts. Since it was clear by 1965, however, that the United States and the government of South Vietnam would not bend to forces loyal to North Vietnam and its supporters in the south, the outcome would have to be decided on the field of battle.

President Johnson appeared to have the advantage. Provided he could continue to gain sufficient public approval for the conduct of his war, there was every prospect of calling up still more troops and ordering yet more air strikes against targets within North Vietnam. Against the might of the United States, the NLF and the Viet Cong seemed almost naked. The Pentagon's planners reckoned that over time the will of even the most dedicated Communist cadre would break before American fire power. Assuming that the number of fresh units was finite and that the morale of experienced fighters would crumble, it was hard to see how defeat could be long avoided. Ho's ragged soldiers equipped with nothing much more than rifles and grenades would soon succumb to enemy mortars, napalm and the appearance of helicopter gunships. The Viet Cong might use nightfall, shallow tunnels and sympathetic villagers as allies to bring in reinforcements, but nerves must surely crack – ideology was not much protection against carpet bombing. In addition, although both the Soviet Union and the PRC were known to be supplying military aid to North Vietnam, the government in Hanoi prided itself on its national independence and tried to avoid taking sides in wider Sino-Soviet ideological disputes. Ho Chi Minh had long disliked being beholden to his fellow Communist states.

Hanoi, in much the same fashion as the Johnson administration in Washington, was obliged to reckon with the regional and international consequences of any widening of the war. There appears to be little doubt that China was more open in its encouragement of the North Vietnamese government to expand the war by committing North Vietnamese regular troops to fight in the south. Yet Hanoi could gain support from different quarters, even from North Korea, by maintaining that it was under attack from the United States and its lackeys. By 1964, for example, the NLF had been able to open its own office in Moscow, seemingly in order to balance the one that was already in existence in Beijing. The Soviet Union, particularly after the demise of Khrushchev in October 1964, became somewhat more positive in its attitude towards Vietnamese reunification under Hanoi, even though this carried a substantial risk of tension between Moscow and Washington. China, while more enthusiastic, continually risked being seen by North Vietnam as having its own ambitions in Southeast Asia by fomenting left-wing resistance in Indonesia, Thailand and the Philippines. There were long-held North Vietnamese fears that any future success in getting rid of the United States might lead to the emergence of the PRC as the next regional supremo. The prospect that this created in Hanoi can be easily imagined, given both the lengthy history of Sino-Vietnamese animosity and the fact that Chinese personnel were currently contributing to the North Vietnamese war effort. Greater Chinese involvement contained the risk of greater postwar influence.

Calculations over Chinese behaviour played an equally important part in the Johnson administration's thinking on the widening of the war. The President had received a short, sharp warning from Senator Mike Mansfield on the domestic and international dangers attached to escalation in January 1964. Johnson had expressed to Mansfield his concern that 'we do not want another China in Viet Nam', to which the senator from Montana had testily added, 'neither do we want another Korea'. Mansfield noted that

a key (but often overlooked) factor in both situations was a tendency to bite off more than we were prepared in the end to chew. We tended to talk ourselves out on a limb with overstatements of our purpose and commitment only to discover in the end that there were not sufficient American interests to support with blood and treasure a desperate final plunge. Then, the questions followed invariably: 'Who got us into this mess?' 'Who lost China?' etc.

Mansfield hoped to avoid both another Korea and another China by refusing to send more US marines and by redoubling diplomatic efforts to hunt for a peace settlement, but twelve months later the dice had been thrown. Johnson decided to expand the bombing of North Vietnam and yet work to minimize any Chinese intervention.

The United States fought in Vietnam knowing that the People's Republic of China would most emphatically retaliate if its territory were attacked, but, as the Vietnam Task Force's deputy director reported from Hong Kong in May 1962, 'they don't want a major war'. This assessment of China stood throughout the decade and was based on 'their economic plight and because they will not have an effective way of delivering the bomb in the foreseeable future'. This did not preclude, however, far-reaching concerns of Beijing's regional ambitions. By the winter of 1965, McNamara would argue that there was 'a long-run United States policy to contain Communist China'. This was essential, since China 'looms as a major power threatening to undercut our importance and effectiveness in the world and, more remotely but more menacingly, to organize all of Asia against us'. Much later, in his memoirs, McNamara would quote these remarks against himself as evidence of sheer folly, but in the months when the Johnson administration escalated the war, this perception of the dangers posed by Beijing was generally accepted by the government. The administration's thinking over Vietnam was invariably shaped by China's support for Hanoi and its actions elsewhere in the Asia-Pacific, yet President Johnson's advisers calculated that the PRC was unlikely to intervene in force in the war.

The administration, however, was constantly aware of what it saw as Beijing's regional ambitions. Unlike the Soviet Union, which had been held by State Department officials from the early 1960s to 'think Communism can make gains without local wars', the PRC 'will back wars of "National Liberation" provided the risks are controllable. The ChiComs think local wars are the best way to spread Communism and will accept higher risks'. The difficulty for Johnson was to estimate how much military pressure could be applied to the North Vietnamese and their allies in order to persuade them to desist and agree to open peace negotiations. The danger, as the deputy director of the CIA explained in November 1964, was that at 'each step the chances of extreme NVN and Chicom reaction would increase'. It was felt, however, that limitations on direct US ground troop activity in North Vietnam might well prevent anything comparable to China's massive intervention in Korea in 1950.

In this instance the administration's judgement was proved correct. China did not intervene directly in force, yet the American war that aimed to create 'an independent and secure South Vietnam with appropriate international safeguards' continued to falter. By December 1964 General Wheeler, chairman of the Joint Chiefs of Staff, had informed General Westmoreland, the commander of US troops in South Vietnam, that both Congress and the public would want to know 'the reasons for our lack of success' and were increasingly 'frustrated that we are not winning the war'. The administration's solution was to attempt to provide the reinforcements that Westmoreland continually requested and simultaneously to shore up the succession of governments that emerged in Saigon. Each new division that arrived from the United States made it increasingly apparent that this was very largely an all-American war. The British Labour cabinet under Prime Minister Harold Wilson refused Johnson's entreaties to despatch even a single regiment, such as the Black Watch, as a token of Anglo-American solidarity. Wilson was careful not to court domestic unpopularity over Southeast Asia, much as he ruled against military intervention in Rhodesia following Ian Smith's unilateral declaration of independence. Certainly the governments of South Korea, the Philippines and Australia did agree to make contributions, but numerically their impact was small and failed to inch much beyond what President Johnson derided as the chaplain and nurse level.

Equally apparent was the continuing political instability in South Vietnam, where Johnson heard himself admitting to his advisers that even a return to the days of Diem might have advantages over the current domestic confusion. By fighting and financing the war, the United States had undertaken the role vis-à-vis South Vietnam that it had earlier criticized France for playing. The parallels, however, were disturbing. Washington might not be attempting directly to colonize South Vietnam but its military and economic power over the latter's fate was pervasive. To save Saigon, it appeared as if the Johnson administration had given itself vice-regal status and was intent on imposing a protectorate on the new state. Yet by December 1964 Johnson could only express his disappointment to Ambassador Maxwell Taylor, a general officer trusted by the White House, on 'the continuing political turmoil in Saigon', and note that there remained a 'lack of progress in communicating sensitively and persuasively with the various groups in South Vietnam'. Johnson, returning to a theme he had first developed during his vice-presidential visit to the country in 1961, felt that American area specialists in shirt-sleeves with the necessary political skills were thin on the ground. The United States, in Johnson's view, was hardly winning the war to gain the confidence of the 'immature and often irresponsible' elites of South Vietnam.

There was little change, however, in either the manner in which the United States dominated South Vietnamese affairs or in the conduct of the war. McNamara certainly grew increasingly sceptical of the likelihood of a military solution, but, though there were occasional bombing pauses and exploratory talks in diplomatic circles, the war intensified. Public opinion supported this action in 1966 and generally remained on the side of the administration until the scale of American casualties began ominously to grow. This was accompanied by what McNamara predicted by 1967 would be a quite unpredictable outcome, even after all of Westmoreland's requested reinforcements had been sent. It appeared that the Viet Cong and its allies from North Vietnam had sufficient numerical strength and sufficiently high morale to continue to defy American calculations that its defeat was only a matter of time. The fighting prowess of the enemy also gained considerable respect from US front-line troops, who had to face them at uncomfortably close quarters. The familiar adage, attributed, among others, to Henry Kissinger, that a conventional army loses if it does not win and that a guerrilla force wins if it does not lose, now came into play.

The international context further weakened American strategy. The Johnson administration had avoided, as we have seen, measures that would involve war with the PRC, while simultaneously reckoning that the conflict was at bottom about preventing the expansion of an ambitious China. Dean Rusk was obsessed with this fear of Beijing, though his critics insisted that China was not in a position to determine the behaviour of North Vietnam. Yet the United States may have made its own position unnecessarily difficult by failing to impose an immediate naval blockade on North Vietnam and by rejecting the idea of preventing incursions into South Vietnam through the Laotian border route known as the Ho Chi Minh trail. This inability to seal off North Vietnamese use of the Laos and Cambodian borders for vital supply purposes cost America dearly. Inside Laos, for example, the Communist-backed Pathet Lao acted as surrogates for the Viet Cong, while portions of Cambodia too came under North Vietnamese control. In neither case, though, can it be said that the United States acted with particular resolve in circumstances that had an obvious bearing on the large-scale war it was conducting in Vietnam. If the infamous domino theory was as important to American foreign policy as its upholders continued to maintain, the relative feebleness of US actions in South Vietnam's backyard remains hard to explain a generation later. However, Walt Rostow, it should be pointed out, suggested long after the event in 1999 that this refusal was determined by President Johnson, 'presumably on the grounds that any movement of American troops to block infiltration on the trails would bring the Russians and Chinese into the war'. Rostow further argues that 'if the alternative might have been a larger war or the risk of nuclear war, it was worth paying' the price, though General Westmoreland disagreed at the time and felt that 'our hands were tied'.

Dissent began to emerge also on more fundamental issues than whether to risk bombing Viet Cong sanctuaries outside the boundaries of Vietnam. The Johnson administration finally began to see the resignation of key officials, which was correctly assumed to be the consequence of rival views on the wisdom of presidential policy. The departure of Johnson's national security adviser McGeorge Bundy in 1966 was followed by major differences on how best to prosecute the war, which verged even on the apostasy of whether the fight could be won. One long-debated issue concerned the difficulties of trying to calculate if the casualties meted out to the enemy indicated genuine progress towards winning the war. McNamara became increasingly isolated as his pessimism grew over this crucial question. He informed President Johnson in January 1966 that 'the odds are about even that even with the recommended deployments, we will be faced in early 1967 with a military standoff at a much higher level, with pacification hardly underway and with the requirement for the deployment of still more US forces'. Military intelligence also reported that, despite the extraordinarily vehement bombing of North Vietnamese facilities, Viet Cong troop infiltration into the south had actually increased. The United States was having to relearn the conclusions reached by Allied bombing surveys conducted at the end of the Second World War on the German and Japanese experiences. It appears that there are indeed limitations on the amount of damage that even vastly superior air power can inflict on military and civilian targets and on national morale.

North Vietnam had one additional weapon in its armoury that gave it an unquestionable advantage over an open society such as the United States. In a protracted war where there were few set-piece engagements and it was hardly possible to quantify military progress, the key to Ho Chi Minh's eventual success was patience. Despite setbacks and miscalculations, the North Vietnamese leadership remained confident that it could take the appalling casualties inflicted on its forces by US gunships, rocket attacks and automatic rifle fire. By 1968 it was hard to envisage that the Americans would remain much longer. Even for a man with the energy and determination of President Johnson, there were limits to going through the punishing daily ritual of telephoning from the White House to yet more parents of enlisted servicemen to inform them that their sons had died in action in South Vietnam. General Giap, the administration's opponent, correctly noted that once 'American boys being sent home in body bags … steadily increase', it was certain that 'their mothers will want to know why. The war will not long survive their questions'.

Yet Hanoi had no intention of merely waiting for the day when the Americans followed the French into ignominious retreat. Historical inevitability might offer its warm consolations when training new cadres, but hardened politicians and military commanders were expected to construct their own reality from the material at hand. North Vietnam might then prove to be considerably more than the 'ragged ass little fourth rate country' of President Johnson's contempt. Similar deprecation, it may be recalled, was employed by General MacArthur when surveying the burnt-out wreckage of post-surrender Japan. It was also the sad case that every GI in South Vietnam appeared to possess identical opinions, invariably expressed in identical language, with regard to America's supposed ally as those that their President had formed of their enemy in Hanoi. Friends and foes could all too easily merge into a vague, largely unknown Vietnam where, as the novelist Tim O'Brien would put it later, it was 'man against gook' and yet in the foxhole the 'vapours suck you in. You can't tell where you are, or why you're there, and the only certainty is overwhelming ambiguity'.

To hold the nation that the United States claimed to be defending from Communism in the same disdain as your military opponent suggests that the American war effort was troubled from the start. South Vietnam was to be saved, almost regardless of its widely held faults, because of its political and strategic worth to the United States. The fact that American officials thought little of its successive governments or the fighting prowess of its soldiers had become almost irrelevant by the mid-1960s. Saigon quickly began to resemble a glorified hotchpotch of US bases, similar to those to be seen in Japan, South Korea and the Philippines with their proliferation of PX stores, bars and brothels. The whole process spawned corruption on a grand scale.

Evidence that the United States was failing in its military struggle to prevent the Communists from overrunning South Vietnam was apparent from 1967 onwards. McNamara finally resigned from the government in the autumn, having informed Johnson in what would become a widely cited note that 'continuation of our present course of action in Southeast Asia would be dangerous, costly in lives and unsatisfactory to the American people'. In the months before McNamara left office, he had seen the near hopelessness of further escalation and instead argued forcefully that, since the US had drawn the line successfully against China, it should now prepare South Vietnam itself for a wider government. On the ground, General Westmoreland could hardly claim that he had cleared more than a portion of the country of Viet Cong units, though the influx of large numbers of refugees from the countryside into more secure urban areas showed that his opponents also were far from victorious.

Tet and the Johnson Administration

The Tet offensive of February 1968, however, quickly clarified the military and, more importantly, the political positions of both sides. The attacks on US and South Vietnamese units may not have had the near total tactical success claimed at the time, but the psychological result on American domestic opinion was profound. The fact that Viet Cong troops could launch surprise attacks and, in some instances, hold key points in South Vietnam belied the claims of the Johnson administration that it was waging war correctly. Despite the extraordinary statistics on American firepower and the deployment of nearly a dozen divisions, the critics appeared to have been right all along. The ability of the Viet Cong to occupy the US embassy and the presidential palace in Saigon for even a few hours was highly damaging to American prestige and valuable evidence to anti-war activists from London to Tokyo that their foe was weakening. If the heart of South Vietnam was as vulnerable as events appeared to illustrate, commentators wondered how serious the situation might be elsewhere in isolated rural hamlets and unprotected provincial towns.

Tet transformed the war. The Johnson administration recognized immediately that its position was now vulnerable and that it would be infinitely harder to explain the war and justify the casualties that it increasingly brought in its wake. Dean Rusk said sadly in March that 'the element of hope has been taken away by the Tet offensive. People don't think there is likely to be an end'. But President Johnson knew that his earlier strategy of approving each request for additional troops and yet more bombing raids could no longer be contemplated and that Tet did indeed point to a way out of Vietnam. His advisers began to shift positions. Distinguished figures who had laid the foundations for American globalism a generation earlier now recommended, as gently as they could, that the administration recognize the inevitable and prepare to disengage. 'Johnson's War' was gradually ending.

Debate within the administration on the prospects for change intensified. Certainly the President had been asking his advisers 'Should we get out of Vietnam?' for several months, but the question had often been posed among several other, quite contradictory, options. After Tet the answers appeared clearer. On 31 March 1968 Johnson announced a succession of policy changes in the conduct of the war and then stated unequivocally that he would no longer be a candidate in the forthcoming November general election. In his speech he said: 'We are prepared to move immediately toward peace through negotiations. So tonight, in the hope that this action will lead to early talks, I am taking the first step to deescalate the conflict. We are reducing – absolutely reducing – the present level of hostilities'. While it is the case, as others have noted, that

Johnson's remarks did not mark an irrevocable change to the war, since there had been earlier bombing holidays and talking about peace also had a lengthy pedigree, it did mean that a new president might bring fresh solutions to Vietnam. Hanoi probably responded under the assumption that its chances for success were now far greater, even though it had not gained control of the cities of South Vietnam and still risked military defeat if it took the American bait and decided to go for large-scale confrontations with the US forces.

After years of warfare, political change was slow. The Paris peace talks began hesitantly amid a background of mutual suspicion and the continuation of fighting. Hanoi, after stating that the US 'has not seriously and fully met the legitimate demands of the Government of the Democratic Republic of Vietnam' or of 'progressive American opinion', disagreed over scaling down its war in the south in exchange for limitations on American bombing of the north. Eventually, in the autumn of 1968, a compromise formula was concocted by President Johnson that agreed on wider talks taking place, in which both South Vietnamese figures and representatives of the National Liberation Front were invited to participate. This face-saving formula was to be accompanied by a halt to American bombing, even though American troop casualties were fearfully high at this stage in an increasingly unpopular war. While the fighting in South Vietnam was clearly far from over, there were at least indications from Paris that substantive talks might now get under way. The inauguration of the Nixon presidency in January 1969 also contributed to a degree of optimism.

The Nixon Years and Vietnam

Yet it was far from certain where President Nixon himself stood. He might claim to have a 'secret plan' to end the war, much as Eisenhower had stated in similar circumstances during his 1952 presidential campaign with regard to the Korean conflict, but the gulf between campaign rhetoric and the more sober dawn of office was indeed wide. While senior figures in his new administration called for an immediate US withdrawal from Vietnam, Nixon was having none of this defeatism. But discovering an alternative route that might sustain American prestige and at least partly disguise the bitterness of defeat was a challenge that the President heartily disliked. He hoped against hope that some arrangements might be found that would console his own nation and stiffen its South Vietnamese protégé against the fate of almost certain conquest once the United States abandoned it. 'Peace and honour' were doubtless the fine words required of a presidential candidate, but they worked to limit his opportunities after he discovered, or perhaps had sensed all along, that these two elements were largely contradictory. It would be some time, however, before this became apparent. In the interim, US force levels were reduced and the 'Vietnamization' of the war continued, on the premise that future wars in Asia would require substantially more Asian forces in the front line as far fewer soldiers could be expected from the United States. Nixon's remarks, known as the Guam Doctrine statement of July 1969, would have major long-term implications for the future of US strategy in the Asia-Pacific region but provided no immediate answer to his prayers on how to satisfactorily conclude the war in Vietnam.

To attempt to escape from this unpleasant box, Nixon in April 1970 ordered American forces to attack Cambodia. The aim was to 'protect our men who are in Vietnam and to guarantee the continued success of our withdrawal and Vietnamization programs' by a show of force. This was designed to reject what the President termed the dangers of letting loose 'totalitarianism and anarchy' across the world. It was a controversial and highly publicized move that angered Nixon's opponents and probably did little to change the complexion of the war. After the fiercest of attacks, the North Vietnamese government continued to deploy troops down the Ho Chi Minh trail and Hanoi increased its support to the dreaded and antediluvian Khmer Rouge, who were fighting the US-backed Lon Nol regime for control of a divided and exhausted Cambodia. The shifting politics of the Cambodian civil war were largely unaltered by Nixon's action. Following the barrage of adverse criticism within the United States at what was seen as a further escalation of the Vietnam War, all of the American units were ordered to withdraw quickly from the country. But since the accompanying South Vietnamese forces, who had given a generally good account of themselves, had failed to capture either the retreating leadership or the purported headquarters of the NLF, there were few spoils on display.

The Cambodian expedition made little difference to the stalled peace negotiations in Paris. Both the United States and North Vietnam continued to talk past each other as events on the ground took centre stage. The US officials in Paris obviously appreciated that the continuing monthly reductions in the number of American military personnel in South Vietnam risked eventually undermining their nation's position, but the political impasse continued until the autumn of 1972. The invasion of Cambodia had, however, further undermined morale among US troops and greatly added to opposition on the home front. One author has even suggested that 'before the Cambodian affair, American morale had fallen almost to zero. Now it sank below zero'. Henry Kissinger, Nixon's national security adviser, persuaded the White House to ignore those who wished for a return to a bombing campaign and blockade of North Vietnam. Kissinger saw that after the uproar over incursions into Cambodia, public opinion would hardly countenance a major new American military offensive.

Nixon Goes to China

Nineteen seventy-two was the year of the Sino-American diplomatic revolution. After over two decades of near total disregard for each other, the two nations at the centre of Asian-Pacific affairs finally agreed to start a process that would eventually end their diplomatic isolation. It was indeed the beginning of a new era that would have profound consequences for all the nations of the region. President Nixon, revelling in the grand political gesture that could wrong-foot his opponents, had announced on 15 July 1971 that he planned to visit the People's Republic of China. Two factors were at the heart of Nixon's decision to seek an accommodation with the Communist state that he had so often criticised throughout his own Cold War political career. Nixon wanted to exploit the international opportunities that he felt were given to Washington by the deterioration of the Sino-Soviet split into open border warfare along the disputed Ussuri River. He hoped also to be able to persuade the Chinese authorities to apply pressure on North Vietnam to be more willing to negotiate in Paris, while reducing their own aid to Hanoi.

Since Nixon's political reputation had been built on a resolute foundation of anti-Communism at home and abroad, his announcement that he would fly to China was an international bombshell. It left the Japanese government, for example, in huge difficulties. Nixon was unsympathetic to its predicament, in part because he held that the conservatives in Tokyo had been particularly reluctant to open markets to American goods and had stubbornly rejected calls to stem domestically sensitive Japanese textile exports to the United States. In addition, since Nixon had for years been a staunch supporter of Chiang Kai-shek, the president had to attempt to placate Taipei. He did so by sending Ronald Reagan as his special envoy to Chiang and promised that ties to Taiwan would not be irrevocably cut by the tilt to the PRC. Yet behind all of Nixon's calculations, as his scribbled notes on the eve of his arrival in China suggest, was a wish for both short-term gain with regard to Chinese assistance in getting the United States out of Vietnam and a recognition that the long-term future stability of the Asia-Pacific required the development of closer and more amicable ties with Mao and his successors. Only Nixon, it was said half in jest, could have had the nerve to transform US foreign policy over China without worrying about Nixon. The bid was extraordinarily brave politically and probably a right-wing, internationalist Republican was the individual best qualified to make this shift, since the Democrats still feared being tarred and feathered with the charge that their leaders had 'lost' China in 1949. Nixon, who had said in 1960 that the Chinese Communists 'don't just want Quemoy and Matsu. They don't just want Formosa. They want the world', was now intent on the reversal of much of postwar American foreign policy in Asia.

In the short term, Nixon's visit to China in February 1972 made some difference to North Vietnam's behaviour. Because of Beijing's anxieties over the Soviet Union (and vice versa), Kissinger could note later that neither state was prepared to look with any particular degree of sympathy at North Vietnam. Both Beijing and Moscow, Kissinger stressed, 'for all their hatred of each other, and perhaps because of it, were agreed on this point'. The Chinese, defined by Kissinger, who ought to know, as 'the most unsentimental practitioners of balance-of-power politics I have ever encountered', were sufficiently alarmed by their hostility towards the Soviet Union to cooperate with the United States. The fact that Chairman Mao had already termed 'the revisionist leading clique' in Moscow 'a mere dust heap' was confirmed, though his remark on the same occasion in October 1966 that the 'US imperialists and all other such harmful insects' were diggers of their own graves would be politely forgotten. For its part, the Soviet Union's dislike of Beijing had already led it to mention to Washington that it was considering a pre-emptive strike on China before the latter's infant missile system became a larger threat. The world was now witnessing what the American scholar Donald Zagoria would aptly term a 'new cold war'. This time, however, it was no longer a strategic contest between East and West but border clashes and dire military scenarios between neighbouring and antagonistic Communist states. The process played into the United States' hands, since Nixon and Kissinger firmly held that the Sino-Soviet fracture was capable of 'revolutionizing world diplomacy'. It was a shift of seismic proportions, important enough for Kissinger to write graphically in his memoirs: 'The bipolarity of the postwar period was over'. The moves by the Nixon administration led next to constructive triangular diplomacy that inevitably worked to the advantage of Washington, given the very substantial differences that existed between the Soviet Union and the PRC. Washington correctly reckoned that it could persuade the Soviet Union to behave in a less threatening manner in global affairs. The United States, relishing its new China card, did succeed in restraining Moscow, though Mao complained that this was achieved only by standing 'on China's shoulders'. Under international circumstances that left the Soviet Union suddenly facing major opponents on two fronts, détente generally prospered. In the process, the lengthy years of Sino-American confrontation in the Asia-Pacific were reversed. President Nixon had succeeded in replacing a generation of implacable hostility between Washington and Beijing with an era of quasi-good feelings. An entire chapter in American foreign policy towards the Asia-Pacific was finally ending.

Progress over Vietnam was assumed to be the largest immediate political dividend that might accrue from the secret diplomacy behind Nixon's summit in Beijing. This was made considerably more difficult by the start of Hanoi's spring offensive. It led the Nixon administration to caution both Moscow and Beijing that much would depend on how each responded to North Vietnam's attacks on a nervous South Vietnam, which by 1972 had been largely obliged to look to its own forces to protect its sovereignty. Near completion of the programme of Vietnamization was widely predicted to provide the ideal opportunity for North Vietnam to test the military and political cohesion of the uncertain Thieu regime in Saigon. So it proved, yet to the surprise of many, the South Vietnamese military, assisted by American airpower, fought back with vigour to defeat the massed attacks designed to overthrow their pro-American government. The White House was also relieved to see that neither the Russians nor Chinese rushed in to increase their assistance to North Vietnam. The PRC told Kissinger through private channels that it preferred to stand aside, while the Soviet Union also gave the impression of washing its hands of residual responsibilities for North Vietnam's fate.

Peace-making in Paris

Kissinger's objective was to engineer a 'process of separating Hanoi from its allies'. Yet the administration knew that Congressional determination to end the war would eventually work to North Vietnam's advantage, unless an imperfect but substantial agreement might be cobbled together before the domestic political clock disrupted events. President Nixon might win re-election in 1972, but funding for continuing the war would assuredly be terminated once a sufficient number of conservatives felt the terms on offer were acceptable to the general public. The administration therefore offered to both sides proposals that would lead to a comprehensive ceasefire, the withdrawal of all troops, supervised elections, and what had by now become the key issue for the United States – the necessary return of its prisoners of war. Le Duc Tho and the North Vietnamese negotiators in Paris preferred to gain a coalition government of national reconciliation after the resignation of South Vietnam's Thieu and worked to ensure that fulsome political rewards would follow from military success. For his part, Thieu responded vehemently through what became known as the multiple nos – there was to be no coalition, no neutralization and no territorial concessions.

The problem for the administration remained, of course, the near impossibility of getting its terms accepted by Hanoi. Henry Kissinger surely deserves some sympathy for writing in his memoirs that 'we had our own imperatives. We had struggled and suffered for four years over a war from which we were trying to disengage. We had accepted nearly unbearable fissures in our society to maintain our honour and credibility'. While the national security adviser was fighting two wars simultaneously, through talks in Paris and on Capitol Hill, he feared that Congress could vote to terminate the war against the wishes of Nixon, thus 'undermining the authority of the American Presidency in every corner of the globe'. Since all presidents from Truman on had argued that Southeast Asia had to be saved both for its own importance and because of its global impact on American foreign policy, it is hardly surprising that even in 1972, after an unpopular war, the Nixon administration feared the Vietnam War's impact on American objectives elsewhere. Getting out without destroying the United States' reputation was as important for Nixon as staying in to safeguard its international credibility had been for his predecessors. Lengthy involvement and delayed disengagement appeared to hinge on similar international factors that at times may have had relatively little to do with Vietnam. The longest war was terminated only after the longest peace process.

Eventually, after scores of unproductive formal and clandestine meetings, a breakthrough was achieved. Much to the surprise even of those at the heart of the talks, Hanoi did give ground and a compromise of sorts was worked out in January 1973. This followed only after an intense US bombing campaign (termed Linebacker II) on its opponents' bases and installations that probably succeeded in persuading North Vietnam to drop its earlier objections to a coalition scheme for the south. The Paris peace accords had also required immense juggling by Kissinger and his staff to gain President Thieu's reluctant consent to arrangements that he detested. South Vietnam's leader was left in little doubt that the United States in the last resort would make its own arrangements with North Vietnam. To sugar the pill, however, the Americans are reputed to have handed over to Saigon what was calculated to be the fourth largest air force in the world.

It is doubtful if the outcome gained President Nixon much peace or honour. He could claim to have ensured that the South Vietnamese regime was still in place and that there were political schemes afoot to produce a settlement acceptable to both sides, but his critics questioned whether much had been achieved. Many were quick to stress the huge costs involved in prolonging the war. Henry Kissinger would maintain that the final accord fitted, if imperfectly, into the long-standing US goals of refusing to abandon South Vietnam's government, of gaining at least a military ceasefire, and of ensuring the return of all POWs. There was, however, no prospect of achieving the withdrawal of North Vietnamese forces from South Vietnam, since 'ten years of war and three administrations' had singularly failed to gain that impossible goal. Instead, Kissinger reckoned 'we had a moral obligation as well to our own people: not to prolong their division beyond the point demanded by honour and our international responsibility; to end the war in a manner that would heal rather than divide'. Yet this hardly constituted the 'decent settlement' that the American negotiators hoped against hope to achieve. There were also bitter disputes with Thieu that stretched the concept of allies almost to breaking point. Only after a 'showdown' that left Nixon threatening to sign the Paris accords regardless of South Vietnam's views was the agreement approved by all sides.

The final playing out of the second Vietnam War began immediately after the envoys had put their names to the settlement. Few doubted that the withdrawal of the United States from the field would lead to further conflict and that no document, however well crafted, could long disguise this reality. The chances of any South Vietnamese regime being able to resist its opponents for more than a short interval were never high. Since the remaining American units were by now so few and promises of future American support already so problematic, it would inevitably be a case of South Vietnam attempting to fend off its opponents on its own. The collapse of non-Communist South Vietnam rounded off a dismal saga. From the United States' 'creeping' containment in the 1940s and 1950s, to the massive involvement of the late 1960s and the attempts of the early 1970s to use diplomacy as a substitute for force, its policies in Indo-China had all ended in ashes. After what is now being termed 'America's longest war' and, far more damningly, 'an unnecessary war', the results were soon very plain to see. The huge toll in lives, damaged minds and mangled limbs had failed to achieve much beyond an only slightly con-cealed defeat in Southeast Asia and a divided, bitter domestic polity. If Hemingway had spoken for the lost generation after the First World War, it would be the task of Philip Caputo and Tim O'Brien to articulate the disillusionment of their times. Songs, movies, memoirs and then the inevitable histories conspired to keep Vietnam in the public conscious-ness to an extent that many politicians could only deplore. It was for this reason that President George Bush found it necessary to boast in March 1991, after a swift and relatively bloodless victory for American forces in the Gulf War, that his nation had finally 'kicked the Vietnam syndrome'. Yet the result of the Vietnam disaster for the United States at home and seemingly abroad was a harvest of rancour. We shall look next at the contrasting and largely unanticipated consequences of the Vietnam War on the Asia-Pacific region and the broader international system.

5   Postwar: Asia-Pacific, 1975–1989

China is outgrowing Asia and trying the world on for size.
Steven I. Levine, *China's Foreign Relations in the 1980s*
(New Haven, 1984)

As long as Japan remains a merchant-cum-industrialist, we must
always defer to the United States. We have to swallow our pride,
accept insults and not argue back. Otherwise, we may lose the
American market.
   If that is too high a price to pay, we have to raise our sights and
become a leader. We would need our own ideology, independent
defense and economic policies, and leaders who can perform on
the world stage.
Amaya Naohira, *Tokyo Shimbun*, 24 June 1987

The United States' humiliation in Vietnam coincided with major alterations to the bipolar world that had existed since 1945. While the Cold
War certainly continued throughout the 1970s and, indeed, 1980s, there
were changes to the fundamental structure of international relations that
led to an enlarged and thereby more complex international system. By
the early 1970s the manner in which the United States and the Soviet
Union had jointly organized and run the world underwent novel and
important shifts. President Nixon, for example, invoked the concept of a
new world order. He identified five power centres: those, naturally, of
the United States and the Soviet Union but with the addition of the
European Community, the People's Republic of China, and Japan. There
were, of course, large discrepancies in the relative political, military and
economic power positions of all five such entities, but even to recognize
these trends publicly within the world system is evidence of how the US
government's thinking was evolving by the early 1970s.
   Central to much of this international debate was the depth of the Sino-
Soviet split. This, as we have seen, had led to opportunities for American
diplomacy that the Nixon administration had relished, both for its probable impact on the continuing Vietnam imbroglio and for its wider global
implications in the long-running Cold War. The Asia-Pacific region was

clearly crucial to this political, ideological and, on occasion, fiercely military confrontation between the two superpowers, and Nixon's moves towards China were intended to gain advantages for the United States by manufacturing a Sino-American rapprochement that could not fail to concern the Soviet Union. The result was to prompt Moscow to adopt a more cooperative posture towards the United States that led in turn to détente between the two superpowers through arms control measures and the stabilization of borders in Europe. It also allowed Richard Nixon and Henry Kissinger to work gradually to change the deep mutual hostility that had enveloped the United States and China since 1949. It followed, therefore, that in the context of America's global strategy, the Sino-Soviet split was undoubtedly a godsend to Washington. The differences between the Soviet Union and the PRC proved to be far more than a theoretical debate between rival armchair cadres in Moscow and Beijing. Instead of merely dissecting obscure points of Marxist doctrine on the correct manner in which to raise revolution in the Third World, the Sino-Soviet split was an intense competition for power over which state was best equipped to manage the international Communist movement and how its business should be conducted. In the process the PRC would gradually move from the periphery of regional affairs to a position of greater prestige and strength as both Washington and Moscow reassessed their earlier hostility towards China.

President Nixon was able to deal skilfully with the PRC because Beijing much preferred a South Vietnam with strong links to Washington to a North Vietnam that professed close ties to Moscow. The thought of a united and successful Vietnam on China's southern flank was more than enough for Mao to welcome Nixon. Yet Nixon and Kissinger could not extend this winning hand for long. Sino-American relations soured once it became apparent that the US Congress would refuse to countenance either the further deployment of US troops or continue military and economic aid to South Vietnam. The failure of Gerald Ford, who replaced President Nixon when the latter was obliged to resign after the Watergate scandal, to win Congressional approval for emergency appropriations was seen shortly afterwards by one vocal critic as symbolic of the foreign policy of an entire era. For Roger Morris, this was 'a last vain, guilt-ridden effort to purchase a nation-state that did not exist in South Vietnam'.

The final months of American involvement in South Vietnam paralleled an earlier moment when hesitancy rather than boldness had been the order of the day. As the evacuation of the remaining US personnel began in April 1975, approximately the same groupings scrambled to leave as had once cautiously made their way into French Indo-China some three decades earlier. Then it had been a handful of marines, some

CIA staff and a few foreign service officers who had begun the process of engagement; now it was their disappointed successors, who waited for the giant helicopters that would airlift them to the safety of US aircraft carriers steaming offshore. Many pro-American South Vietnamese, however, were not so fortunate. There were scenes of near panic as guards at the US embassy used any means at their disposal to restrain the thousands of desperate Vietnamese who, sensing their fate with scores about to be settled, fought to get on the last flights out of Saigon. Almost immediately afterwards, on 30 April 1975, the capital fell. Some South Vietnamese forces had attempted to resist, while others had thought discretion the better part of valour and had simply shed their uniforms, abandoned their boots on the pavement and melted into the crowds that began cheering the arrival of the first highly disciplined North Vietnamese units. General Khoi of the defeated South Vietnamese forces would recall later: 'It was 1025 hours, 30 April 1975 by my watch. This was the end, I was most sorry for the outcome of the war, but I had done my best. I was, of course, arrested by the Communists and held captive in various concentration camps for seventeen years'. Amid the turmoil and looting, the few remaining Western journalists who had vowed to stay on watched nervously as North Vietnamese tanks encircled the presidential palace. Suddenly they saw their jubilant crews race to raise the blue, red and yellow flag of the National Liberation Front over what would shortly be renamed as Ho Chi Minh City. Although Ho did not live to witness this moment, it was indeed appropriate that, after a lifetime of incessant campaigning to win the independence of his country, this honour should be bestowed posthumously on its determined leader.

After decades of conflict, it appeared that finally, in the early summer of 1975, Vietnam was at last to be united and its people seemingly freed from endless civil war and external intervention. The process of decolonization and reunification had been brutal and the costs in lives lost can still only be guessed at, but the final collapse of the discredited Saigon regime marks a milestone in postwar international history. The United States and its erstwhile protégés in South Vietnam had lost to an infinitely poorer and less developed nation. Advanced technology and military might had proved in the end to be no match for determined nationalism and ideology. It was a reminder that in war, as the victorious General Giap would explain to the *New York Times* much later, 'there are two factors – human beings and weapons. Ultimately, though, human beings are the decisive factor'. It was a case of miscalculation by the United States. General Westmoreland, noted Giap of his opponent, had been 'wrong to expect that his superior firepower would grind us down. We were waging a people's war – *à la manière Vietnaminienne*. America's sophisticated arms, electronic devices and all the rest were to no avail in the end'. Giap stressed that 'if we had focused on the balance of forces, we would have been defeated in two hours'. North Vietnam had won a resounding victory and confounded the policies of the greatest of contemporary powers.

It was a humiliation that would haunt and divide American society for a generation. The construction of the simple, non-heroic Vietnam Memorial in Washington DC stands in contrast to the more conventional military figures depicted in its sister Korean War memorial, as if to remind the nation of past controversies and doubts. The black stone wall with its listing of the names of all the dead from the Vietnam War remains a focal point of homage for many veterans. Twenty-five years after the fall of Saigon, the correspondence pages of American journals still resound to the claims and counter-claims of angry participants and commentators. The Vietnam War record of presidential candidates (or the lack of it) has been a factor of considerable debate in recent general elections, though this type of scrutiny is of little importance among most younger voters. Yet there has been and, it is safe to predict, will continue to be major disagreement both over whom to hold responsible for the debacle and what, if any, might be the appropriate lessons to draw from the experience. Outside the United States, the gloating over America's failure has long since faded, though it was once widespread; even nations usually friendly to Washington had found it hard not to disguise their delight at the fate of the colossus.

The Americans left Vietnam with few accomplishments to their credit. Although they might claim to have prevented the immediate fall of South Vietnam and could boast that their military had imposed enormous damage on its Communist and neutralist neighbours in the process, there was no guarantee that this situation would endure for long. Wider factors had also to be assessed. It was far from clear how the rest of Southeast Asia would cope with the departure of the United States and the formal establishment in July 1976 of the newly united and militarily tested Socialist Republic of Vietnam. It remained to be seen whether the many new and decidedly weak nations of the region might now be subjected to similar experiences to those recently undergone by South Vietnam. The oft-predicted domino effect was about to be tested.

Pro-American regimes in the region had long expressed deep fears of possible American retreat from Asia. The United States' allies could hardly be expected to remain locked into military and economic relationships with Washington if substantial evidence were to emerge of any significant reduction in the United States' overall commitment to the vast Asia-Pacific region. Such thinking also stretched to more self-confident nations, such as Japan and Australia, where conservative voices also could be heard expressing reservations over the possible long-term staying power of the United States. Public opinion had inevitably been influenced by periodic mass demonstrations against the Vietnam War in Tokyo, Osaka, Seoul, Manila, Melbourne and Sydney, though in none of these cities did the immediate political damage lead to any permanent fracturing of relations with Washington.

The Birth of ASEAN

It was ironic that President Nixon, who had laboured hard to explain to the American public that the United States was now a major Pacific power, had to shore up his own nation's resolve in the region. To improve the chances of the non-Communist states, Washington worked to encourage far greater cooperation between countries that at first had little in common but shared colonial pasts and a wish to maintain their independence in an era where Communism appeared to be on the march. The Association of South East Asian Nations (ASEAN) had been formed by Indonesia, Malaysia, Thailand, the Philippines and Singapore in August 1967 as an anti-Communist regional organization to promote some sense of political and economic solidarity. Its birth was far from auspicious, however, and few would have prophesied that the embryonic structure would eventually display such later strength. Yet the rise of North Vietnam and the retreat of the United States in the early 1970s acted as a powerful spur towards the encouragement of common goals and a discussion of common values that might eventually underpin the movement towards greater regionalism. These aspirations began by taking the form of cautious discussion rather than precipitative movement. This led to the frequently invoked 'ASEAN way' of pursuing a consensual approach to pressing problems. The result was an uncertain American bloc constantly looking over its shoulder to Washington that gradually formed itself into a cohesive organization able to articulate the concerns of its fellow members with fewer and fewer inhibitions. The process may have been slow and interrupted by border disputes but the entity did gain in unity and confidence. The unexpected, such as the American overtures to the PRC and the expulsion of Taiwan from the United Nations, could, however, quickly reveal differences among ASEAN's founder members that required fast diplomatic footwork to prevent disruption. Yet institutional developments were generally assisted by alterations in Big Power relations after the mid-1970s. Many of these swift changes in international politics during the 1970s were unwelcome, of course, to a new and divided grouping, but ASEAN was obliged to grow up fast. Events were in the saddle. It was essential, therefore, to consider how to respond to Sino-American rapprochement, the withdrawal of British forces from Southeast Asia in 1971, followed shortly afterwards by those of the

United States, and the soon apparent ambitions of a reunited Vietnam. ASEAN was never a military organization, yet even the crafting of a common political stance was immensely difficult, since the five founder member states had varying objectives and harboured suspicions of each other. Sceptics indeed had doubted from the outset whether several long-standing rivalries between, for example, Indonesia and Malaysia could ever be adequately papered over. It was noticeable too that Indonesia, regarded as the most ambitious of the ASEAN states, was the only founding nation not to have collective defence agreements with either Britain or the United States.

Progress was uneven. ASEAN members had major domestic political and social problems to contain as well as reckoning on appropriate economic modernization strategies that inevitably held priority with its leaders. Yet regional developments simply would not permit ASEAN the luxury of merely cultivating its own garden and neglecting the behaviour of its closest neighbours. The final defeat of the South Vietnamese regime by North Vietnam in 1975 required a collective response to a moment that appeared to confirm the worst fears of ASEAN members.

The consequences of Hanoi's victory were felt first, of course, in the various countries of Indo-China. It quickly became evident that blood would flow to some extent in South Vietnam and Laos but more particularly in Cambodia, where the Khmer Rouge's brutal behaviour was indefensible. Following in the dreary pattern established by the Tamburlaine of legend, their victims' skulls were piled high in mounds. Two decades later, when the regime had been thankfully destroyed and its leaders had gone to their natural deaths, all Cambodians were invited to inspect the Khmer Rouge's torture chambers and killing fields. The word 'genocide' may be overused on occasion but surely not when it comes to accounting for the fate of very many in Cambodia after 1975.

The course of later events in Indo-China has led Henry Kissinger and others to seek to justify the United States' actions in Vietnam. Such commentators can rightly point out that the mass murder begun in Cambodia once the Khmer Rouge took over in April 1975 led to barbarism on a scale that the world has rarely seen even in a century noted for its cruelty. Yet the connection between the atrocities committed by the Communist Khmer Rouge in Cambodia and the motives for American intervention in Vietnam is tenuous, since the former country was invariably a strategic sideshow. What happened after 1975 in Cambodia, however, was an extraordinary category of evil. It led, as Kissinger has noted in his autobiography, to the execution of all government officials and their families, while urban dwellers were simply ejected from their homes and ordered to fend for themselves in an inhospitable countryside that could not begin to support such a mass influx. Democratic

Kampuchea, as the country was renamed, experienced revolutionary change as its party leadership united under the banner of 'Enemies without continue to approach; enemies within our frontiers have not been eliminated'. It is estimated that between one and two million Cambodians were murdered before Hanoi occupied Phnom Penh in 1979, though this in its turn merely triggered a further decade of civil war.

While these dismal scenes were being enacted during the 1970s, the rest of Southeast Asia had no choice but to respond to the new political realities of Communist accomplishment in Indo-China. The speed of the takeover was remarkable. From the spring to the autumn of 1975, Cambodia, South Vietnam and finally Laos all fell successively into the Socialist camp. This suggested that the region faced an uncertain, divided future, even if the superpowers were able to engineer a relaxation of tension among themselves. ASEAN responded as it had in the past by annual consultations that aimed to demonstrate solidarity and by proposing a muted form of economic cooperation. Instead of continuing to be pawns in the Cold War, Southeast Asian nations now appeared to contradict the spirit of détente that Washington and Moscow intended to develop in their new global relationship. The world might be becoming less divided and dangerous but this did not necessarily apply to Southeast Asia.

The Rise of China

The continuation of Sino-Soviet divisions further complicated the situation. In December 1971 Chou En-lai had dismissed the Soviet Union as capable of little more than 'a pompous but empty show of power', while equally uncomplimentary remarks were muttered in Moscow to the effect that the Chinese were racially inferior and deserved to be taught a lesson. Since the Soviet ambassador to the United Nations had already, at the time of the border clashes along the Ussuri River in 1969, reputedly shouted: 'Who do they think they are? We'll kill those yellow sons of bitches', it was only to be expected that China's leaders would return the compliment by calling 'Soviet revisionist social-imperialism' the 'most direct, the most perilous and the most practical enemy'. Chou En-lai had confidently held in 1971 that Soviet revisionism at home and abroad was bankrupt. The PRC rejoiced at Moscow's domestic economic problems, noted its social decadence and predicted the loss of its empire in Eastern Europe, while claiming that Beijing alone was the rightful leader of the Third World. Yet Chou saw that the European front was of far greater strategic importance to both the Soviet Union and the United States and that therefore China should only expect 'some skirmishes' along the Sino-Soviet border. 'It is', suggested Chou En-lai, no more than 'fanfare and an intimidating pose for them to "concentrate troops on the frontier" of China. We must not be ensnared by them'. Yet the inevitable withdrawal of US forces from Vietnam was regarded as certain to prompt Soviet adventurism from the nation that was China's 'most threatening enemy'. The USSR might, in Chou's view, 'both struggle against and collude with the US' but 'they maintain completely antagonistic relations with us'.

When debating Southeast Asian questions, the PRC attempted to place its regional policies within the overall global framework of this deteriorating Sino-Soviet relationship. Beijing, as was suggested earlier, was wary of close ties between Hanoi and Moscow, preferring to under-mine such developments by increasing its own contacts with the United States during the 1970s. If the Soviet Union were the declining hegemon and newly united Vietnam the 'Cuba of the East', it was clearly in China's national interest to criticize 'the Soviet revisionists' who, as Chou had predicted, would offer economic assistance to Hanoi 'to countervail our influence in Vietnam'. Once Hanoi had successfully annexed South Vietnam, however, the question of how Beijing should handle relations with this new and stronger nation became of greater importance. After April 1975 Sino-Vietnamese relations had a more pressing life of their own, where the earlier perspective which determined that Vietnam should be seen through the prism of Sino-Soviet ties was less in evidence. Beijing's long-term concerns over a larger Vietnam appeared well founded. In March 1975 Mao's wife, Chiang Ch'ing, quoted him as having asked the Vietnamese ambassador to inform the leadership in Hanoi of his statement, 'To oppose imperialism without opposing revisionism will eventually lead to a second revolution'. Major Chinese complaints in-cluded the brutal manner in which Vietnam expelled the large minority of ethnic Chinese, the vexed question of disputed sovereignty over the Paracel and Spratly Islands in the South China Sea and, most important of all, Hanoi's handling of its relations with the two neighbouring states of Cambodia and Laos.

The deterioration in Sino-Vietnamese relations culminated in China's invasion of northern Vietnam in February 1979. This was widely viewed as being the Chinese response to the impudence of Vietnam in aspiring to a regional role that might put Beijing in the shade. Greater powers invariably take unkindly to being upstaged on their own turf. Beijing's wish to belittle Vietnam was certainly conditioned by the Vietnamese invasion of Cambodia on Christmas Day 1978. This episode was itself the result of Hanoi's determination to end the rule of the Pol Pot regime, which had become a contemporary byword for barbarism and anarchy. Vietnam despatched 120 000 troops which were welcomed enthusiastic-ally by the Kampucheans as they pushed back the Khmer Rouge forces.

The Vietnamese were therefore able to claim to be the liberators of Cambodia at a time when the West and China had elected to recognize the murderous Pol Pot government in preference to being seen to be dealing with Hanoi.

The Sino-Vietnam war was yet another in a long succession of frontier engagements that the People's Republic of China had fought since its inception in 1949. It followed in the pattern set by the hugely expensive intervention in Korea, the conquest of Tibet, and border clashes in the Himalayas with India. In the case of Vietnam, the PLA mounted a massive force of 300 000 troops to make its point. Officially the contest was claimed by Beijing to be centred on border disputes, but few observers doubted that this was merely part of the far wider issue of China's insistence that it be seen as the regional hegemon. Yet China failed to prove its point. While the PLA military made some gains near Hanoi, its equipment was shown to be out of date and its opponents had the twin advantages of knowing the terrain and being battle-hardy. China's war against Vietnam was precipitated by Beijing's anxiety over strong Soviet–Vietnamese ties that had Moscow supporting Hanoi over border violations and urging ASEAN to admit Vietnam as a member. The dominant factor, however, in at least the timing of the Chinese response, was Hanoi's invasion of Kampuchea. Before launching its attack, Vietnam had received substantial Soviet military equipment and the United States claimed to have identified numerous advisers from the USSR on the ground. Since the invasion also coincided with the signing of the Soviet–Vietnamese friendship treaty in November 1978, this diplomatic offensive was seen by Beijing as justifying its fears of encirclement. China repeatedly stated that Vietnam was the 'Cuba of Asia' and that it deserved to be taught a lesson.

Paralleling China's stridency in the region was a temporary weakening in American–Chinese exchanges. In part this may have been an unavoidable reaction to the euphoria that followed President Nixon's visit to Beijing, but later commentators have noted that the ensuing years also saw major differences over the entire question of détente. Henry Kissinger's expectation that his nation could maintain decent relations with both the Soviet Union and PRC proved wishful thinking. The Chinese authorities heartily disliked the Helsinki agreements over the recognition of all postwar European boundaries and were not prepared to help in letting the Americans casually swallow what Kissinger assured Nixon could be potent drams of both mao tai and vodka. Differences over the status of Taiwan further added to Beijing's unease with the United States, leading Chinese diplomats to wonder whether Washington preferred to shore up its links with Taipei rather than work towards its professed goal of the eventual normalization of relations with the PRC.

Lengthy debates now followed where domestic events in the United States and China contributed to a decidedly cooler atmosphere between the two nations. Leaders in both countries had to avoid measures that would provide ammunition for opponents who were critical of the direction of Sino-American ties. President Ford faced sniping from Ronald Reagan and Republican right-wingers, who sensed that Taiwan was being sold down the river, while the ageing figures in China who had promoted the sea change with Washington had to contend with attacks from the left-wing 'gang of four' led by Jiang Qing. These critics insisted that the United States was already too closely linked to Taipei through political, military and trade connections.

Yet the anti-Soviet strategic imperative that tied the United States and China into a closer relationship still held. Sino-American differences were patched up and new efforts made to build on past successes. The American side, for example, publicly pledged its support for China after the death of Mao Tse-tung in September 1976 in order to deter any meddling by Moscow, while the PRC instituted modest bilateral trade flows and permitted cautious cultural exchanges with the United States. Although hardly answering Henry Kissinger's mock complaint to Chou En-lai that US businessmen were disappointed that they still had not achieved their target of selling 'one billion pairs of underwear' to the China market, it was evidence of a sort that Sino-American ties would both survive and strengthen.

This was emphatically underlined in the political process that led to the normalization of relations between the two nations on 1 January 1979. For President Jimmy Carter this was one of the major achievements of his four somewhat unhappy years in office. The process, which required lengthy and tedious Sino-American negotiations, was intended to strengthen ties between Washington and Beijing and weaken Soviet antagonism towards the United States. The increasing difficulties in American–Soviet relations in the late 1970s, prompted by Soviet conditions for a second strategic arms limitations treaty and its interventions in Africa, certainly contributed to closer American–Chinese ties. Yet the Carter administration approached the normalization issue knowing that domestic public opinion was still sympathetic towards Chiang Kai-shek's Taiwan and uncomfortably aware too that the Nixon and Ford administrations had made agreements with Beijing that might box in their successor. Exploratory discussions only added to the difficulties and led Deng to claim that Carter's cabinet had reneged on earlier accords, thereby encouraging a cautious president to make haste slowly. Eventually a compromise was cobbled together that incorporated portions of past US commitments and yet did not grant Beijing all it had hoped to obtain. Although their joint communiqué spoke flatly of agreeing that this would contribute 'to the cause of peace in Asia and the world' and noted in the briefest possible manner that 'there is but one China and Taiwan is part of China', the text was supplemented by separate statements from the US and Chinese governments that hinted at the hurdles that had been faced initially and then finally ducked in the protracted process. The Carter administration noted its pledge to terminate all official ties with Taipei and the withdrawal of all remaining military personnel but noted also that it still possessed 'an interest in the peaceful resolution of the Taiwan issue and expects that the Taiwan issue will be settled peacefully by the Chinese themselves'. Washington also made it apparent in the negotiations that it would continue with its sensitive policy of permitting the sale of arms to Taipei. For its part, the Chinese side explained in decidedly louder language that the Taiwan question was 'the crucial issue obstructing the normalization of relations between China and the United States' and cautioned that 'the way of bringing Taiwan back to the embrace of the motherland and reunifying the country ... is entirely China's internal affair'. The pill was suitably sweetened, however, by the final paragraph of the statement, which announced a forthcoming official visit by Vice-Premier Deng Xiaoping to the United States. This, it was hoped, would further promote 'the friendship between the two peoples and good relations between the two countries'. This soon proved to be generally the case.

The 1980s saw a further improvement in Sino-American relations, assisted both by Deng's determination to ignite an economic revolution in China and the continuing failure of Beijing and Moscow to repair the rifts caused by a generation of deep hostility. While many Chinese officials feared that the opening of their country to foreign influences might encourage instability and thereby threaten the dominance of the all-important Communist Party, Deng's insistence on rapid modern-ization remained state policy. Those in the CCP who reckoned that this unprecedented experiment would leave their nation at the mercy of unscrupulous foreigners lost the argument, since Deng rejected any historical parallels with the nineteenth-century misfortunes that had befallen China. Then it had been obliged to open up its territory to Western merchants, who, in their bid to exploit markets, had enjoyed the twin advantages of legal protection by treaty-port consuls and emergency support from the Royal Navy's flat-bottomed gunboats. A hundred years on, however, China was held to be in a more advantageous position, since it was in the process of supervising foreign trade and had its own, if incomplete, legal system. This time China reckoned it could avoid the humiliations of the Open Door era. It intended now to reap the rewards of regulating inward investment from the industrialized First World and, more importantly, from its neighbours, through encouragement of the 'patriotic' actions of overseas Chinese long settled in the Pacific Basin. The diaspora was to be turned round and portions of the accumulated wealth and skills of China's millions of *émigrés* returned to benefit the motherland.

Deng warned that there could be no future for China (or its ruling party) without substantial economic growth, which in turn would require massive foreign loans, a whole series of complicated joint ventures, and technological imports. Chinese citizens began to talk of 'catching up' with the industrialized world. They employed terms that had spurred an earlier Japan forward, first to modernization and then to what the Japanese public of the 1980s delighted in referring to as the 'overtaking' (or even 'taking over') of its complacent North American and Western European rivals. However far-fetched some of these ambitions might at first have appeared in the case of China, the relaxation of state controls did produce an invigorating mood, particularly in those coastal regions of the country fortunate enough to be officially designated as special economic zones. If contemporary Japan could be seen as an economic superpower, then in the heady atmosphere of the 1980s it was possible to dream of the day when China too might again aspire to dominate the Asia-Pacific region. Yet whatever long-term ambitions China might possess, little could be realized without the further expansion of its still fledgling private sector economy. It was a thesis that many in the United States were delighted to endorse. One cover cartoon of the *New Yorker* wryly captured this vision of a new China when it displayed a traditional brush painting to which the artist had added a series of golden arches. McDonald and Coca Cola were indeed eager to acquire a stake in any aspiring Chinese consumer culture, much as American aviation and energy corporations hoped to build parts of the key infrastructure required for successful modernization. Chinese ministers endorsed these aspirations. Minister Chen Muhua, in charge of foreign economic relations and trade, spoke in April 1984 of aiming to quadruple her nation's trade flows by the end of the century. It was the case, she emphasized, that overseas funds and technology would continue to be as important as ever and that the 'open-door policy will be implemented unswervingly'.

Not everybody in the West, however, responded with quite the same enthusiasm to this rhapsodic vision of post-Maoist China. Senior Chinese officials and eager foreign entrepreneurs might repeat the mantra of end-less economic growth, but others recalled that little more than a decade earlier the official New China News Agency had predicted that 'the 70s of the Twentieth Century will be the era in which imperialism will rapidly approach its extinction'. Many of the proponents of 'Dengism' – including, of course, its chief architect – had themselves been subject to the indignities and violence of the Cultural Revolution. It was difficult, therefore, to find much reassurance in mere statements from on high that the turbulence of the recent past was over for good. Indeed, among the more unpleasant consequences of the new economic reforms was an increase in crime and social unrest that boded ill for those quick to predict a forthcoming capitalist nirvana in China. Yet although human rights activists in the United States might protest at the repressive nature of the CCP and pro-Taiwan groups continue to keep up a fierce denunciation of the shift in China policy, the broad goals behind the American engagement of China went unchanged. Domestic critics, such as liberals who despised China's human rights record, religious leaders who spoke up against Chinese intolerance, and trade unionists who were anxious to safeguard their members' jobs, failed to turn back this tide. The best they could hope to achieve was at least to draw attention to what were seen to be glaring defects within Chinese society and apply sufficient pressure to postpone, if not overturn, US actions.

The cooperative policies of the United States remained largely intact until the Tiananmen Square massacre of 1989. Yet the American–Chinese relationship over much of this period ultimately depended more on the attitudes proclaimed by Deng Xiaoping than the work of successive US administrations. Capitalism, Deng stated, was a system that 'already has a history of several hundred years, and we have to learn from the peoples of the capitalist countries. We must make use of the science and technology they have developed and of those elements in their accumulated knowledge and experience which can be adapted to our use'. But Deng was careful to underline that the importation of advanced technology would proceed, albeit 'selectively and according to plan', only on condition that 'we will never learn from or import the capitalist system itself, nor anything repellent or decadent'.

While the official media now trumpeted the slogan 'To Get Rich is Glorious', there was still plentiful concern that the end result would be largely a society of rampant bourgeois profiteering and party corruption. American commentary from China, however, spoke breathlessly of the first sightings of the new shoots of proto-capitalism. Reporters hailed the popularity of 'American-style white bread' in Beijing with the bakery staffed by those who had attended the twenty-week course offered by the American Institute of Baking in Manhattan, Kansas, though it cannot have been to the taste of croissant-loving Deng. Pierre Cardin went a stage further in this battle for the stomach by boasting of his success in opening a Maxim's in China's capital and predicting that within a decade 'this country will be like Japan'. By both advocating economic reform and acknowledging simultaneously that this process contained potentially serious risks for many within the Chinese state, Deng was able to retain the support of the West and carefully sidestep many of his domestic critics. His popularity in the United States was such that *Time* magazine selected him as its 'man of the year' in 1978 and again in 1985. The praise may have been excessive and the prose slightly jarring, but Deng's successful visits abroad and his determination to alter China suggested that he was a leader of courage and vision – the fact that he aimed to maintain the one-party apparatus and that most of his subjects were little better than peasants trapped in rural poverty could get forgotten amid the euphoria. Yet Deng reassured many in the West that their past images of an erratic and ideological China deserved to be thrown on the bonfire of history. This time the Open Door would remain at least half open, with foreign direct investment much preferred to foreign ideas and belief systems.

The 1980s proved to be a generally sound decade for American–Chinese relations. Differences were far from always solved, but agreements to disagree were employed to avoid any head-on collisions. The successes gained in the intricate dance that had led to the normalization of Sino-American relations by 1979 served as encouraging evidence that even highly sensitive issues might be resolved in a like manner in the future. The precedent could have its uses when negotiators next met to iron out their differences, but equally it was seen also by some members of the US Congress as an act of bad faith towards Taiwan. For this group it therefore served as a reminder on how not to mend fences at the expense of an old ally. The passing of what became known as the Taiwan Relations Act by a Congress that had doubts over the Carter administration's handling of the normalization process is a reminder of how divisive the issue was for American domestic opinion. The huge majorities for the bill (89:4 in the Senate and 339:50 in the House), while not crippling the administration's freedom to interpret legislation, would soon have consequences. Beijing, for its part, detested references to the US commitment to sell arms 'to ensure that Taipei enjoyed a sufficient self-defense capability, and that the United States would maintain the capacity to resist any use of force or coercion that would threaten Taiwan's security'.

Carter Changes Tack

Yet the Taiwan question, however disruptive for both governments, could not obscure the new closeness of American–Chinese ties. The change in American perceptions of Beijing is perhaps best personified in the policy decisions approved by President Carter. During his administration there gradually emerged an entirely fresh appreciation of the global geopolitical advantages that might accrue to the United States from befriending the PRC. The shift in policy, however, was far from unanimous. The State

Department under Cyrus Vance, in particular, was fearful that any signs of fawning on Beijing would jeopardize American–Russian relations, and it took considerable persuasion from National Security Adviser Zbigniew Brzezinski before Carter himself was persuaded. Once won over, he reacted with all the fervour of a born-again convert. Brzezinski from within and Deng from without worked to change the President's mind. The former bombarded Carter with memorandums that stressed enduring hostility to all things Soviet, while Deng reinforced this picture by informing the world that China and the United States must unite 'to place curbs on the polar bear'. It was a double-barrelled volley that convinced Carter that the China card should be played and played for all its worth. A new strategic relationship with China, along the lines that Brzezinski had urged on the President in his weekly report of 7 July 1978, would lead to 'a major change in the international balance'. By the end of the Carter presidency the US government had become sufficiently concerned at the increasing strength of the Soviet Union to abandon many of its earlier initiatives that had been intended to defuse tensions with Moscow. Carter had hoped to be seen as a figure who could work with his rival superpower to ensure a more stable world where human rights would be more widely respected, but, as Gaddis Smith has noted, the result by 1979 was 'the return to containment' both in Asia and elsewhere. The conventional solution, as Brzezinski had recommended in a minute to Carter in March 1980, was to demonstrate American resilience against 'Soviet assertiveness'. Brzezinski had long maintained that it was necessary 'to exploit politically our relatively favourable position in the US–Soviet–Chinese triangle' and was ever anxious to avoid 'a further deterioration in the US global position'.

The eventual success of this battle for the President's ear was further assisted by international events in the region that American analysts termed Southwest Asia. The Soviet invasion of Afghanistan was greeted in the most strident language by President Carter. He went so far as to suggest that the United States and its allies were now facing their worst crisis since the end of the Second World War, but then rather spoiled his case by offering little in the way of specific measures to cope with the ensuing situation. While events in Kabul certainly provided evidence of Soviet designs that appeared to confirm the views of Brzezinski, Afghanistan was hardly an area that the American public had been accustomed to regarding as possessing vital strategic importance to their nation, and besides, the US locker was almost empty. It was also far from clear in 1980 what the cumulative effect of such Soviet expansion in the Third World might prove to be. Only later could authorities state with confidence that Soviet behaviour in Afghanistan, the horn of Africa and the Middle East led inevitably to an intensification of internal problems for Moscow. Henry Kissinger, the rival international political authority to Brzezinski, would write in the mid-1990s, when the total collapse of Communism had become a reality, that 'Soviet overextension produced, not catharsis, as it did in America, but disintegration'.

The Reagan Presidency

In the early 1980s, however, it was rare to discover many such Western figures willing to bet their own money on the improbable demise of the Soviet Union and its empire within a few short years. It was rather more common to read of alarming prognostications by Western authors on the build-up of the Soviet Pacific fleet and to hear dire predictions on the weaknesses of the US strategic deterrent and the glaring failings of the American economy in the face of its newly confident Japanese rival. The decade began after all with the sweeping presidential victory of Ronald Reagan, who was able to win office by denouncing the alleged faults of American foreign policy and by stressing the need for a larger military to offset the purported strengths of the Soviet Union and its allies. Concern at the United States' very public inability to solve the Iranian hostage crisis and the contortions exhibited during the Carter years in dealing with the Kremlin led to a Republican once again capturing the White House. This time, however, the United States had elected an individual who made it clear from the outset that he would not be tailored in the drab cloth of détente. International relations would now change. The zigzagging detours and cul de sacs of his predecessor were not intended to be part of Reagan's road map. The cartoonist's view of an America in decline, seen in the depiction of a pair of warships that were cleverly named USS *Intrepid* and USS *Insolvent*, would soon be replaced by a more triumphalist era.

The new president employed very different language from that of Carter, Ford and Nixon. Reagan's news conferences may not have been particularly articulate, informative or frequent but the message that came across was one of serene confidence in his own ability to exploit the deep structural faults of the Soviet Union. Reagan delighted in claiming that the USSR was doomed and deserved to collapse He stated too that this process of decline and fall awaiting Moscow must be assisted by the United States, through the strengthening of America's own military and political positions. Instead of merely following the conventional doctrine of holding fast, Reagan pressed ahead with massive arms build-ups that inevitably left the Kremlin struggling to reconcile its geopolitical need to counter the United States with the economic discomfort and worse that this would cause to the Soviet Union's peoples and allies.

Reagan's political career had been constructed on anti-Communism. He had nominated Barry Goldwater at the Republican convention in

1964 and it was this reputation for contempt towards Moscow that largely ensured that later comment on Reagan's own frequent meetings with Soviet leaders would be so muted. The critic of détente escaped censure for building bridges to his sworn opponents. President Reagan made no bones about what he intended, but few of even his most fervent supporters could have anticipated the speed with which his speeches on the desirability of a new era would be translated into political reality. The strategy of the new administration was to begin with confrontation and thereafter switch to reconciliation. The result, as Henry Kissinger would later acknowledge with a mixture of admiration, bemusement and envy, was that 'Reagan was the first postwar president to take the offensive both ideologically and geostrategically'.

Reagan's advent also coincided with important shifts within the Kremlin, where the inner leadership of the Soviet Communist Party had long been seen as a collective gerontocracy. Its membership put itself through a giddy succession of changes following the end of the Brezhnev era, before a relatively youthful Mikhail Gorbachev emerged against the odds in March 1985 to gain power through the routing of the old guard. Gorbachev recognized from the outset that change in the Soviet system was urgently required to correct the faults of Communism. It ought to be underlined, however, that the new man, grossly overconfidently as events would soon prove, reckoned that any such alterations would lead to the prompt reinvigoration of the Soviet Union rather than its equally sudden strangulation. Yet the fact that both Gorbachev and Reagan were prepared to negotiate and reconsider the superpower relationship was an encouraging beginning. Of course, each hoped to gain from these widely publicized diplomatic events, but outsiders could draw some comfort at least from the fact that serious discussions on what divided their two nations were to be arranged. Summits might fail but, given their exceptional rarity during the Cold War, agreement even to hold any such venture was a useful omen.

Changes within the Kremlin gave Reagan his chance. It was no coincidence that Gorbachev too saw the necessity of a new approach to the divisive East–West issues that had been gingerly touched on over the past two generations. When writing in 1987 in the preface to the revised English-language edition of his essays, simply entitled *Perestroika*, the Soviet leader was quick to stress the pressing need for dialogue. This, he contended, could lead to cooperation through a far greater understanding of the USSR's reformist goals, though he acknowledged that it 'has proved more difficult than we at first imagined'. It was also hard to shake off the suggestion that behind the 'new political thinking [and] the philosophy of our foreign policy' there were claims that perestroika was the father of Gorbachev's bid to alter the Cold War. The General Secretary responded by agreeing that 'we need normal international conditions for our internal progress' but added that an end to the arms race was 'an objective global requirement that stems from the realities of the present day'. Such remarks no doubt appear somewhat tame by today's standards. Yet until the mid-1980s it would have been hard to recall any other postwar Soviet leader who had risked speaking out so frankly and openly of the faults of his own society and the need for Washington and Moscow to reckon with the defects of the superpower relationship. President Reagan famously had dubbed the Soviet Union as 'the evil empire'. Gorbachev astutely claimed the higher ground and spoke instead of mankind's urgent agenda to halt nuclear proliferation and warned that an increasingly interdependent world would expect joint solutions to common political and humanitarian questions.

At times, however, as a degree of mutual trust grew between Gorbachev and Reagan, the two leaders found themselves using passages in speeches and statements that could have been extracted almost verbatim from the other's remarks. Initially, many of the negotiations had been necessarily exploratory, but the pace quickened rapidly as greater understanding between the two men developed. President Reagan held to simpler and potentially more far-reaching views than his American predecessors, who had seen the Cold War as the means of maintaining rather than scrapping an approximate global balance of power. Henry Kissinger would note that the Republican President 'did not in his own heart believe in structural or geopolitical causes of tension', thus making for 'extraordinary tactical flexibility'. The President's confidence in the virtues of the American way of life had been a theme he had repeated on the political stump and in sponsored speeches for private enterprise over the decades, and he instinctively drew on this philosophy in his dealings with the Soviet Union. He was certain that the United States had a superior political and economic system; all that was required was to convince his opponents of this self-evident reality. Reagan wanted to replace the endless crises that had surrounded US–Soviet relations by a new international order where there could be nothing to disguise both the imminent ideological and economic bankruptcy of Communism and the affluence, power and benevolence of the United States.

Assisted by substantial new weapons programmes to strengthen his diplomacy and reports on the weakening of the Soviet economy, Reagan pressed on. The Reykjavik summit came close to agreeing on hugely substantial nuclear arms reductions by the two superpowers (50 per cent over five years for strategic weapons and all ballistic missiles within ten years), though ultimately it failed through Gorbachev's insistence that testing on the Strategic Defense Initiative ('Star Wars') be halted as well. Yet the message was clear. The Reagan presidency did indeed aspire to the elimination of nuclear weapons and anticipated a fresh international system where old political rivalries would dissipate.

The United States and a Changing Asia

The implications for the Asia-Pacific region were necessarily substantial. If the United States and the Soviet Union could achieve an improved relationship in Europe, the initial fear was that this might contribute to less rather than more international stability in Asia. What concerned the allies of the United States in the region was the possibility that once the USSR's SS-20 missiles had been decommissioned on the European front, in line with recent American–Soviet agreements, they might next be moved to the east. This would certainly be conducive to reducing tension between the Warsaw pact and NATO members, but only at the expense of South Korea and Japan. The energetic and eager spokesman for this widespread but rarely expressed Asian anxiety was Prime Minister Nakasone Yasuhiro of Japan. He had long prided himself on possessing a realist's perspective on international security, something that most of his peers in Tokyo deliberately shunned as being fundamentally at odds with their reactive, 'trading state' approach to every potentially disruptive foreign policy crisis. Instead, however, of subscribing to this minimalist 'do nothing' approach, which led to the instinctive knee-jerk reply that it was invariably the responsibility of other and greater powers to solve regional problems, Nakasone was quick to voice an alternative view. He asserted that since security was indivisible, it followed that threats against allied countries had to be countered everywhere or the entire global system devised and underwritten by the United States would lose its vital credibility.

While Nakasone's thesis saw Japan on the side of the angels for a change, his statements were predictably unpopular with many in Tokyo. His own Liberal Democratic Party thought it counter-productive to be associated in any firm manner with anti-Communist communiqués. Japan, unlike the United States, had to live in close proximity to a host of flashpoints. The Japanese establishment knew only too well that its neighbours might be tempted to embroil Japan in such crises. As the only affluent, long-standing democratic Asian state who, in addition, had for two generations possessed uncomfortably close security ties to Washington, Japan stood out conspicuously in the region. The more that Japan confirmed its membership of the Western camp, the more vulnerable it became, at least for those in Tokyo who questioned the reliability of the United States' security guarantees.

In the event, the swift ending of the Cold War in Europe eliminated many of the more feared military consequences. Yet the Reagan–Gorbachev movement towards détente did underline the fact that the then two superpowers were deciding how to alter the structure of international relations with little input, at least in any discernible public form, from the member states of the Asia-Pacific region. Others, it appeared, would have to wait until Washington and Moscow had reached their joint conclusions. In the autumn of 1986, for example, members of the joint Trilateral Commission, drawing on the advice of its North American, European and Japanese membership, could only reckon that watchfulness might be the best policy. They concluded limply that the difficulties of calculating how the grouping might respond collectively to Soviet initiatives would accumulate and sensed too that the centrality of resolving the American–Soviet relationship might be at the expense of specific European and Asian interests. Similar points were made by the analyst Nishihara Masashi, who warned of the Soviet Union's desire to play off the West's diverse positions but could only loyally recommend that the United States' paramount role be recognized, 'once consultation has taken place' with its allies. How novel coordination mechanisms might be devised to take note of the views of the pro-American states of the region was left to the future, though the emphasis on widening and deepening regionalism would indeed be a feature of the next decade. In the specific case of threats to East Asia in the mid-1980s, Nishihara noted the impressive build-up of the Soviet fleet in the Asia-Pacific region. He quickly added, however, the reassuring riders that its aircraft carriers were little more than floating helicopter platforms and pointed out that 'Soviet ships are often seen being towed because of mechanical breakdown'.

During the lengthy Nakasone era, Japan nailed its colours to the American mast. The immediate advantage that accrued to the ambitious premier and his rather more cautious citizenry was the considerably enhanced international profile granted to Tokyo. Yet what was seen initially to be a decided plus was soon transformed into a long-term problem for Japan. Rising overseas expectations, based on Nakasone's most un-Japanese delight in formulating allied responses to the Soviet menace, were rarely realized. It might have been wiser for Nakasone to have delivered on more modest promises before bragging that he held a royal flush. When the West asked to see Japan's real hand, the cards eventually turned over proved to be pitifully weak.

To add to Japan's difficulties, its foreign policy makers faced a second, equally uncomfortable test. In addition to demonstrating its professed solidarity with the West on political and strategic issues, successive Japanese governments found themselves explaining, prevaricating and defending their behaviour over what was understood on all sides to represent the emergence of a new economic superpower. The international attention to the rise of Japanese trade and finance in the years from the first oil crisis of 1973–74 to the eventual derailment of the Japanese economy in 1990–91 proved highly divisive on all sides. It led to massive claims and counter-claims as to the nature of Japanese capitalism and it would come close to destabilizing the entire US–Japan partnership that

Nakasone had so recently trumpeted. *Time* magazine, to give but one illustration of the seriousness of the issue, put a giant sumo wrestler up against a rather weedy-looking Uncle Sam on its cover for 13 April 1987 under the simple headline of 'Trade Wars: The US gets tough with Japan'. The simplified message peddled overseas was that Japan had either broken the accepted rules of international trade or had created a bureaucratically controlled political economy that gave the nation unfair advantages. Japanese spokesmen, for their part, were quick to respond in kind by insisting that their country was being pilloried through foreign ignorance, misunderstanding or blatant prejudice.

The US administrations during the 1970s and 1980s found it difficult to unify policy towards Japan. In the earlier post-occupation era, it had been standard operating procedure for the State Department to oversee the direction of the relationship. Working in reasonably close conjunction with the Pentagon, they had understood that Japan's geopolitical importance to Washington necessitated a relatively relaxed trade policy. This was now near impossible. The criticisms from a host of enraged US manufacturing interests turned Japan into a football ready to be kicked by every industry that faced hard times. Japan became a very visible scapegoat for valid and spurious criticism alike. Tokyo was charged with cheating, dumping and unfairly manipulating markets abroad, while zealously protecting its own domestic turf from unwelcome foreign goods. Critics stated categorically that the Japanese economy bore virtually no resemblance to capitalism as practised in the United States, and executives returned from Tokyo and Nagoya with lurid tales of the all-embracing tentacles of bureaucrats big and small. From the docks at Yokohama to the customs inspectors at Narita and on to the dreaded officials in the Ministry of International Trade and Industry (MITI), a stereotyped picture quickly emerged of a leviathan that was intent on conquering the world by administrative force and guile. In such a politicized atmosphere, the truth or otherwise of such charges was irrelevant.

Yet the Japanese state made its task of explaining its behaviour and then negotiating with its bruised trading partners infinitely harder by its own disappointingly dilatory response. Tokyo gave ground slowly and reluctantly in its trade diplomacy. It feared, doubtless with some justification, that any arrangement made with one nation would lead swiftly to similar requests from others. The result was bad tempers all round and a litany of excuses from corporate bosses in the West for their ineptitude and ignorance, and equally soggy remarks from Japanese management, industrial federations and MITI spokesmen. Eventually, in contradiction of talk of market-based capitalism, Western governments were able to persuade Japan to bend international trading rules and devise agreements that restrained specific sectors such as electronics and cars in order to grant some relief to beleaguered manufacturers in North America and Western Europe. Although Japan complained bitterly, the fact that such 'voluntary' restraints in a large number of politically sensitive trading areas were necessary was a remarkable endorsement of Japan's economic achievements. The common Western stereotype that somehow Japanese industry and its associates had conspired to conquer the globe through unprincipled activities would have been laughable if it had not been so widespread. For far too long Japan had been grossly underestimated by its trading rivals, who found the necessary readjustment to the much-derided 'samurais with suitcases' particularly difficult to accept. Forty years on and the pupil of the occupation era had become the management guru and quality control authority to his former masters. In addition, as if to add insult to injury, the US Congress began holding committee hearings on the feasibility of the United States adopting its own brand of industrial policy, complete with 'national development banks' and proposals for 'a US MITI' and what the financial press termed as 'an America, Inc.'

Japan's efforts were even more remarkable when the changes in currency values are taken into account. Despite the huge appreciation in the yen, the juggernaut simply failed to slow down. The trade surpluses continued to grow and the best that Western governments could do was try to persuade Tokyo to assume wider responsibilities more commensurate with its much-envied affluence. Washington urged Japan to use a portion of its newly acquired balances for the benefit of the international system that had set the preconditions for Japan's rise to riches. It was not, however, a particularly popular thesis in Tokyo. It took time before the permanent bureaucracy and the equally permanent political leadership of the LDP would accept that in areas such as foreign aid and educational assistance there might be legitimate claims on Japan. The public, recalling its own individual efforts in scrambling to find work and then rebuilding the nation's blitzed cities after the Pacific War, was frequently either unsympathetic or at best apathetic. The world beyond the Japanese islands remained largely unknown and potentially dangerous. Gradually, however, the United States and Japan collaborated over an informal division of labour in the Asia-Pacific region. By the 1980s an unwritten agreement had been devised that allowed Washington to concentrate on the political and strategic arena and left Japan as the region's banker and aid donor. The result was that Japan, at long last, was back in Asia as the generally welcomed provider of financial, economic and technological services that were largely unavailable from other overseas sources. The adoption of this new role by Tokyo had the added advantage of showing Japan to be an obviously non-aggressive nation that would this time work with, rather than against, the interests of its neighbours in areas of common concern.

Evidence for the cooperative nature of Japan's economic foreign policy was quickly demonstrated. Tokyo became the world's largest provider of foreign aid (Overseas Development Assistance was the euphemistic phrase employed by the Japanese government) and greatly increased the number of overseas studentships for young Asians. These were encouraging indications that Japan was serious in rebuilding its regional ties, though the good news was qualified by the widespread suspicion that a considerable portion of Japan's foreign aid was merely channelled back to its own manufacturing industries and giant trading companies in the form of 'tied' aid.

Japan's greater contributions to regional issues were prompted by the United States and much encouraged by the West in the light of the deterioration in relations between the two rival superpowers. It is most unlikely that the Japanese state would by itself have been persuaded to become a major burden-sharer, since few observers regarded increased tension as anything but the perfect moment to draw in one's horns and behave with renewed circumspection. The change was the product of Mr Nakasone's limitless self-assurance, the extraordinary successes of the Japanese economy, and the careful diplomacy that persuaded Tokyo that it would be in its interest to prop up the region rather than look on from the sidelines since instability curtailed both imported energy supplies and trading opportunities. Ezra Vogel, the American academic who had been feted in some quarters for his laudatory work *Japan as Number One*, would return in 1994 to describe this new policy shift under the title of 'Japan as Number One in Asia'.

Greater cooperation between the United States, Japan and Asia, despite the seemingly endless issue of serious trade friction, was now shown to be possible. Japan was the only advanced industrialized nation that was willing and able to extend the vast loans and sink the necessary capital into the host of projects that the entire Asia-Pacific region was eager to promote in the 1980s. In the process, Tokyo acquired a higher profile and a greatly enhanced status in the region. There was quite simply no alternative to looking to Japan, if South Korea, Taiwan, the People's Republic of China and Southeast Asia were to modernize successfully. The result was certainly not comparable to the infamous Greater East Asia Co-Prosperity Sphere of the Pacific War years but rather should be seen as the provision of vital social infrastructure and an intermediate manufacturing base in parts of the region. Japanese finance and industry, in the process of recycling its large trade balances with the West, made possible some of the preconditions for the so-called 'tiger' growth economies and the 'takeoff' for parts of coastal China. Japan's role in sponsoring the emergence of the new East Asian market economies held parallels to what the United States had done to encourage Japan during its own occupation era. By the 1990s the results were sufficiently impressive to cause concern in Tokyo that Japan had possibly erred in working so assiduously on behalf of what were nascent industrial rivals.

The Strengthening of ASEAN

Southeast Asia now exhibited much of the self-confidence of an earlier Japan. The West, however, was in no mood for celebratory banquets; it intended rather to sidestep the policy mistakes of the past and maintain a cautionary approach towards international trade. The memories of the difficulties created by Japan's rapid and unexpected rise to global economic power were not quickly forgotten and acted to encourage a more reciprocal system. Ironically, it was now possible to hear Japanese officialdom and trade federation spokesmen denouncing the very protectionist and labour cost practices of Southeast Asia and South Korea which only a generation before had helped propel Tokyo swiftly down the same road to modernization. It appeared that Japan wished to avoid the emergence of a second Japan.

Yet the United States also had to reckon with the advantages that successful industrialization would bring for its friends in Asia. Clearly the advent of a degree of prosperity was in the interests of American foreign policy and might in the longer term offer lucrative fresh markets for its corporations. What needed to be achieved more immediately this time, however, was stricter adherence to multilateral trade practices and insistence on more open domestic markets. The Cold War strictures that had allowed the United States to turn a blind eye to Japan's flouting of the rules had long gone by the 1980s. Trade would now have to follow GATT regulations or Western politicians would find themselves swiftly facing the wrath of their electorates.

Aside from trade issues, it was apparent that Southeast Asia was increasingly becoming a region of lesser importance to the West. The United States, as we have noted, was eager to see Japan take over much of the facilitator role that underpinned the 'tiger' economies' impressive roar into growth. Washington and London were also greatly relieved to watch from the touchline as the region strove increasingly to solve its own state-to-state problems. The central mechanism to this end was ASEAN. Membership of this organization was eventually to be shared by all the non-Communist nations of the area and it gradually evolved into an institution that warranted considerable respect from abroad. In an organization designed to stress solidarity, its leaders attempted to work informally among themselves, without resorting to overt cajoling in the manner of some of their colonial predecessors. The end of the United

States' involvement in Vietnam had of course concentrated ASEAN's mind on regional security matters. There was little choice, since by September 1976 President Ford's assistant secretary of state for East Asian and Pacific affairs would confirm the remarks of Lee Hamilton, chairman of the House Foreign Affairs Committee, that Southeast Asia was 'an area of more limited interest to the United States as a result of Vietnam and the changes that have occurred'.

The relative lack of involvement of all administrations from Carter to Clinton in the complex question of Cambodia's stability and independence is evidence of Washington's reluctance to be closely tied to regional issues of secondary importance. The United States has generally left Cambodia's fate to bodies such as ASEAN, Japan and the United Nations. It was therefore not surprising that one US diplomat, accompanying Secretary of State Warren Christopher on his visit to open the US embassy in Hanoi in August 1995, would summarize American foreign policy to Southeast Asia in the new language of commerce: 'In the old days we wanted to make Asia safe for democracy, these days we want to make it safe for American exports'. All that Washington officials, therefore, could propose were polite words of encouragement for ASEAN's assumption of new responsibilities. It was hoped that increased aid, trade and bromides on the importance of human rights would suffice. Unfortunately, any such gentle strictures could be ignored almost at will by President Suharto in Indonesia and by President Marcos in the Philippines. Ferdinand Marcos, until he was toppled in February 1986 by the first instance of what has become known as 'people power', was the beneficiary of the United States' wish to protect its important military installations at Subic Bay and Clark. President Suharto survived considerably longer, enjoying the extraordinary total of thirty-three years of personal rule and family largesse, during which period his invasion and permanent occupation of East Timor in December 1975 was generally overlooked by Washington.

China, the USSR and the Region

China, for its part, advocated a foreign policy based on what it termed 'the principle of antihegemony'. It preferred to be forthright in stating its position in opposition to both superpowers, reckoning that it stood to gain by being regarded as the underdog in a region bristling with tension and mistrust. The PRC had strong words for both the Americans and the Russians. Throughout the second half of the 1970s and the early 1980s, Beijing was discovering that its teething problems with the United States, most notably over the status of Taiwan, were lingering; it was discovering also that the Communists in Moscow were slow to respond to requests for an improvement in Sino-Soviet ties, soured because of the strong Russian support for Vietnam's invasion of Cambodia. China may have had hopes for a fresh start in its relationship with the politburo in Moscow, but any warming was decidedly slow to emerge. The bitterness of the past could not be easily brushed aside, particularly when China made very public stipulations on what the USSR had first to accomplish over Cambodia, as well as ending the Soviet occupation of Afghanistan and ordering substantial troop reductions along the sensitive Sino-Soviet border, if it were to gain Beijing's official stamp of approval.

Moscow responded forcefully to Beijing's statements by underlining what the Novosti press agency publishing house defined proudly as the Soviet Union's own 'growing political vigour in Asia and the Pacific'. By the mid-1980s, through the initiative of Mikhail Gorbachev, the newly appointed reformist general secretary of the Communist Party of the Soviet Union, the region was reminded that Moscow had substantial claims to untangling 'the Asia-Pacific knot'. Gorbachev would insist that his nation was 'an Asian, as well as European country', and he predicted that the region would become the centre of world politics in the twenty-first century. Gorbachev, in a well-received speech at Vladivostok in July 1986, defined the Soviet Union as a major Asian power which had a responsibility 'to look at international policy issues from the Asian-Pacific standpoint'. The region's 'impressive diversity' and 'colossal human and socio-political massif' were identified by Gorbachev as forming 'yet another renaissance in world history', where 'a huge potential for progress' was under way. It was, of course, a view of Asian dynamism widely shared by those in other chanceries, but Gorbachev's articulation and timing were deservedly applauded.

The Vladivostok speech contained specific proposals for rethinking the Cold War framework that the region had endured for four decades. Gorbachev noted that the process of détente, then well under way in Europe thanks to the Helsinki accords, had barely begun in Asia. While speaking kindly of the USSR's friends in the region and attempting to draw Beijing back into the fold, Gorbachev acknowleged categorically that the United States 'is a great Pacific power' and that a peaceful and prosperous Asia-Pacific would require the active cooperation of Washington and its allies. In an ambitious five-point programme, Gorbachev outlined how the integration of the region into 'a comprehensive system of international security' might be attempted. Through the settlement of local issues, the reduction of conventional military levels, nuclear missile arsenals and regional naval forces, plus the creation of a zone of peace in the Indian Ocean and the beginnings of confidence-building measures, Gorbachev demonstrated a rare ability to think regionally and encourage others to respond with a comparable vision. Certainly, one intent was to recall the influence of the Soviet Union but, as Gorbachev noted with understandable satisfaction in 1987, the 'insinuations from the West over Moscow's objectives displayed an already familiar "caveman-like" response to our initiatives'. Outsiders might well ask when the region had last heard of a comparable programme from an American (or Chinese) leader that outlined such an optimistic and inclusive vision for the future. Portions of the Soviet Union's proposals on working towards arms reduction and encouraging regional cooperation would be echoed over the next decade in scores of public forums and academic papers throughout Asia. Certainly Gorbachev was stronger on rhetoric than substance, but his intentions were widely felt to be both timely and positive. The fact that neither Washington nor Beijing was prepared immediately to offer a comprehensive alternative to the Vladivostok initiative suggests that the Soviet Union had regained at least part of its regional reputation by the mid-1980s. Yet the growing military and political deficiencies of the Soviet Union could not be disguised by oratory alone. The Western tag that the USSR was merely 'Upper Volta with missiles' had more than an element of truth to it, particularly as the military posturing of the Soviet Union severely dented any hopes of improving its lacklustre domestic economic performance.

Decade's End

Throughout the 1980s the power centre of the Asia-Pacific region remained unchanged. The United States confounded many observers by putting its débâcle in Vietnam behind it, without losing its elaborate Cold War alliance structures in the region. While it negotiated in the second half of the 1980s with Gorbachev's Soviet Union over nuclear and conventional arms reductions, it was able simultaneously to keep its diplomatic ties with China in reasonable order. The highly competitive triangular relationship between the United States, the Soviet Union and the People's Republic of China that had been apparent a decade earlier was now reckoned to be somewhat a thing of the past. It was no longer the case that rapprochement between any two of the nation-states necessarily led to suspicion or, worse, to dealings with the slighted third party. During the 1980s the strategic waltz certainly continued, but the position of Washington as the hegemonic power was rarely in question; vocal concerns over American economic competitiveness would, however, become more pronounced, with Japan being frequently seen as an unwelcome and possibly unscrupulous industrial and commercial rival. The United States began and ended the decade as the arbitrator of the region. It found itself afforded the luxury of observing the unexpectedly sudden disintegration of the Soviet Union and adopted the noncommittal view that the PRC was a strengthening but still aspiring regional power. After the watershed of 1989, however, much would suddenly change both in the long-seated confrontational relationship between Washington and Moscow and in the entire Asia-Pacific region's necessary reassessment of the domestic and foreign stances of China. There was to be no respite as new problems and complexities now emerged to take the place of the old, familiar, bipolar landscape.

6   Post-Cold War: Asia-Pacific, 1989–2000

America today is by any measure the world's unchallenged military and economic power, having completed the first peacetime expansion of our global reach since the days of Theodore Roosevelt. The world counts on us to be a catalyst of coalitions, a broker of peace, a guarantor of global financial stability. We are widely seen as the country best placed to benefit from globalization.

> Samuel Berger, national security adviser to President Clinton,
> *Foreign Affairs*, November 2000

Japan is our principal friend, ally and partner – not China.
That doesn't mean we are not anxious to improve our relations with China.

> Ambassador Thomas Foley, *Asahi Evening News* (Tokyo),
> 11 December 2000

Is America going to end its presence in Asia and listen to its own interests? Or is it going to continue to face resistance if it were to intervene too much? But there is also a dilemma in this region, that if America were to abandon Asia completely, it would create numerous problems.

> Yamamoto Mitsuru, panel discussion on China in the twenty-first century,
> Tokyo, November 1994

The End of the USSR

The collapse of the Soviet empire and then the sudden demise of the Soviet Union astounded the world. The speed and finality of this process caught nearly everyone off guard. Few Great Powers have surrendered their dominions and then committed suicide in quite such a dramatic and unexpected manner. The Berlin Wall fell on 9 November 1989; less than a year later Germany was reunified and by December 1991 the USSR was no more. One moment Moscow was the overlord of Eastern Europe and a recognized superpower equipped with intercontinental ballistic missiles; very soon afterwards it was nothing but a shell of its former self.

Within the space of a few months, its sprawling subject nations were free and the USSR had ceased to exist. Its ideology, collective values and red flag, which had survived for seventy years to create a modern state, defeat the might of Fascism and earn equality with the United States at the negotiating table, were viewed now as despised relics of a bygone age. Triumphant statues of Lenin were pulled from their pedestals by jeering crowds in every town square in the land, as commemorative handfuls of stone from the once infamous Berlin wall were instantly peddled in the West. These unholy relics of totalitarianism quickly found a market, confirming in the process what Marx had known only too well, that capitalism is ever ready to grab an opportunity to turn a profit.

Gorbachev had begun as a reformer, yet he remained a loyal Communist. While he most certainly said to his confidant and foreign minister Edwarde Shevardnadze on gaining office that 'We can't go on like this', it is far from clear if he could ever have ridden the tiger he had unleashed. To want to change his country but to stay true to the Communist Party proved an impossible contradiction. While Gorbachev was indeed prepared to jettison his European empire, if it came to a choice between deploying force or permitting freedom, this was not intended to undermine the Soviet Union itself. Yet the process of attempting to reform the Soviet Union in order to shore it up was quickly seen as an impossibility. Police repression and the threat of tanks on the streets had long kept order in Eastern Europe, but once removed it left Moscow's politburo dangerously naked at home. Party members immediately complained bitterly that their patrimony was being lost, while liberal elements demanded that the freedoms granted in Eastern Europe be transferred to them. Politics in the Soviet Union quickly became a witches' brew of Communists attacking Nationalists, who in turn hated the emerging democrats. To make things even worse, Gorbachev failed in his economic reforms and frightened citizens saw that the old familiarities of an inefficient Communist system might well be replaced by the even more uncomfortable world of international competition and gangsterism. Queuing for subsidized vodka and surviving on state pensions had traditionally led to a life of complaints, but a country with only rudimentary order and a new elite of flashy entrepreneurs hardly appeared much of an improvement. Whereas Soviet politicians had been used to enjoying an insulated, protected life, now their Russian successors must wear bullet-proof vests and answer to the electorate for their deeds.

Since Gorbachev had told the East German leader Erich Honnicker that it was 'impossible' to deploy riot squads and water cannon against peaceful mass demonstrations, it followed that the Soviet Union had little left with which to defend itself when challenged on all sides. Gorbachev could only plead for patience. His position, however, was destroyed by the Communist-inspired coup of August 1991 and he finally resigned in December as the last general secretary of the Communist Party and the first and only president the Soviet Union would ever know. When asked four years on by the writer David Remnick if he was shocked by the tawdry glamour and stark poverty of the newly emerging Moscow, Gorbachev replied, 'What on earth could ever shock me now?'

The Soviet leader's position had been further undermined by two skilful and adroit opponents in the West. President George Bush and West German Chancellor Helmut Kohl made Gorbachev's hopes of surviving much weaker by playing a game of diplomatic nicety towards Moscow, while all the time reckoning on how best the USSR could be quietly wrecked. The short period from 1989 to 1991 was indeed to witness what Bush and Brent Scowcroft would later term 'A World Transformed', through an unexpected and largely peaceful shift that Bush and his national security adviser have described as a 'down-and-dirty, hands-on' process. It led to the attainment of the basic goal of US foreign policy over the past half-century and the beginning of a new era in world politics. This was quickly apparent when, after living next to the Soviet empire in Europe for two generations, the West German state and its people had displayed their overwhelming determination to achieve both the eventual American-sponsored reunification of Germany and its in-clusion in a modified NATO structure. Yet their success and the extra-ordinary and extraordinarily swift removal of the Soviet Union from, in turn, Czechoslovakia, Romania, Hungary and Bulgaria had relatively limited impact on the map of the Asia-Pacific region. Whatever the sub-terranean processes at work, the surface features remained very largely untouched. No Communist state in Asia moved to scrap its domestic political arrangements or considered shifting into the opposition's camp in terms of security alignment. There was no knock-on effect.

The contrast between Europe and Asia was indeed pronounced. The People's Republic of China, North Korea, Vietnam and Laos reaffirmed their Socialist heritage. The Chinese Communist leadership in Beijing was quick to assert that the collapse of the Soviet Union simply demon-strated the thoroughly deserved consequences of apostasy for Moscow in deviating from Marxist-Leninist thought and practice. This was, of course, a long-held stance which Mao, for example, had adopted when criticizing Nikita Khrushchev in the mid-1950s. China had for decades maintained that the Soviet Union's revisionist behaviour ought to serve as a precautionary tale on how not to run a Socialist state, organize its people or conduct international affairs. The Soviet model was deemed irrelevant and worthy of contempt. Moscow's fate led to rejoicing in China both on the grounds that the Soviet Union was no more and because its demise afforded new opportunities for the PRC to stake a claim to greater regional influence. The fall of the USSR provided both relief and delight for a China that had long feared Moscow more than Washington in the Asia-Pacific. The Soviet military build-ups of the 1980s are now being seen, at least in hindsight, as designed more to intimidate the PRC than to weaken the grip of the United States in the Western Pacific. The American concern over Soviet naval deployment in the region simply resulted in even greater US naval superiority through extensive and domestically popular shipbuilding programmes. Yet for the Chinese Army, the need to increase battalion numbers along the endless border with the USSR to match Soviet actions was most unwelcome. It deserves also to be recalled that for the thirty years between 1958 and 1988, there is no proven record of a single encounter between the most senior leaders of the two most powerful Communist nations on earth.

The replacement of the USSR by the Russian federation made little immediate difference to the structure of international relations in the Asia-Pacific region. Moscow's collapse hardly came as staggering news to those accustomed to observing its long-drawn-out decline in Asia. Although Gorbachev had employed fine rhetoric and a rustbucket fleet to give the impression of strength, the tangible results had been less than impressive. A bravura performance remains a performance. His successors will doubtless wish to do better, but at present it is surely a case of attempting to make bricks without straw. Analysts are certainly required to consider the day when Moscow may perhaps return to a position of greater strategic importance in the Asia-Pacific region, but the contemporary historian can only respond that it did not happen on his watch.

The West and China

The major changes that followed in the international politics of the 1990s concern the newly enhanced status of the United States and the reaction of strengthening regional powers, notably China, to this uncomfortable reality. The end of the USSR and its replacement with a weaker and poorer Russian federation automatically left the United States as the sole remaining superpower in the Asia-Pacific region. The collapse of Communism might lead to a notable absence of euphoria and victory parades in the capitals of the West, but victorious the United States undeniably was. The Soviet Union and its subject empire was gone for good and there was no prospect of the successor state to the Soviet Union being able to mount a fresh challenge to the United States and its allies. International history has few general axioms but it remains a crude rule of thumb that once great powers are seemingly incapable of raising themselves from the dead to regain lost glories. The contrasts between the achievements of Imperial Spain, the France of Louis XIV and mid-

Victorian Britain with their later diminished circumstances all strongly suggest that national reincarnation is well-nigh impossible.

The objectives of the People's Republic of China in a now unipolar world that it intensely dislikes deserve to be identified and assessed. To start with the unpalatably obvious, Beijing had little choice but first to recognize and then to live with the consequences of the strengthened status of the United States. It might (and frequently did) complain against this gross injustice, yet its ability to alter the international dominance of Washington was much less than its shrill bark. The venom of China's criticism of a seemingly expansionist and power-hungry United States served only to leave outsiders sensing that crude propaganda masked a general insecurity. The almost universal Western criticism heaped on the PRC over the Tiananmen Square massacre of student demonstrators in June 1989, when combined with the simultaneous ending of the Cold War, placed Beijing at an obvious disadvantage. Events shortly afterwards in the Middle East further underlined the political and military weaknesses of China. The quick and almost painless success of the American-led coalition in defeating Iraq in the Gulf War of 1990–91 left the Chinese military in no doubt as to its own technological backwardness. The spotlight was uncomfortable for China's leadership and the unease showed.

The student protests in China that led to the violent military intervention coincided with the presence in Beijing of Mikhail Gorbachev. The fact that the Soviet reformer was in China on an official visit to improve Sino-Soviet relations gave hope to the students, as did the intense foreign media coverage that ensued. Such attention infuriated the Chinese authorities and allowed the world to compare the repression that followed in Beijing with the unexpectedly pacific steps being taken in Eastern Europe and the Soviet Union to transform the Socialist system. While China was clearly committed to extensive economic reform, most commentators held that the PRC leadership had reckoned that an improvement in living conditions would be sufficient to deflect any large-scale demands for political liberation. The dream of a better life was intended to smother dissent. Awareness throughout China of the gold-rush atmosphere of Shenzen and Shanghai suggested that the authorities might be correct. To get rich was an improbability for most of the internal migrants who flocked recklessly to the booming, polluted and noisy cities, but as an aspiration it frequently precluded much thought of existing party controls. Despite the claims of politicians and political scientists in the West, it did indeed appear that a semi-open economy could operate hand in hand with a repressive police state. Reagan and Thatcher might proclaim that Marx and Madison Avenue could not cohabit, but contemporary China thought otherwise. Affluence was all.

Events in Tiananmen Square may have served to prompt a temporary reassessment of basic state policy, but with the advantage of a decade's hindsight, it appears that the Communist Party's calculations were correct. Although Beijing was rightly criticized by the West for its gross mishandling of the demonstrations, the longer-term consequences for China's international reputation were slighter than its critics had hoped. The condemnation and curses showered on China had little impact since trade boycotts and selective sanctions rarely work. Isolation did not last. Beijing was also helped by the lack of unity among its critics and by the continuing lure of the China market that left governments reluctant to damage their own corporations' involvement by instituting tougher sanctions than rival powers. Boeing, for example, to take one important American exporter to China, had no wish to be deprived of its place in the sun by its European rivals. There was, and there remains today, invariably an anxiety among all who do business with China that contracts could be quietly discarded as retaliation for bilateral political quarrels and that the awards might be passed on to more cooperative sources. Deng Xiaoping also defiantly told Richard Nixon after Tiananmen that China would never 'beg the United States to lift the sanctions. If they lasted a hundred years, the Chinese would not do that'.

Britain and Japan were the first powers to break ranks. Much against his known wishes, Prime Minister John Major was persuaded by the Foreign Office's China watchers that it was in the furtherance of overall Anglo-Chinese relations, and in particular to the sensitive question of the reversion of Hong Kong, if he made a visit to Beijing. China, of course, was delighted at the decision but had no intention of assisting the British government in its difficulties over explaining and defending the Joint Declaration of September 1984, already in place as the Sino-British blueprint for determining the future of Hong Kong after 1 July 1997. It had been accepted by both governments that China would then regain sovereignty over what would be designated as the Special Administrative Region (SAR) 'directly under the authority of the Central People's Government of the People's Republic of China'. For Britain to be seen to be so publicly courting China when memories were so fresh was a useful gain for the PRC. The diplomatic momentum was then reinforced by Japan, whose heart had never been in extensive sanctions.

Sino-Japanese Ties

Tokyo argued throughout that its preferred way forward was to maintain a dialogue with the Chinese authorities rather than to create obstacles by isolating its formidable neighbour. Japan maintained that the nature of its special relationship with China entitled it to handling Beijing as it saw fit, and this priority was endorsed by the fact that Prime Minister Kaifu in August 1991 became the first G-7 leader to fly to Beijing after the Tiananmen Square massacre. Considerably earlier, on the fortieth anniversary of China's National Day, the director-general of the Asian Affairs Bureau of the Foreign Ministry had already been quoted as saying that any move to chastise the PRC 'could lead to the emergence of an introvert or a bitterly combative China, a prospect not in the least relished by either Japan or other Asian countries'. Similar stances are traditionally adopted by Japanese bureaucrats when proposals from overseas governments and private organizations are received to outlaw other renegade regimes in Asia and beyond. A general reluctance to speak out against the current military junta in Burma (Myanmar) is a sad case in point.

Formal improvement in Sino-Japanese relations was rapid. To celebrate the twentieth anniversary of the normalization process begun by Prime Minister Tanaka Kakuei, the Emperor was sent in 1992 on a meticulously planned state visit to Beijing. Spokesmen from both nations went to great lengths to note how the two Asian societies exhibit shared cultural traits and maintained that a 'special relationship' would replace the dreary invocation of appalling historical clashes in the first half of the century. Instead of being opponents in the Cold War, the expectation on both sides was that an improvement in relations would assist bilateral ties and contribute to the relaxation of international tension in the wider Asia-Pacific region. Events, however, have taken a different path. Japan and China have certainly avoided any repetition of the unhappy postwar era when relations moved hesitantly at best, but the lack of cordiality in their relationship remains apparent. Ministerial discussions are now more frequent, yet some of the old uncertainties remain. China still regards Japan's strengthening security links to the United States as a barrier to progress, while Japanese governments, of whatever hue, look with increasing annoyance at what is widely seen by the man in the street as Chinese arrogance as its rise in international stature continues.

The 1990s proved a disappointment to those expecting broad co-operation between China and Japan. Both sides may have thought that substantial future improvement could flow from the first-ever visit of a Japanese emperor to China, yet in retrospect, 1992 marked the high point of the new relationship. Prospects for economic ties in particular looked promising. Japan wished to assist in the economic reforms taking place in China by encouraging its own trading houses and corporations to devise long-term investment strategies that might benefit both nations and thereby avoid the charge, frequently voiced of other industrial nations, that Japan was only in China for immediate gain. Yet the warmth in Sino-Japanese ties was temporary. The prolonged recession that first hit Japan in 1990–91 was to lead to disappointing growth throughout most of the decade and inevitably curtailed both the foreign policy aspirations of the Japanese establishment and the free-spending practices of the corporate sector. The maximization of profits suddenly became a necessity, and projects previously undertaken in part to purchase future goodwill were slashed as management faced unprecedented pressures to correct dismal balance sheets. It followed that if the economic relationship were in difficulties, the entire Sino-Japanese edifice would appear vulnerable. Massive yen loans that had been initialled before the Tiananmen Square massacre were taken up in the early 1990s, but the results were less than encouraging for Japanese capitalism. While investment levels reached record levels in 1992 and the import-export trade between the two nations also grew rapidly, the reality was more troubling for Tokyo than the raw statistics might suggest. China's modernization inevitably presented challenges to the less productive and weaker portion of the Japanese industrial sector, characterized by subcontracting family firms. Small companies that form the backbone of Japan's dual economy did not take kindly to being squeezed out by new Asian competitors, and the trade bureaucrats in Tokyo were anxious not to provide advanced technology to China (and elsewhere in East Asia) that might be used against Japan's own struggling domestic manufacturers. Difficulties over contracts, the repatriation of profits and the uncertainties of an opaque bureaucratic system all added to Japan's problems. Outsiders were tempted to compare some of the difficulties that Japanese businesses now experienced in China with the administrative nightmares and red tape common to those attempting to break into the Japanese market. The boot was now on the other foot.

Such reservations hardly accorded with Prime Minister Kaifu's claim in June 1990 that the ending of the Cold War made it possible to 'go out into the world and if there is a need, if there is a request from another party, we should not hesitate in meeting it'. It remained less than clear whether the economic ties between Japan and China could carry the heavy political baggage that Tokyo had traditionally placed on this relationship. To encourage domestic stability inside China through close economic links was an admirable aim, but for Japan to appear as Beijing's financial patron was probably an unrealizable goal. Once China's economy had begun to modernize at speed and Beijing's range of options had grown correspondingly, it was difficult even to persuade the PRC leadership to acknowledge in public that Japanese aid had greatly assisted in this great leap forward. Yet to expect Japanese aid and preferential loans to do serious diplomatic duty was unrealistic, particularly when other nations could also offer similar financial and commercial packages. The concept of a shared Sino-Japanese economic sphere in East Asia remains an illusion when China has no intention of becoming over-dependent on

Tokyo's economic might, and China has to be cajoled into noting the extent of Japanese aid.

Sino-Japanese ties might well have had setbacks without wider political problems, but when the uncertainties of territorial and strategic issues were also factored into the relationship, it became harder still to recall the optimism of less than a decade earlier. Japanese public opinion is wary of the new assertiveness displayed by Beijing in the Asia-Pacific region, both because it arouses concern over China's long-term objectives and through a sense of disappointment that Tokyo has failed to lay claim to at least some of the influence now ascribed to the PRC. Japan has fewer options to play than ten years ago. Its hopes of a more independent role are circumscribed by the continuing domestic economic difficulties it still faces and by the prospect of regional crises on both the Korean Peninsula and the Taiwan Straits.

The greatest risk for Sino-Japanese relations concerns Taiwan. Governments in Tokyo continue to be hesitant about being seen to offer any overt support to the United States in defence of Taiwan which might draw Japan into a major crisis with the PRC. To avoid this possibility Japanese diplomats continue to urge restraint on all parties, though the existence of the US–Japan security pact and the size of Japan's financial and commercial stake in Taiwan suggest that being all things to all men is a near impossibility. What is clear, however, is that Japan wishes to avoid giving the slightest indication of assistance, even in the form of logistical support to US forces, if there were to be a military confrontation in the South China Sea. The present interpretation of Japanese law with regard to deployment of its Self Defense Forces is to maintain that even indirect security cooperation in a combat zone is not permissible. Japanese maritime self-defence minesweepers and oilers are apparently to sever all links with allied shipping at the slightest hint of a crisis and sail immediately to their home ports, regardless of the consequences for US vessels. The probable results of such inactivity on the part of Japan are not difficult to imagine; it would then be immensely difficult for any American administration to curtail the hue and cry from its public at Tokyo's perceived perfidy. The fate of the alliance might next be placed in question and the long-term Chinese strategic objective of detaching Japan from the United States brought considerably nearer realization.

The Korean Question

The Korean Peninsula is the point of contact for all major powers in the region. Indeed, it is the sole geographical area where the vital interests of the United States, China, the Russian Federation and Japan coincide. The complexity and interrelationship of these factors has ensured that

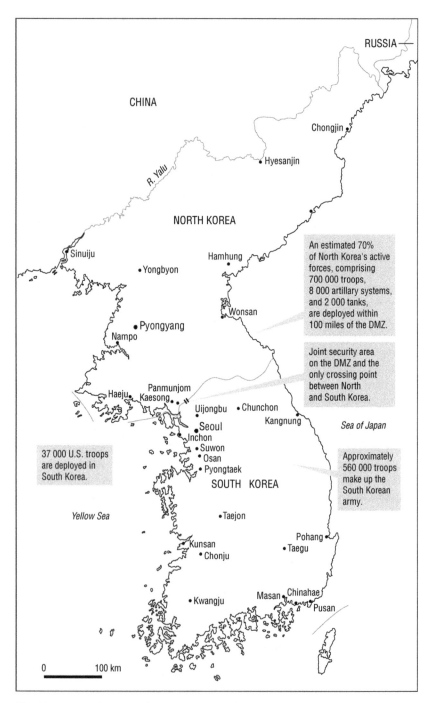

The Korean Peninsula, 2000
Based on The International Institute for Strategic Studies, Strategic Survey,
2000–2001 *(Oxford, 2001).*

events on and around Korea would long warrant the highest priority in international affairs, since instability on the peninsula runs the considerable risk of igniting first regional and then global tensions. During the 1990s the erratic and stubborn policies of North Korea were a constant anxiety to Seoul, Washington and Tokyo. The end of the Soviet Union did, of course, raise hopes initially that North Korea might adopt different foreign policies. There were indeed intergovernmental talks between Seoul and Pyongyang and the two Koreas were able to enter the United Nations simultaneously in 1991, while agreeing in the following year to make the peninsula a nuclear-free zone. Since the Russian Federation and then the PRC had moved quickly to begin formal diplomatic relations with South Korea, it was apparent that North Korea risked near complete isolation, since it could no longer hope to rely on its former friends for sustenance and support in a rapidly changing region. The United States for its part hoped that a joint approach with South Korea and its allies would restrain North Korea. For a brief moment, following the collapse of Communism across Eastern Europe and the USSR, it did appear that the Asian headlines on the improvement in North–South Korean relations warranted the cliché of the new morning calm across the peninsula. The end of the Soviet Union and the inevitable weakening of Russian–North Korean political and economic links seemed to suggest that Pyongyang's overtures to its former adversaries would quickly bring dividends in the shape of enhanced stability for the region. Since the United States had responded with a swift decision to withdraw its nuclear weaponry from South Korea and Kim Il Sung had announced his willingness to open North Korean nuclear facilities to international inspection teams and terminate his country's uranium enhancement programme, it appeared that reciprocal gestures could lead to a breakthrough. This soon proved to be a false spring.

Yet regardless of what would be a difficult decade of alternating hopes and setbacks, it was clear that Washington would continue to play the major role in Northeast Asia. The United States, it may be recalled, has had the greatest influence on Korean affairs since the end of the Pacific War. From its initial involvement in the autumn of 1945 to the early 1990s, its approaches were determined by a strenuous military policy of limiting North Korean expansion. In the last decade, however, the United States, as the military and economic sponsor of its South Korean ally, has been required to negotiate at length with North Korea, in order to prevent the expansion of both its nuclear and ballistic missile programmes. In this decade-long process, Pyongyang has doubtless had the satisfaction of finding itself being taken very seriously indeed by the world's only remaining superpower. For a small Asian nation of limited economic strength this is a considerable – if for others unfortunate – accomplishment. It would also not be surprising if the North Korean leadership had developed a certain fascination with such red carpet diplomacy and might therefore be tempted to perpetuate the process. To be treated to the hospitality of the State Department and then to be able to negotiate as an equal with the other powers in Northeast Asia may well have its attractions. Although any end to Pyongyang's isolation is likely to be an extended and arduous experience, it is difficult to envisage how the eventual outcome can be postponed indefinitely.

Given the armament build-ups by the government led first by Kim Il Sung, until his death in July 1994, and then by his son Kim Jong Il, Japan clearly had no choice but to support the Clinton administration's efforts to persuade North Korea to exercise restraint over military and nuclear policies in exchange for food and humanitarian assistance as the North Korean economy deteriorated and the region faced the prospect of a crisis being ignited out of desperation. Yet again, it was a case of Japan taking its cue from other powers and then reassessing its own stance as regional circumstances altered. Japan adopted a relatively low-key approach to improving what initially were its almost non-existent ties to Pyongyang during the decade. Both the historical legacy of Japanese imperialism and the intense divisions of the Cold War served to restrict even informal contacts between two nations without diplomatic relations or a peace treaty. Discussions between Japan and North Korea were rare and raw as the North Korean government insisted that Japan make restitution for the colonial era before entering into talks on the present. Japan, for its part, demanded that the North Korean authorities offer full explanations over past terrorism and the bizarre abduction of Japanese citizens. In addition to these serious and long-standing bilateral differences, the relationship was further worsened by the launching of a North Korean Taepodong-1 missile on 31 August 1998, which underlined the strategic vulnerability of Japan. Although the North Korean authorities insisted that the venture was intended to launch a satellite, the test was widely regarded as a reminder of the increasing military power at North Korean disposal. The Japanese Defense Agency stated in its 1999 white paper that the government would immediately counter the threat of more advanced, longer-range North Korean ballistic missiles by launching new information-gathering satellites in the near future and by closer coordination with its allies. The fact that two North Korean vessels were discovered inside Japanese territorial waters in March 1999 and that all attempts to intercept these probable spy ships failed has only added to public unease over Pyongyang. These very considerable Japanese anxieties over North Korea also helped cement closer ties between Tokyo and Seoul, though this was something of an unintended 'own goal' on Pyongyang's part.

The international complexities of the Korean question are worsened by the different domestic agendas of the various participants. Links between Japan and North Korea have remained extremely tenuous, and domestic opinion in Japan is unlikely to forgive fawning by its own government if it were in the future to appear excessively apologetic and display any particular generosity in achieving an eventual rapprochement. Equally, in South Korea the strenuous efforts of President Kim Dae Jung's courageous engagement policies towards North Korea need to bear considerable fruit before too long or the reaction in Seoul to setbacks could jeopardize Kim's own position.

After President Kim came to power in Seoul in 1998 as head of a coalition government, he took considerable risks. Kim had for decades been involved in the vigorous world of fluctuating civil and military South Korean politics, where his reputation was high as a determined reformer who had experienced prison terms, kidnapping, death sentences and exile. His bold approaches to Pyongyang were quickly known throughout Asia as South Korea's 'sunshine policy'. Kim's determination to engage the north through non-provocative dialogue and the offer of economic cooperation were far from popular with many sceptical South Koreans, who retained bitter memories of the Korean civil war of 1950–53 and of Pyongyang's frigid responses to earlier attempts at national reconciliation. Conservatives in South Korea remain eager to criticize their prime minister for not taking a harder line with Pyongyang, while adding for good measure the fact that Kim Dae Jung is guilty of neglecting the economic difficulties facing his nation as he concentrates all his energies on achieving a breakthrough with North Korea. Yet sufficient progress was being made by June 2000 for North Korea's Kim and South Korea's Kim Dae Jung to meet in person and to at least begin what is being regarded even by its strongest supporters as an immensely complicated and lengthy process that may end in the reunification of two highly diverse societies. The awarding of the Nobel peace prize to Kim Dae Jung in October 2000 was an important psychological boost for the peace process and a reminder of how closely the rest of the world is viewing developments. In addition to praise for Kim's lengthy and outspoken campaigning for greater democracy within South Korea, the Nobel citation spoke of Kim's visit to North Korea as having given 'impetus to a peace process which has reduced tension' between the two Koreas and suggested that there 'may now be hope that the Cold War will also come to an end in Korea'. It is hardly fanciful to suggest that, if this were eventually to occur, the result might well be a similar award to honour Kim Jong Il.

Efforts by the Clinton administration played a key role in persuading Pyongyang to moderate its earlier policies with regard to missile testing and nuclear reactor programmes. The United States spent much of the 1990s attempting to establish sufficient trust with the North Korean leadership to gain a series of accords. It led to what then Secretary of

Defense William Perry would later tell an audience in Tokyo was 'the only time that I believed that the United States was in serious danger of a major war'. The June 1994 crisis arose from concerns that the North Korean nuclear facility at Yongbyon was about to start processing nuclear fuel, which, in Perry's words, 'would have provided them with enough plutonium to immediately make a half-dozen bombs'. It was only after the United States and its regional allies, South Korea and Japan, had announced their intention to impose sanctions and Washington had moved to increase its troop deployment levels on the peninsula that negotiations were able to begin. Perry, rarely given to hyperbole and conscious of the need to work with South Korea and Japan in determining an appropriate engagement policy, called this 'truly a close-run operation'. By the Agreed Framework agreement of October 1994, North Korea stated its willingness to stop its suspected nuclear programme in exchange for US assistance with two light-water 1 million kilowatt reactors and alternative energy sources. This was a considerable accomplishment. To implement these substantial dealings an international consortium was formed under the title of the Korean Peninsula Energy Development Organization (KEDO) in March 1995. This body, composed initially of South Korea, Japan and the United States, has the still unfinished task of financing and arranging the construction of the proposed substitute plants and also of storing and removing the spent fuel rods from the North Korean reactors. It is, however, much too early to predict the final outcome of this nuclear diplomacy, since there are major financial difficulties over the financing of the KEDO consortium and these already substantial delays could be compounded by fresh tensions on the peninsula.

Washington was assisted too by the weakening of links between North Korea and its former allies, Russia and China. The economic deterioration that Pyongyang has had to cope with for most of the past decade has been made worse by the sharp reduction in aid from its traditional friends. Since evidence is rarely forthcoming on the precise state of domestic conditions within North Korea, it is difficult to reconcile the persistent claims of famine, bankruptcy and cannibalism with the fact that North Korea, however poor and repressed its people may be, has managed to survive to negotiate at length with the United States and its more powerful neighbours. It is probable that the United States, at least in the near and medium term, will be satisfied in gaining what is frequently termed as 'peaceful coexistence' with North Korea. It is also the position of Lee Joung Binn, the South Korean foreign minister, who stated in an interview with the *Los Angeles Times* in February 2001 that 'we are trying to promote reconciliation and co-operation on one track and a reduction in military tension on another track, so that we can create favourable conditions for peaceful unification – eventually'. He added that he hoped that Washington might 'continue to stay even after unification on the Korean peninsula'. Yet to gain the first goal of genuine understanding would in itself be a considerable accomplishment and might greatly improve the entire regional security position, though of course still falling far short of the ultimate South Korean goal of peaceful reunification. President Kim Dae Jung's aspirations could well take a generation to be realized.

As the region's diplomacy with North Korea has evolved, it appears that Pyongyang has appreciated that it stands to make considerable gains by showing greater willingness to talk and compromise. In the face of severe, debilitating famine, hugely expensive military build-ups and a rigid domestic political structure without parallels elsewhere, North Korea has been rewarded with substantial food aid. Demonstrating a modicum of goodwill towards Seoul is all part of the process of accepting alternative energy arrangements. Yet its leadership must know that moves towards a gradual opening of North Korea would create immense strains for a state and society that has been isolated both diplomatically and domestically. Indeed, some Korean analysts in the United States sense that any substantial rapprochement would be tantamount to Kim Jong Il signing his own abdication papers, since greater awareness of the outside world could undermine the entire state structure.

The summit meeting in June 2000 between the two Kims, however, has been seen as a turning point in the history of the divided peninsula. High-level meetings began within Korea and wider diplomatic moves followed immediately afterwards, with President Clinton receiving the vice-chairman of North Korea's National Defense Commission, Jo Myong Rok, at the White House in October 2000 to underline the thaw in past hostilities. The meeting led Clinton to claim that tension had eased and that Jo's visit was 'an important way to continue to engage'. Although it may take decades to realize national reunification, it is significant that symbolic gestures, such as family exchanges and the beginnings of postal and telecommunicational links, have also commenced. It too is intended to engender confidence-building and mutual trust in a region where such moves have been lacking for decades.

Much must remain speculative, and it is impossible to provide more than approximate outlines of recent developments. It is clear though that North Korea's neighbours have attempted to coordinate policies with those of the United States to ensure that tripartite cooperation between Washington, Seoul and Tokyo prevents opportunities for North Korea to split its erstwhile opponents' united front. But the United States and South Korea have to recognize that Japan is almost certain to be more hesitant in dealing with North Korea, since Tokyo is in no mood to press ahead with precipitate action, both because of the reservations long held by public opinion and through the need to find solutions to its separate bilateral issues with Pyongyang. The former Japanese diplomat Okazaki Hisahiko noted in October 2000 that the North Korean economy has continued to shrink since 1994 and that without the importation of capital and technology on a substantial scale from the United States, Japan and South Korea, the danger of implosion will inevitably grow. To counter these alarming consequences, North Korea appears to have accepted the need for constructive dialogue. It has been vividly suggested that the changed behaviour of Kim Jong Il himself reflects a willingness to discuss long-standing issues, whereas in the past 'Pyongyang replied to overtures from the outside world with total silence'. It is also probable, as Okazaki suggests, that Kim has deepened his confidence politically and psychologically in the six years following the death of the 'great founder' of the nation, Kim Il Sung, and as a result his power base has solidified, thus making the new approaches to opponents overseas more readily acceptable within the party leadership.

Yet coordination among allies is unlikely to be simple, if Japan's behaviour to date is any guide. Tokyo appears less than consistent in its stance towards North Korea; it gives contradictory signals at times over the size of food aid on offer and over its attitude towards past terrorism, and it is likely to lag behind others in the protracted normalization process. The fact that domestic party-political factors could dictate the announcement in the autumn of 2000 of both the extraordinary size and the content of rice shipments to Pyongyang is hardly a useful omen. The ruling Japanese coalition cabinet led by the Liberal Democratic Party's Mori Yoshiro suddenly reversed earlier concerns and agreed to ship 500 000 tons of highly expensive home-grown rice to North Korea without any stated preconditions. The gesture was intended to demonstrate Japanese goodwill before scheduled normalization talks, which have been making little progress since their inception in 1992. Cynics would claim that this also served as a convenient political method for getting rid of a great deal of surplus rice but contributed little to the solution of ongoing issues. It did not appear to have had much effect on dealing with the alleged abduction of Japanese nationals by North Korean agents or smoothing the tortuous path to any agreement on compensation for Japan's past colonial rule. As of November 2000, the North Korean authorities were refusing to countenance a Japanese proposal that would offer a financial and economic package to Pyongyang which had distinct similarities to that used to broker a normalization arrangement in 1965 between the ROK and Japan. Kim Jong Il's government was quick to reject such suggestions out of hand, and the Japanese were equally insistent that it should continue pressing such schemes in future talks.

President Clinton's expressed wish to visit Pyongyang never materialized, but his hopes for the establishment of a new relationship 'free from
past antagonism' could prompt far-reaching changes in Northeast Asia.
The expectation in the winter of 2000 was that the United States and
North Korea might follow in the wake of the North–South Korean
summit and thereby 'radically improve the bilateral relations in favour
of consolidating the peace and security in the Asia-Pacific region'. The
'new orientation', which was intended to build on earlier US–North
Korean joint statements, would require cooperation and compromise on
a scale quite unknown in the past. One early test of the depth of the new
relationship would be whether the two parties could eventually agree
on what the US–North Korean communiqué of 12 October described
as 'denuclearization'. Pyongyang, for its part, was prepared to make a
gesture to this end by promising not to launch any long-range missiles
during forthcoming talks and by offering inspection of its Kumchangri
underground facility. The subsequent follow-up visit by Secretary of
State Madeleine Albright to Pyongyang in the same month appears to
have sustained the diplomatic momentum. The US government, however, was cautious in public over the future, beyond pleasantries such as
Mrs Albright's remark that the United States and North Korea were
nearer the end than the beginning of their remarkable diplomatic
journey. This may well prove to be far from the case. The difficulties
should not be underestimated of persuading Pyongyang that the West's
enticements are sufficient to alter the basic foreign and domestic foundations of the North Korean state. It will also take considerable skill to
maintain an approximate policy coordination between Washington, Seoul
and Tokyo as each nation will be tempted to go its own way and attend
to its particular interests. Any unseemly scramble to Pyongyang might
improve Kim Jong Il's hand and. weaken the present common front.

Taiwan

The question of the future of Taiwan bedevilled Asia-Pacific relations
throughout the 1990s. Whereas the powers had greatly increased their
cooperation over tackling the North Korean issue, there was far less solidarity on the long-standing and sensitive case of Taiwan. The explanation,
of course, is that the People's Republic of China is most unwilling to
regard the Taiwan debate as anything but a domestic issue that deserves
to be managed in its entirety by Beijing. Given that the PRC has persisted
in claiming such exclusive rights, the approaches of the United States and
other nations have been regarded with the highest suspicion by Beijing.
By 2000, semi-official voices were repeating what Beijing had long
insisted, namely that Taiwan had no choice but to revert to the mainland
under the promise of a high degree of local autonomy. Only then, so

the Chinese authorities insist, can there be reasonable expectations for regional stability and closer Sino-American relations.

The fact that most nations no longer accord full diplomatic recognition to Taiwan has led to increasing isolation for Taipei. Even scholarly texts published in the West have begun to adopt the view that Taiwan, for example, should not be listed as a separate entity and that indexes will merely note 'Taiwan, see under China'. This is unhelpful. It contributes to a general perception that Taiwan is in the process of returning to the fold of the PRC and is in clear contradiction of events over the past two generations. It might be best to begin with the obvious. Taiwan exists as a relatively affluent, well-armed and reasonably open society. It appears unwilling to accept repeated offers from Beijing that it should bow to the inevitable and rejoin the Chinese peoples on the mainland. The leadership of the Chinese Communist Party has long found the truculence of Taipei a national embarrassment, and successive heads of the PRC have vowed that they will ensure the return of Taiwan. None, to date, has had much luck in this important national goal. The 'one country, two systems' approach, though granting local autonomy to post-colonial Hong Kong and in place since 1997, has yet to prove much of an enticement to Taiwan, where sentiment favours greater stress on the increasing divergence of Taipei from Beijing. Yet open statements on the imminence of a 'two countries, two systems' reality by politicians in Taiwan would be unhelpful and may well transform what is obviously an uncomfortable position into one where the PRC would feel obliged to respond to Taiwanese taunts. Silence might better assist Taipei and make it more probable that Beijing would feel less required to assert its national will. It should also be recalled that China lived with the existence of the colonial enclave of Hong Kong on its doorstep for nearly half a century. While this was an undoubted political embarrassment to Beijing, the PRC was able to benefit substantially in economic, financial and technological terms from the anomaly. The case of Taiwan, of course, is in many ways more pressing and less easily solved to the advantage of Beijing than was the diplomatic process that led to the reversion of Hong Kong, yet it might suggest the possible virtues of patience and caution. Hong Kong's transformation from British colony to Chinese Special Administrative Region is far from a complete success story, but the fears of many overseas that the PRC would quickly wreck its newest acquisition have so far proved false.

Taiwan is losing friends but it is not yet friendless. It has gained in self-confidence through enjoying an era of rising prosperity and has the satisfaction of knowing that the United States remains committed to holding the ring. Taipei has reason to believe that if there were to be any future political realignment of Taiwan and the PRC, Washington would seek to ensure that this be on the basis of equitable negotiations rather than crude force. The general attitude of the United States is clearly crucial to the safety and stability of the small island republic. However formidable the Taiwanese military may appear to be on paper, the long-term fate of Taipei depends on security guarantees from the United States. It follows, of course, that any suggestion that Washington might wish at some future date to reassess its commitments to Taipei would have immediate and drastic implications for Taiwan's security. Today, as in most of its uncertain history, Taiwan has to be content with the uncomfortable reality that it continues to survive and, indeed, prosper on the slopes of a live volcano. It may be unpleasant at times, but much like the villagers on Mount Etna, there are compensations, provided the oft-predicted catastrophe is postponed. Taiwan also has the satisfaction of knowing that any eruption would not only severely damage the island but presumably create havoc over portions of China, and leave the PRC standing almost alone in the region.

Yet the potential dangers should not be overstated. The frequency of crises over Taiwan since 1949 has not deterred its impressive economic modernization or the more recent, and still fragile, democratization process that followed on after 'Island China' had achieved an impressive standard of living. The beginnings of legitimate cross-strait trade flows between Taiwan and the PRC offer one positive indication that more normal commercial and financial linkage could lead to a greater degree of cooperation between the two Chinas. Undoubtedly the PRC has been an important beneficiary of Taiwan's new prosperity. Although Taiwan's economy was badly mauled by the 1997 Asian economic crisis, its long-term prospects remain generally strong. Analysts in 2000 noted, however, that in order to maintain its substantial growth record it will be necessary to continue to alter the once dominant manufacturing basis of the economy to one more reliant on higher technology and the service sector. The fact that Taiwanese corporations are now establishing subsidiaries in China has accelerated the process of adopting more capital and know-ledge-intensive industries domestically and thereby outsourcing much of its manufacturing of electronic components. Such suggestions have not been well received by some in Taipei, who fear that further declines in the production of relatively unsophisticated industrial items would result in entire industries being based offshore. Concern that a downturn in global demand for computer products might leave the present Taiwanese economy particularly vulnerable, with few alternative sectors to take up the slack, has yet to be addressed by the government.

The United States and China's Policies

Hong Kong remains one yardstick by which the United States and other Western powers can gauge the behaviour of the PRC. It is, of course, in many ways thoroughly atypical, since the Sino-British arrangements that prepared for the reversion of Hong Kong make constant reference to democratic forms that have few parallels in the rest of China. Yet despite a zealous attempt by the local and international media to report every item that might be viewed as critical of Beijing, it has to be said that the Chinese authorities have generally stuck to the broad framework of the Basic Law of April 1990. While there have indeed been political errors, most notably perhaps the fiasco over the attempts to muzzle research on public opinion conducted by the University of Hong Kong, and heavy-handed threats against the Falun Gong sect, it would be difficult to prove that Hong Kong's freedom of expression and respect for the rule of law have been seriously eroded since 1997. Many, however, reckon that the covert influence of Beijing has grown substantially. Open and vocal public disapproval with Tung Che-hwa (C. H. Tung), the thoroughly unpopular chief executive of the SAR, is evidence that the peoples of Hong Kong expect to speak, demonstrate and organize in an open manner that, short of widespread physical intimidation, is too deep-rooted a political characteristic to be easily abolished. Certainly there are flaws in the system of government and pressure has been used against journalists of the calibre of Willy Wo Lap, then of the *South China Morning Post*, but informal nudges by the authorities were hardly unknown in the colonial era. Tung's difficulties have been made worse by such concerns and, if the farewell remarks of his deputy Anson Chan are to be believed, he has made the going harder by a general reluctance to confront Beijing and a personal unwillingness to consider improving the slow movement towards the introduction of a democratic system of government for the SAR. Tung has, however, some reason to argue that he has generally upheld the constitutional arrangements established before his appointment. It may be that any substantial improvement in Hong Kong's economic fortunes by 2002 could yet see a belated boost to his sagging reputation.

More serious, however, than Western attention to events in Hong Kong is the sensitive and far-reaching question of China's trade policy. It has long been a central issue in Sino-American relations and is certain to remain a subject of controversy for the foreseeable future. The likelihood of China's admission to the World Trade Organization (WTO) can be assumed to resolve some long-standing issues, though it may in turn create a host of new ones. The question of whether the United States should actively support Beijing's wish for its inclusion in the WTO (and its predecessor the GATT) had been a source of domestic political debate for over a decade. Many trade unionists and their leaders had campaigned strenuously against China's membership, even when the Democratic Party had won back control of the White House and President

Clinton was determined to endorse the PRC's membership. Other nations also were divided over the implications for their societies of admitting a country whose reputation had been severely damaged by its failure to comply with trade agreements that it was already a party to and by fears that China's labour costs were such as to undercut much of the rest of the world in such sectors as mass-produced textiles and inter-mediate electronics. Chinese export concentration on certain politically sensitive areas parallels the postwar experiences of the West when obliged to adjust to unwelcome and particularly strenuous competition from first Japan and then the 'tiger' economies. By the 1980s, however, some American manufacturing industries often felt that the only way that might ensure their future survival was by outright opposition to China. After attempting to cope with a succession of Northeast and Southeast Asian economies, the thought of yet another potential onslaught from the Pacific Rim was particularly unwelcome.

For the Clinton administration the China trade issue was an important part of the challenging general question of how best to deal with the new strengths being demonstrated by Beijing. While the possibility offered by Harry Harding in 1992 that US–China trade relations could face 'cease-less controversy' – fomented by Chinese trade barriers and Congressional retaliation – has not materialized, there remain major difficulties between Washington and Beijing across the entire economic, political and security spectrum. The fact that the United States and China signed a WTO accession agreement in November 1999 and that the same autumn the US Senate approved permanent normal trade relations with the PRC was welcome news for those who saw the wave of globalization as the best way to integrate Beijing into international economic and political structures. Success was achieved through Clinton's actions and the tenacious fight put up by President Jiang Zemin and Prime Minister Zhu Rongji to gain general acceptance from recalcitrant Chinese ministries that feared the domestic political and social consequences of joining the WTO. If China's eventual accession to the WTO is to be seen as one of Clinton's finest hours, part of the praise should be given to Jiang Zemin for driving through an unpopular measure at home. Individual responsibilities aside, it is clear that increasingly close Sino-American economic ties should work to enmesh China with the wider world. Extensive investment flows, technological agreements and the attractions of new consumer markets now possess their own dynamic. Statistics that indicate how China's foreign trade was ten times larger in 1995 than in 1980 give comfort to those who maintain that China's sense of inter-dependence will gradually act to reduce friction, not only over economic issues but also in the political and security arenas. Greater Chinese compliance with international trading standards and Beijing's wider appreciation of how others conduct business and diplomacy are surely positive developments.

The Clinton administration had good reason to defend its overall record in the fields of trade and commerce. Its spokesman argued in November 2000 that the two terms of the Clinton presidency demonstrated how its efforts to form NAFTA, its China trade policy and the success of the Uruguay trade round constitute 'the most significant liberalization of world trade in decades'. Yet whether the current Sino-American trade imbalance, which leaves the United States with a yawning deficit that could parallel earlier uncomfortable clashes with Japan, would be sustainable over the medium term remains to be seen, as does the question of how cooperative Beijing may be over the implementation of a large range of unwelcome WTO commitments.

Sino-American trade questions are made more complicated by the fact that they can rarely be isolated as merely questions of trade. Economic issues have been used frequently by American opponents and supporters of China alike as platforms from which to speak out on other topics. Human rights activists within the United States have often asserted that trading arrangements should not be granted unless the PRC substantially improves its record over a raft of political and religious freedoms. This would prohibit, for example, the export of products made in Chinese labour camps and the use of capital punishment in corruption cases. Equally, those who wish to see an open China that might show greater and more cooperative involvement within the Asia-Pacific region maintain that trade is one legitimate means to this end. Beijing, of course, has its own views and would not wish to give any impression of even indirectly accepting linkage between economic matters and other arguably unrelated questions.

By the end of the Clinton years it would appear that the United States had reason to feel more satisfied with its relations with China than at any comparable point in the past decade. In a widely quoted remark in April 1999, President Clinton maintained that a greater spirit of Sino-American cooperation would prevent a series of dangerous possibilities, arguing that there were 'risks of a weak China, beset by internal difficulties, social dislocation and criminal activity, becoming a vast zone of instability in Asia'. This, however, could not be taken to suggest that an era of good feelings was automatically in the offing, since the Taiwan issue remains as a near permanent obstacle and that further modernization of the Chinese military will lead to questions within the United States on what the purpose of such programmes might be. Washington and Beijing may be able to work for closer economic and financial ties but neither regards the other with much beyond suspicion on the political and security fronts. The existence of such mutual sentiments may then feed upon itself and thereby contribute to the further exacerbation of tension. Future American administrations will have to face harder decisions if, as appears likely, China's economic advance continues successfully and Beijing's greater wealth enables the pace of as yet unsophisticated defence programmes to be accelerated. Difficulties in Sino-American relations would then increase, since aspiring Great Powers do not take kindly to being instructed by their rivals on how the region ought to be managed.

The debate over how the United States might best engage or 'enmesh' with the PRC is one that will grow. It is complicated by differences within the American political system and by the need to reckon with the attitudes of other nations in the region, in addition to the highly problematic future of China itself. Yet responsible governments can hardly take refuge in such imponderables, and the United States will hope to persuade Beijing that working with itself and its Asian neighbours holds out more pleasant prospects for all. Such hopes, however, can be little more than professions of faith and are likely to be revised by the next generation of leaders in Beijing and Washington in the light of later developments.

Since contemporary Chinese academic opinion broadly reflects government thinking, it can be assumed that public statements to overseas audiences will rarely deviate far from the party line. It follows, therefore, that remarks by Professor Wu Xinbo of Shanghai's Fudan University in November 2000 on the necessity of solving the Taiwan question on terms dictated by Beijing is the absolute precondition for US–Chinese rapprochement. It also follows that little will easily be improved until the United States pulls back its military presence in the Asia-Pacific region. Wu Xinbo next predicts that changes in the security arrangements of the region over the next decade will result in the decline of the US military posture and 'a pluralistic security community will very likely emerge'. Only then would Beijing magnanimously accept that there might still be 'a significant role' for Washington as a member of a nascent Pacific security grouping that could evolve 'over time into a more effective means for promoting regional co-operation on security issues'. As a description of the Chinese authorities' objectives, these remarks are consistent and indicate how eager the PRC is to weaken the United States' grip on the region. Beijing will not desist from suggesting that American military alliances and regional basing arrangements are anachronistic hangovers from the Cold War era which should be replaced by forward-looking economic and political institutions that better reflect more recent trends and thinking. Clearly, under such circumstances, the effective crafting of Sino-American relations is a challenge that the entire Asia-Pacific region is obliged to follow with the greatest of attention. The hope, of course, is that probable disruptions will not lead to major crises and that constructive engagement becomes more of a reality in the next generation.

Southeast Asia

For Southeast Asia the 1990s were years of economic expansion, followed by a severe financial crisis that underscored the domestic weaknesses of several nations and confirmed the difficulties of regional cooperation. Until the sobering events of 1997, the decade had proved to be one of economic expansion and political consolidation; thereafter it was a largely a case of salvaging what could be saved from the wreck and redoubling efforts to stabilize the situation. Some commentators, who had mercilessly spoken of 1997 as the most severe economic depression in generations, had been obliged by 2000 to admit that their prognostications had been generally followed by an equally rapid recovery. It remains the case, however, that neither the severity of the crash nor the speed of the recovery had been fully anticipated. The later rebound was of little consolation, however, to those whose livelihoods had been lost and whose futures were now bleak. It was also a most uneven recovery that left several nations trailing far behind with huge government budget deficits and massive non-performing corporate loans. The bizarre sight in downtown Bangkok and Jakarta of abandoned, half-completed skyscrapers serves as an unintended memorial to both the aspirations of the boom years and the massive consequences of the crash of 1997.

Before we ask what prompted the crisis and trace how it was able to create such havoc among what were widely trumpeted to be the most vibrant of the world's new economies, it is necessary to review the 'tiger' economies' performances in the earlier portion of the decade. By any standards, the 1990s were remarkable years that nailed the myth that only Japan had discovered the Asian holy grail of high-speed modernization. The economies of Southeast Asia and South Korea emerged into the limelight displaying many of the same characteristics that had seen Japan achieve its own hyper-growth. Against somewhat less difficult odds than those that occupied Japan had faced, the new nation-states had developed in the 1970s and 1980s the social and political infrastructure that made possible the achievements of the early 1990s.

The role of the United States must also be recalled. As with postwar Japanese industrialization, it would have been virtually impossible even to consider economic growth without Washington's commitment to regional security and an open trading system. Although frequently ignored amid the hyperbole, it was the United States that provided much of the support that gave the preconditions for modernization. These factors in themselves hardly ensured that the 'tigers' would advance, but the stabilizing presence of the US military in Asia and the American willingness to accept almost limitless exports from Asia were crucial, if generally unsung, advantages for the developing nations in the region.

The successes of the 'tiger' economies were evident in the prosperity of their new professional classes and the speed with which overseas investment poured into the region. Southeast Asian funds on Wall Street and London were particularly attractive to investors, who might well have little knowledge of the nations and their growth industries but were eager to realize quick profits. Stock exchanges and banking houses in Bangkok, Singapore and Jakarta thrived in this atmosphere. It appeared that the fundamental structure of the 'tiger' economies justified the high share prices and the substantial borrowings by local banks. Entire cities were transformed in the process. The boom continued as fresh employment opportunities encouraged rural migration, which in turn placed new pressures on inadequately planned (if at all), substandard housing and rudimentary social services. Urban populations doubled as the world's press reported on the construction frenzy and the inevitable traffic jams that followed in the wake of the Asian economic 'miracle'.

For a brief moment the future of the Southeast Asian economies appeared limitless. Commentators rushed out instant works on the Asian success story and whole shelves in the region's bookshops were reserved for tomes devoted to the inevitability of the forthcoming Pacific Century. The region's self-esteem disappeared, however, in the summer of 1997. News of events in Thailand's financial sector set off a wave of selling across the region which very quickly demolished the dreams of societies that had become accustomed to greater opportunities and at least the prospect of affluence. The crash of 1997 was a jolt to the system. It dashed the region's inflated confidence in its ability to engineer wealth and drew massive attention to the faults of most Southeast Asian regimes. It was a salutary reminder that speculative finance can be instantly re-patriated at the touch of a keyboard in New York and served as a warning that the much-heralded era of globalization has particular risks for its weaker partners.

What began as merely a local difficulty very quickly became a regional disaster. Panic selling led to the calling in of business loans, the collapse of corporate groupings and the contraction of entire economies. The 'tigers' suddenly became unwanted strays. As the impact on not only the region but the wider international trading system grew, Southeast Asia had to go cap in hand to institutions such as the much-maligned International Monetary Fund (IMF) and the World Bank for emergency aid. This, much to the surprise of many of the more naïve within the region, came with a large price tag attached. But hunting for foreign scapegoats, while useful for domestic political purposes, did little to ease the pain of economic realities. Salvation would require surrender to overseas prescriptions and busybodies. It all smelt rather familiar to the older generation, who had memories of not so distant colonialism. Instead of direction from Europeans, however, this time the commands came in more elliptical, economic language. Still, the distinction was largely academic as the advice, even when nicely dressed up in polite form, had to be followed if the required bailouts were to be forthcoming. Put at its crudest, the shock waves of 1997 were a reminder that smaller economies are ever vulnerable to global forces and that the street demonstrators who held up placards claiming that the acronym IMF stood for 'I'm Fired' were at least half correct.

Yet the domestic faults of the Southeast Asian economies should not be played down. Much was jerry-built, both literally and in terms of organizing a viable modern economic system. The crisis began with the banking sector in Thailand and quickly spread throughout the region. The speed and pervasiveness of this so-called 'Asian contagion' was extraordinary. While it may well have trapped many undeserved victims, it did expose in a brutal manner the faults of rapid and at times entirely unregulated growth. There were immediate and severe losses of employment, financial sector collapses and corporate restructuring on a scale that threatened to undo many of the recent achievements. Workers who had rushed from the countryside to the cities lost their jobs overnight, banks closed their doors, and the value of local currencies was instantly reduced on the foreign exchange markets. Trade slumped and politicians found it hard to devise effective policies for correcting the economic mess and deflecting the scale of public anger.

The immediate panic hurt the entire region, but it quickly became clear that some nations would suffer far more than others. Those states that had generally open financial sectors and at least semi-transparent economies where financial reporting was reliable, emerged relatively unscathed. Others, given the inadequacies quickly exposed by the crisis, were chastised mercilessly by financial operators overseas. Western investors bailed out as Asia discovered that markets are unforgiving. International financial institutions then sent in their experts to examine the wreckage and recommend draconian action plans to revive a battered region. The findings were disconcerting and generally confirmed initial reportage on the weaknesses of the banking sector across much of the region. The 'knock-on' effect from this was to force major corporations into insolvency and to sharply increase what are coyly termed 'non-performing loans'. Inevitably these faults led to runs on many of the overvalued currencies of Southeast Asia and to a severe downturn in trade. This then fed into greatly increased balance of payments deficits when the region had to service ever larger amounts of foreign debt at precisely the moment when it was least equipped to do so.

Worse was to follow, since the economic and financial mess could hardly be expected to be isolated from the region's political and social environment. It quickly became evident that some states faced not only significant economic dislocation but the distinct possibility of serious political instability and the fear of national fragmentation. The worst strains were seen in Indonesia, the region's largest and most diverse and ambitious state. President Suharto, its veteran leader, failed both to contain mass street protests against the cronyism associated with members of his wealthy family and to halt the dangerous militia groups which had instituted violence in the former Portuguese enclave of East Timor. Indonesia risked imploding into rival territorial groupings. From 1997 onwards, Indonesia experienced its worst political crisis since the ferocious domestic violence of 1965–66, which ironically had brought Suharto himself to power as the military successor to President Sukarno. Three years and two presidents later, Indonesia is still in turmoil. The rupiah is decidedly weak and it will take years to restore an effective economy, given that it shrank by 15 per cent in 1998. Even today, memories of the initial anti-government rioting in Jakarta and the communal brutalities in East Timor are raw and it remains difficult to predict either the economic or political future of a badly demoralized and diminished Indonesia.

Other states escaped more lightly. With the possible exception of Thailand, the instigator of the regional chaos, most could claim with some justification to have ridden out the storm within approximately one and a half to two years. Singapore's senior minister Lee Kuan Yew, for example, was able to claim in August 2000 that the self-evident economic disarray was being replaced, at least in the cases of his own country and that of Malaysia, by a new self-confidence, though he cautioned that overall regional growth prospects still appeared to be slim. Lee's faith in Singapore and Malaysia was based on their willingness to embrace new technologies, but even he has had to acknowledge that Northeast Asia has a greater propensity to innovate and that the likely reduction in political tensions on the Korean Peninsula will further accelerate its growth rates.

The problems associated with the crash of 1997 and its aftermath have hardly been helped, however, by the anaemic performance of Japan over the past decade. Since Tokyo suffered its own economic bust at the start of the 1990s, the entire region has had to reckon with lesser investment and minimal leadership from contemporary Japan. The idea of Japan as a 'locomotive' force driving the world economy belongs to history. Disappointments at home have further contributed to a massive contraction in interest and involvement with Japan's Asia-Pacific neighbours and with the wider world beyond the Straits of Malacca. Under these circumstances Southeast Asia has had to fend for itself or discover new partners further afield. Such adjustment has not been easy but there have been few alternatives, given the assistance required to recover from the drenching caused by the mega-typhoon of 1997. The crisis undoubtedly spawned public statements on the need for greater intra-regional cooperation, but it is less clear how much was actually achieved to this end. What appears to have happened is that most of the region's economies were refloated on the fresh tide of liquidity encouraged by international institutions in the autumn of 1998 to prevent a fresh global crisis. This was an unexpected and undeserved blessing for Southeast Asia. It had the effect of helping corporations out of their post-crash difficulties (those that had survived, that is), but it also postponed much of the financial discipline required to correct malpractices and create a more transparent banking culture. Thus the financial misfortunes of Russia and Japan in 1998 worked to the advantage of the Southeast Asian economies in the short term, while probably ensuring that any eventual reform will be both harder to formulate and more painful to accomplish.

Some attempts were made to assist the humbled Asian economies from within the region, yet it was largely a case of every nation for itself once the full ferocity of the crisis erupted. Japan, having been among the first to repatriate its massive investments, did offer help in the form of a substantial rescue package. This was certainly appreciated within the region and was to be recalled on frequent occasions after the worst of the storm was over, but it was global financial institutions, such as the International Monetary Fund, that led the way to recovery. At a price. Regimes that had seen their much-vaunted growth economies left in tatters were delighted to deflect public anger onto the broad and unpopular shoulders of the IMF and World Bank. Since many governments had been obliged to conduct intricate negotiations with the IMF, it was politically convenient for newly unemployed demonstrators to vent their anger on foreign bureaucrats rather than their own beleaguered governments. Indeed Michel Camdessus, the former head of the IMF, would note in retirement that 'there is a direct proportionality between the volume of criticism and the success of our actions'. This may be the case but it is not yet certain that the IMF programmers, who urged structural reform on the Asian economies despite the ire of protestors and lobbyists, have won the day. Camdessus might claim in September 2000 that 'the response to the Asian crisis has been an outstanding success', but it is far from clear if the old practices and participants are gone for good. To stamp out cronyism it would be necessary to radically change the nature of government in much of Asia. Camdessus sees the IMF as having fought to dismantle 'the conglomerates, the chaebols in Korea, the family monopolies in Indonesia, and nepotism, collusion and corruption everywhere', yet this is one campaign that would take a generation to succeed. The danger, of course, is that the traditional means of doing business and sharing out lucrative state contracts will quickly re-establish themselves as the crisis recedes.

No country in the Asia-Pacific region was immune from the crash of 1997. Some moved much more quickly to correct faults and therefore were able to recover much faster, but the crisis hurt every financial and economic sector in every state. Even the supposedly safest havens, such as Singapore and Hong Kong, experienced downturns. Hong Kong's currency came under pressure from speculators, while Singapore too experienced the flight of capital and faced dollar depreciation. There was no escape. There was, however, an approximate link between the speed of recovery and the capacity to openly recognize the faults in particular banking and corporate systems. In a very rough and ready way, it appeared that governments and officials who acknowledged the need for greater disclosure of bank information and adopted international accounting standards were the first to rebound. Western bankers were obviously more prepared to start lending again when they had greater confidence in such regimes, though this still begs the question of European, American and Japanese irresponsibility before and during the crisis. In the early 1990s overseas investors often failed to critically examine companies' balance sheets in the rush to gain quick profits. International capital mobility both worked to assist the region (and, of course, both Wall Street and the City of London) before 1997 and helped to exacerbate the subsequent panic.

Asia's standing in the world suffered from the crash. The only state to be able to point to a consistent record of economic growth throughout the 1990s proved to be the People's Republic of China. It had, however, created a strict financial and economic system that deliberately left it able to guard against the instant computer-driven consequences of globalization. The Chinese currency was not generally convertible and therefore could not be hunted down by and massacred by overseas speculators, while foreign bankers had little of the clout they possessed in Southeast Asia. China could also congratulate itself on a fairly healthy economic performance during the 1990s, which further strengthened its defences against the Asian crisis. Its growth record and balance of payments position were impressive, and the fact that foreign direct investment continued to flow into China after 1997 is a positive reflection of its economic stability and future prospects. President Clinton and his economic advisers were indeed grateful for the ability of the Chinese authorities to avoid the mess elsewhere and thereby contribute substantially to preventing a pan-Asian crisis. It remains to be seen whether a more open China, committed to trade liberalization and international labour standards, can implement domestic structural reforms in state enterprises and thereby adjust to a global system.

China's recent economic performance stands in contrast to that of its neighbours in both Southeast and Northeast Asia. The PRC had proved itself able to withstand a regional financial crisis, albeit by deploying mechanisms that discouraged openness, and its economy has continued to grow at very substantial levels. Yet, as Joseph Stiglitz noted in his opening address to the World Bank's annual conference on development economics in 1998, it is ironic that it was the more successful and more transparent Asian 'tiger' economies that experienced the greatest shocks in 1997. Equally, Japan's relative failure to grow during the 1990s was a further blow to the once popular belief that the twenty-first century was almost guaranteed to see the advance of the Pacific to the centre of the international system. The 'Asian model' of fast growth had been derailed to the extent that academic assessors were quick to ask if East Asia had moved 'from being a miracle to needing one'. The result was no end of conferences and commentaries on the immediate explanations for the crash and the still unclear fate of the region's economies. It is likely, however, that the differences in economic policy and behaviour since 1997 make it improbable that a collective label can be applied any longer to what has proved to be an increasingly diverse set of nations with differing responses to the shared crisis.

While Asia suffered as a whole, its nations have diverged on how best to respond to their troubles. Economists have identified at least three distinct reactions to the calamities of 1997. One school, comprising Thailand and South Korea, has adopted the prescriptions of the IMF and done as it was told to deflate and restructure, whereas those in the second category (Malaysia and both Chinas) have rejected external suggestion and gone their own way; Indonesia has been obliged to shift back to the IMF camp after failing in its bid for an independent economic policy stance. The results to date have been equally diverse, with those prepared to accept overseas instruction probably performing the best, though economists continue to warn that substantial increases in world energy prices and the possibility of a downturn in the United States would inevitably hurt the recovery of the entire region. What is less conjectural is the unfortunate link between the East Asian economies and Japan, since, as Lim Hua Sing has claimed, the 'crisis has in fact postponed Japan's economic recovery'. This statement can also be reversed, however: Asia surely has reason to feel disappointed by the very limited improvement in the Japanese economy by 2001, which has inevitably acted to restrict Asia's return to economic health. Lack of consumer demand within Japan has both delayed any significant upturn in Japan's prospects and served to stall Southeast Asia's opportunities for a substantial revival in its own export-led growth.

Clearly the region and the wider world is expecting Japan to put its house in order and restore its reputation as a centre of prosperity. Yet despite the announcement of countless government-sponsored emergency stimulus packages throughout the past decade, so far little has been achieved beyond the prevention of an economic and financial meltdown. Optimism is still unwarranted as the different economic arms of the Japanese state spar over rival assessments of the present condition of their long-suffering patient. It is probable that the emergence of at least a small recovery is on the cards, but much will depend on a future upsurge in consumer confidence at home and the avoidance of a 'hard landing' for the US economy in the early 2000s.

What is immensely more difficult than charting the whirlpools of the past decade is considering how Japan might generate a sustainable economic recovery that would finally leave the stagnation and disappointments of the post-bubble era behind. For years now authors have been adding their recommendations on the best way forward for Tokyo: tax cuts may be the answer, but this is certain to be resisted by the Ministry of Finance, which already faces huge problems in funding the unprecedented level of government indebtedness and has to reckon with ever larger social security costs as the population continues to age. Prescriptions from the United States have tended to be rejected by the Japanese state as economically inappropriate or politically impractical. In an attempt to avoid such an approach, Adam Posen has argued that it might make better sense for critics to concentrate on Japan's domestic realities rather than rehearse already familiar hectoring from US officials on what is urgently required of Tokyo. This may be the case but it has to be said that neither the nation's economic bureaucracy nor successive Japanese governments have found the magic elixir. Attributing blame for Japan's lengthy era of stagnation is an enjoyable spectator sport but the nation has still not discovered the best way forward. Until unemployment begins to decline, deflation is arrested and demand rises, there would appear to be a plentiful supply of possible culprits. For the present, it appears to be the case that Japan is patiently waiting for better times and has limited energy to spend on what is happening beyond its own borders.

The sharp contrast between the remarkable performance of the US economy throughout the 1990s and the relative failure of Japan since the early 1990s has become a commonplace of international political economics. More recently, outsiders have also drawn similar conclusions between the impressive US economic record and the failure of many former 'tigers' to regain their vitality. Equally, expectations were also disappointed over the role played by ASEAN as a collective organization to cope with the crisis and its aftermath. The inability of the region to work closely together when submerged by debt and potential political and social disruption revealed the faults that a generation of officials had tried to paper over. When faced with a crisis of the magnitude of 1997, ASEAN failed to respond with coherent policies. It too looked beyond the region's borders for assistance and appeared unable to discover salvation from within Southeast Asia. By the autumn of 2000, commentators were asking in public whether indeed ASEAN even had a future, given that Indonesia, for long its most powerful member, was still trapped in cycles of communal and subregional violence and that no other member state had shown either the political leadership or economic strength to replace Jakarta. The alternative suggestion that ASEAN must now 'reinvent' itself and devise a more diffuse pattern of leadership, whereby member states would be prepared to be more assertive on particular issues where they had greater experience and resources, remains untested. Certainly ASEAN's failure to respond to the East Timor crisis confirmed that the organization is most unwilling to break ranks and actively intervene in domestic matters, even when the result is that non-ASEAN nations take the initiative in humanitarian and peace-keeping operations that concern the stability of neighbouring states. The problem with insisting that ASEAN should determine policy through joint discussion is that it virtually guarantees a veto on any precipitate action against delinquent member nations. A talking shop that keeps to its rule of sovereign immunity and rules out even emergency humanitarian intervention is unlikely to be taken too seriously in the twenty-first century.

ASEAN's difficulties are compounded by its inclusive membership. The entire region has joined the grouping, but while this may be desirable on political grounds, it has created major problems of coordination. The result, as perhaps may happen with the European Union, is the likelihood of a two-tier set of arrangements whereby there may be an inner core of founder members and a peripheral group comprising the four states of Vietnam, Laos, Cambodia and Myanmar. The economic difficulties that all these recent members of ASEAN face is certain to restrain their involvement in wider issues. The continuing restrictions on human rights within Myanmar, for example, hardly suggest that ASEAN sees itself as a crusading body working for a more open and tolerant regional identity. For the medium term at least, it is hard to imagine that ASEAN can transform itself into an Asian Union. The huge disparities in wealth, population, size and political systems ensure that even obtaining a minimum of agreement from the leaders of ASEAN will remain difficult at best. The attempt to formulate common financial standards and to regulate transnational issues that would weaken vested domestic interests is bound to be controversial and provides clear evidence of the gap between laudable goals and harsher realities.

Yet alternatives to the work of ASEAN are hard to discern. There would appear to be only two organizations that offer some encouragement for greater regionalism. These are APEC (the Asia-Pacific Economic Cooperation forum) and ARF (the ASEAN Regional Forum). It is highly significant that all members of ASEAN are supporters of both APEC and ARF; this, in its turn, accurately reflects the consensual, non-confrontational approaches adopted by both bodies, along the lines long established by the founding fathers of ASEAN. It has to be said, however, that there remains an air of uncertainty about the prospects for APEC and ARF. Both fledgling institutions have received considerable publicity and are the recipients of possibly unwarranted praise, but neither body can yet be held to have effectively proved itself. Great expectations can be an unhelpful burden.

APEC and ARF are both recent, post-Cold War institutions. APEC encompasses virtually the entire Pacific region in an amorphous, unstructured grouping stretching over four continents. It holds an annual summit among its heads of government at a different, often glamorous, location on each occasion. This procedure had generated a great deal of favourable publicity on specific programmes for trade liberalization, but commentators have complained that the need to feed the media has led to the announcement of often unrealistic goals. There are, of course, other, more substantial and less reported committee meetings among specialist staff, where efforts to flesh out the large policy statements must take place behind closed doors. The ARF is more modest in membership and has, to date at least, not been required to approach its work with anything comparable to the frenetic pace exhibited at APEC's media-driven gatherings. Since its creation in Bangkok in 1994 it has attempted to discuss issues involving the powers of the region in a post-Cold War atmosphere of amicable dialogue rather than through threats of confrontation.

APEC's duties are hardly defined in its unwieldy title. Indeed, one former Australian minister has been frequently quoted as describing APEC as 'four adjectives in search of a noun', yet the imprecision appears to make a virtue of necessity. The organization seems fated to exist in its present loose shape because this reduces the chances of nations such as the United States from running the show at the expense of the smaller economic entities across the region. The modest initial objectives of APEC, originally promoted by ASEAN and Australia in the late 1980s, have since been greatly widened by highly inclusionary practices and by a deeper commitment to freer trade and financial services across both sides of the Pacific. Today APEC is committed to achieving these twin goals by 2020, though liberalization is far from assured in politically sensitive areas such as agriculture, information technology and intel- lectual property rights. The picture is also complicated by the fact that there are other, overlapping, international institutions, such as the WTO, ASEAN's own efforts to create some semblance of free trade, and the United States' wish to broaden the North American Free Trade Area (NAFTA) to include Latin America. President Bush, for example, in 2001 has been particularly forceful in calling for speedier and stronger free-trade efforts in his bid for an ambitious Free Trade Area of the Americas (FTAA), which could yet incorporate thirty-four nations.

The 'Return' of the United States

The 1990s provided a series of warning shots on the economic and political fragility of the region. While the 1997–98 Asian financial crisis was contained and difficulties over North Korea, the Taiwan Straits and the possible break-up of Indonesia were resolved, at least in the short term, commentators sensed that such events hardly presaged much confidence in the frequently invoked dawn of the 'Pacific Century'. By 2000 the mood was clearly different, not least because of what can be seen as the centrality of the United States to regional affairs. After the hype of the Japanese model and the new 'tiger' economies had been severely eroded by the events of the past decade, the Asia-Pacific region was reminded that trade flows and investment patterns had a crucial American dimension. Equally, it was the United States' political strength that was responsible, if not for the inauguration of APEC in 1989, then for its subsequent strengthening through the initiatives of President Clinton; use of the phrase the 'Perry Process' underlines the role of his Secretary of Defense in patching together a compromise that defused the Korean nuclear crisis.

In reality, of course, the United States had never 'left' the region. But the aftermath of its defeat in Vietnam, and the successes of first Japan and then the new economies served to belittle the American role in Asia during the late 1970s and the 1980s. After all, President Carter had wished, until he was persuaded otherwise, to remove US forces from South Korea, and the elimination of American troop deployment in Southeast Asia appeared to underline what was perceived to be a weakening of US interest in the Asia-Pacific region. Widespread Japanese criticism of the 'unhealthy performance of the American economy' in the 1970s and a sense in the following decade that the United States was fated to decline in a manner ascribed to all once great powers suggested that the American era was waning. Even Ambassador Mike Mansfield, who constantly reminded American audiences that the Pacific Basin is 'where it all is, what it's all about, and where our futures lie', was obliged on the same occasion in October 1985 to urge his listeners to roll up their sleeves and get more involved in the region. The huge size of the US balance of payments deficit with Japan and the apparent scale of Tokyo's direct investment in US real estate and manufacturing plants worked to demoralize a nation.

The past decade, by way of contrast, might be defined as the 'return' of the United States to the heart of Asia-Pacific affairs. The fact that the post-Cold War years have coincided with an era of unprecedented American prosperity and parallel discomfort for many within Asia has made for a major shift in public attitudes on both sides of the Pacific. It has been relatively easy, against this economic and strategic backdrop, for both the Clinton and George W. Bush administrations to demonstrate their commitment to the maintenance of troop levels overseas and to discuss, consult and act decisively when perceived national interests are at stake. Recent presidents have been afforded luxuries not known to their immediate predecessors, who had to wrestle with the progress of highly unpopular wars on the ground and then tackle the bitter recriminations of trade wars in Asia. At the start of the new millennium, however, the Asia-Pacific was able to bask in what may yet prove to be a rare interlude of relative peace and stability. Whether this benign moment would continue depends in large part on the actions of the United States. The future of Sino-American relations will be examined next; it would appear to be the one outstanding issue of comparable difficulty to the challenges of the recent past and is almost certain to test the skills of US foreign policy-makers to the hilt over the next decade.

7   Future: Asia-Pacific, 2001–2020

There are at least as many designs and strategies for an East Asian partnership as there are countries in the region.

Fred Bergsten, *The Economist*, 15 July 2000

East Asians now know that given the time and the opportunity to engage in trade, investments and technology transfers, they, too, can industrialize and catch up with the West. This self-confidence arises from an understanding of the factors that gave the West their lead, and the self-confidence that we, too, can make the grade.

Lee Kuan Yew, *The Nation* (Bangkok), 21 August 2000

In our experience, young people are much more likely to have confidence in their future if they have a share in shaping it, in choosing their governmental leaders and having a government that is accountable to those it serves.

President Clinton, Hanoi, 18 November 2000

We must now reckon with the more likely prospects for the Asia-Pacific region in the first decades of the twenty-first century, recalling that historians are unqualified by trade to offer any but amateur readings of the international horoscope. Their efforts at divination run the risk of assuming that the recent past is necessarily prologue, and they can all too easily discount the likelihood of sharp caesuras over the next generation. Predictions based merely on the continuation of comforting trends may soon be fit only for pulping. While doctors are said to be able to bury their mistakes, contemporary historians and political scientists have little choice but to live with theirs. The list is long indeed of distinguished individuals who suggested before the fall of the Berlin Wall that the Soviet Union would be able to cope with the unpleasant choices of guns or vodka. In the case of the Asia-Pacific region in the next generation, it may pay to discount a sizeable portion of the assumed good news. Recollection of the violent wars and revolutions of the immediate post-Pacific War period ought to serve as a reminder of the ideological divisions, economic disparities and sharp power rivalries that the region has been subjected to over the past half-century. A vast, loosely organized arena, whose postwar era began with the atomic bombings of Hiroshima and Nagasaki in 1945 and where severe pan-Asian financial disruptions were witnessed as recently as 1997, might reckon it wiser to approach its future with considerable caution. Little is foreordained. Events can humble the best laid plans of even the most experienced of bureaucrats and the wiliest of politicians.

Yet, on paper at least, there would appear to be grounds for a degree of optimism. In contrast to the acute divisions of the Cold War era, the area is now beginning to be criss-crossed by formal and informal regional organizations, though in most cases these are of but recent vintage. The

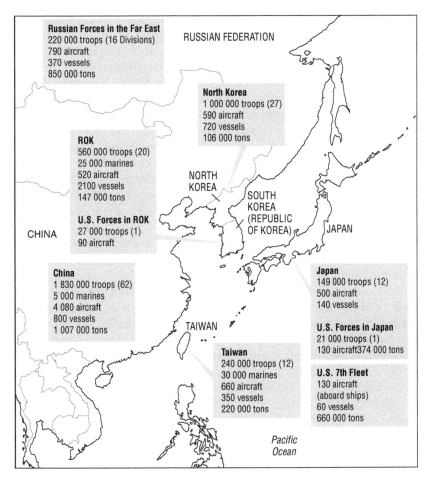

Military balance in the Asia-Pacific, 2000
Based on 'Defense of Japan, 2000', published by the Defense Agency (Tokyo, 2000).

Asia-Pacific region in 2001 possesses an array of forums and associations that suggest a willingness to recognize the necessity of greater political and economic cooperation. This in turn clearly implies a reluctance to resort to violence in the resolution of the inevitable disputes that will continue to buffet an international system composed of a multitude of semi-sovereign states. It would be foolhardy, however, to take refuge from future political uncertainties by placing excessive reliance on Asia-Pacific regionalism. Too much remains untested for any but the naïve to imagine that mission statements, good intentions and lavish hospitality will offer sufficient shelter from the storms that may lie ahead. The lack of effective regional coordination during the 1997–98 Asian financial crisis surely serves as an object lesson in how not to manage a sudden issue of the first magnitude. Equally, the reluctance of most states to publicly criticize the gross injustices recorded recently in many parts of Indonesia and the human rights violations of the military regime in Myanmar should not be overlooked or excused out of fear of impolite interference in the domestic affairs of fellow member states of ASEAN or APEC. The gulf between the mere endorsement of international conventions on civil and political rights by most Asian governments and the actual enforcement of many such agreements remains disturbingly large, while the People's Republic of China, unfortunately, has yet to fully ratify international human rights covenants that it signed in the 1990s. Few states in the region have displayed much enthusiasm for permitting anything but highly circumscribed political dissent; few have agreed to abolish capital punishment, acted to discourage the use of torture to gain confessions, or done much to ensure religious tolerance.

These deficiencies have rarely been guided by a wish to uphold amorphous 'Asian values', but rather by the political imperatives of states that are determined to curtail domestic freedoms that might jeopardize their rule. Concern for wider humanitarian action, such as efforts to stamp out child prostitution and sexual trafficking across borders, has rarely received governmental priority. Nations with enviable records of economic success, such as Japan, have yet to be greatly persuaded that women, the disadvantaged and minorities might be made the subject of special legislation with teeth to correct widespread discrimination. External pressure is probably the best means of achieving social reform in those portions of the region that allow the relatively free exchange of ideas; elsewhere the near absence of civil society leaves the fate of many in the hands of arbitrary power. The public execution of smugglers, drug dealers and corrupt bureaucrats may be one way to encourage better social behaviour in the PRC, but the absence of protests at such action from its neighbours is deafening.

Yet perhaps even more disturbing for the future health of the Asia-Pacific region is the weakness of history. The horrors of the past are frequently brushed aside in a conspiracy of silence that links state and society. Uncomprehending Japanese students continue to approach their lecturers to ask why Japan was such a source of hatred to its neighbours after 1945, while only a little more than a decade ago South Korean academics could arrive for conferences in Kyoto surprised to note that the Japanese government permitted the activities of a legally recognized Communist party on its territory. Likewise, in much of Southeast Asia, it may be safer for criticisms of European colonization to take the place of any strenuous attempt to examine the already lengthy period of independence from London, Paris and The Hague. Old whipping boys, however, are no substitute for full and accurate information on the transformations of the near half-century since the Europeans folded their tents. Contemporary history ought to be too important to be left to government spokesmen, yet nowhere in Asia is there the possibility to consult and quote at will from adequate archival sources. Only when students gain the opportunity to read in untrammelled detail of the activities of their own leaders can Asia be said to be intellectually free. Anyone interested, for example, in Japan's postwar foreign policy is obliged to make a pilgrimage to the National Archives in Washington DC to discover what successive governments in Tokyo were saying in private to their American counterparts. Open access to comprehensive state papers is a litmus test that every government of the region at present fails.

It must also not go unnoticed that the United States was itself guilty of a damning share of atrocities during the Korean and Vietnamese wars – for example those at No Gun Ri and My Lai – while also being generally unwilling to speak out publicly at the rampant human rights violations exhibited by several of its closest Asia-Pacific allies at the height of the Cold War. The impact on Vietnam and Cambodia of US carpet-bombing with chemical defoliants that were widely suspected from the outset to have massive long-term consequences for human beings and the environment is a further charge against the Johnson and Nixon administrations. The several prison sentences and near executions in the lengthy political career of President Kim Dae Jung serve too as a reminder of the brutalities that were not unusual until recently in South Korea when martial law was the norm. Equally, the incalculable deaths within China during the Cultural Revolution, the massacres of the Communists in Indonesia during General Suharto's rise to power in the mid-1960s, the bleached skulls, bones and bits of clothing preserved in Cambodian villages on the sites of merciless killing fields, and the acres of identical white-stone graves in Vietnam, stretching to the horizon like the cemeteries of the Somme, are further reminders of the horrors of recent history.

The first and most important regional entity that may offer a way of working a passage out of the past remains ASEAN. What began as a hesitant anti-Communist regional vehicle had by the 1990s shown enough confidence to invite the PRC to its meetings. Professor John Wong of the National University of Singapore could maintain in 1997 that 'ASEAN's relations with China have come through transformation from Cold War to détente' and that 'for everybody in South-East Asia, if you talk about security, peace, and stability, it will be meaningless to neglect China. China in whatever terms is most important, just as Japan in economic terms is most important for the region'. Wong noted that ASEAN regarded 'economic growth as the most important bottom line: with growth you can have change, democracy, peace, and stability; without economic growth, there will not be stability'. The fact that external groupings, such as the European Union, have recognized the value of ASEAN and in turn have joined forces for the now regular Asia–Europe Meetings (ASEM) is indicative of the perceived strength of Asia's most enduring organization. Whether ASEM, which began through the initiatives of ASEAN's member state of Singapore, can provide a useful and broader perspective for both subcontinents is still unclear, but a start has clearly been made. It is significant that voices in Washington have repeatedly given ASEM their blessing and welcomed what could become a permanent addition to the growing number of forums reckoning with the Asia-Pacific.

The most promising of these loose pan-regional institutions remains APEC. Progress, however, on consolidating and expanding the reach of APEC had slowed by 2001. Explanations for the decidedly low level of current expectations appear to hinge on the lack of collective confidence within the region to promote fresh goals. It has been easier and safer to recall that the optimism of the early 1990s was quickly overtaken by the severe disappointments of the crash of 1997 and thence to draw the conclusion that it was still premature to resume work on highly ambitious programmes that risked collapse a second time. The stalling of APEC's original hopes of obtaining wider free-trade arrangements for an area that comprises twenty-three nations on both sides of the Pacific has left the grouping in danger of losing not only its momentum but even its rationale. Efforts to gain a consensus on more modest goals for APEC have yet to be realized. APEC's aspirations risk being further undermined by uncertainties over the positions of several major trading nations in the region, notably the United States and Japan, whose economic power greatly exceeds that of all other members combined. As with the ten-nation grouping of ASEAN, the diversity in size, population and economic strengths of APEC members conspires to make further movement difficult at best. New programmes, for example, over the reduction in the technological gap between states will be hard to implement, since the poorer nations have few resources available for computerization and certainly confront more pressing issues than the introduction of sophisticated information technology.

One indication of the current weaknesses facing APEC is the predilection for nations such as Japan to initial bilateral trading agreements that avoid the complexities of multilateral arrangements and yet work to increase regional prosperity. The trend towards bilateral pacts will be hard to resist and is most unlikely to shore up APEC's unity or strengthen its political stance. If Japan, South Korea, Singapore and Australia were to successfully organize a new series of mutual trade and financial agreements, this could only bring into question the future of APEC and its claims to being what the Clinton administration in November 2000 termed 'the single most important institution in the Asia-Pacific region'. Cynics had reason to note that if this were indeed the case, then it provided substantial evidence of the paltry progress made so far on constructing an effective regional entity.

To date, few would deny that the Asia-Pacific region's record on establishing and developing organizations that can provide forums for dialogue and then implement agreed policy decisions remains decidedly limited. The obvious difficulties pan-Asian institutions have of coping with such a vast area of disparate states, cultures and economies strongly suggests that any results over the next generation are likely to be qualified at best. The intensity of present and past competition between neighbours is unlikely to subside. No one individual nation located geographically within the region is able at present to command sufficient power or respect to act as a recognized spokesman, let alone potential leader. With Japan still shackled by its past and China widely held to be excessively ambitious, it is difficult to imagine how this position can be swiftly altered. Military rivalries on a scale unknown elsewhere in the world have long persisted on an Asian continent that instantly recalls past imperialism, regional conflicts and civil war. In the mid-1990s five million troops were calculated to be deployed in the four Northeast Asian nations surrounding Japan, while the United States at the end of the twentieth century could boast of its determination to maintain approximately 100 000 men in an often dangerous and disputed region. Given these realities, the United States Pacific Command would therefore continue to remain the largest unified command in the US defence structure, justifying its existence by explaining that the Asia-Pacific region contains 'some of the most serious potential flash points and the fastest growing economies in the world'. It stoutly argues that 'the United States is a Pacific power and will remain so well into the future', in order 'to protect its national interests and those of its friends and allies, and to assure regional stability'.

Under such circumstances, the position of the United States is still vital to the security and prosperity of Asia. Washington alone possesses the political and military strengths to deter aggression and thereby provide the essential foundations for nation-building, economic advancement and regional bonding. Any future Asia without America is widely seen to be a recipe for possible chaos, though this would be contested by Beijing and by opponents within the United States and abroad who maintain that post-Cold War Asia deserves a new security foundation. The efficacy of the US military presence in Asia, however, has been acknowledged on various occasions by both the PRC and, more recently, by North Korea. Beijing, though, would certainly not wish to be associated with views of this nature today with regard to the remilitarization of Japan, which it sees as being unnecessarily close to Washington.

Merely to recall incidents from the supposedly post-Cold War era of the 1990s is a further reminder of the present and future dangers that surround the region. In June 1994, for instance, the United States was, in the later statements of Secretary of Defense William Perry, 'in serious danger of a major war' over the North Korean nuclear facility at Yongbyon. President Clinton was apparently 'within hours of authorizing military actions' before learning that President Kim Il Sung was prepared to negotiate a diplomatic settlement, in contradiction of his earlier threat to reduce Seoul to a 'sea of flames'. Then, less than two years later, US forces in the region were once again placed on the highest alert as the White House responded to the latest in what has been a disturbing series of crises in the Taiwan Straits over the past half-century. The issue centred on the visit of Taiwan's President Lee Teng-hui to the United States in June 1995 and led to the despatch of two carrier battle groups off Taiwan in the largest show of US naval force in East Asian waters since the Vietnam War. The crisis was defused, but Washington has still to tread cautiously between discouraging the PRC from any military action against Taiwan and making it clear to Taipei that it will not countenance any unilateral declaration of independence. Whether such high-wire balancing acts can be sustained indefinitely or will be tested by further confrontations by the two protagonists and near neighbours is certain to remain a formidable challenge for future US administrations. Those who note that ambiguity can best serve as a way forward may be correct, but attempts to engage China in the hope that this might over time reduce its suspicions and gain its cooperation in the Asia-Pacific still have to wrestle with the Taiwan question. When asked by both American and Chinese audiences how the Clinton administration might respond to threats to Taiwan's security, there was much citing by Perry and his advisers of the remark that 'We don't know what we would do, and you don't – because it is going to depend on the circumstances'. No doubt the intention was to muddy the waters, though the complexity of the issue virtually guarantees errors and misperceptions. The hope that Taiwan and the PRC can peacefully and amicably solve their differences is no more than a somewhat remote hope; any realization surely requires intricate and calibrated statesmanship by the United States. Presidents George Bush and Bill Clinton worked assiduously to gain the understanding of Beijing, while attempting to keep to existing commitments made to Taipei, and it is probable that the United States will endeavour to act along similar lines in the future.

However, the continuation of a substantial American commitment to the Asia-Pacific region should not preclude efforts by the United States to move more strenuously to reduce power disparities and encourage a greater sense of cooperation among its allies in the region. This will be a difficult task. Disagreements have yet to be resolved, for example between Japan and both the USA and South Korea over the appropriate united response to North Korea; Japan is presently suggesting that its national interests may preclude any immediate tripartite schemes between Tokyo, Washington and Seoul for engaging North Korea. Yet it is hard to overlook the suspicion that the rather limited scale of Japanese diplomatic initiatives in postwar Asia has served to strengthen its bilateral ties to Washington. As a result of stark political, constitutional and social divisions at home, postwar Japan still finds coming to terms with its own record of past imperialism most difficult, and therefore has yet to achieve any particularly deep relationship with its Asian neighbours. This has played directly into American hands. Japan has been left dependent on Washington because it possesses few genuine friends abroad and is hampered by a hesitant public that refuses to reckon with the concept of international responsibilities where the lives of its civilian and military personnel might be at risk. While instituting a large defence establishment with plans for anti-missile warships and helicopter-equipped destroyers in the future, Japan appears most unlikely to deploy its so-called Self-Defence Forces for anything much beyond the rescue of its own citizens in emergency situations abroad. Collective security is still regarded as taboo. So long as successive Japanese cabinets continue to see both public opinion and the postwar Constitution as forbidding anything but rear-area support for crises in an ill-defined area surrounding Japan, the United States will be highly reluctant to make major concessions over its valuable basing rights. The citizens of Okinawa have long felt that their prefecture, in particular, is host to far too many US installations that vary in scale, noise and importance from massive airfields to firing ranges and golf courses. Yet a portion at least of their complaints – excluding the persistent delinquency of some US servicemen – should be directed at the central government in Tokyo. The American presence on Okinawa will only be reduced significantly if Japan signals its willingness to assume wider regional security responsibilities, though the caveat remains that neither the PRC nor a reunited Korea would take kindly to a Japan whose security policies are moving from 'defensive' to wider regional tasks. Until the day when the United States' wish to encourage greater burden-sharing with Japan is realized, Japan's contribution to the security pact will continue to be a burden largely placed on the shoulders of Okinawa and one rarely shared with the rest of the nation.

In the rare instances where Japan's non-economic handiwork is iden-tifiable in the Asia-Pacific, it is often seen to be complementary to that of the United States. Tokyo's foreign aid has for many years been con-centrated too much on the Asia-Pacific region at a time when other devel-oping societies in Africa and Latin America are surely more deserving of what is likely in the future to be a less munificent process. 'Strategic' aid by Japan to Asian states that were traditionally supported by the United States serves only to leave Japan being seen as an American poodle. Equally, Japan's all-important links to the United States have resulted in a poverty of thinking on what it might do in the region, beyond strenuous efforts to develop economic, financial and commercial links that would ensure the maintenance of Japanese corporate affluence. Japan still prac-tises a minimalist foreign policy, seemingly content to allow the United States to act as protector of the Japanese archipelago and stabilizer of the entire region.

Commentators who argue that the future of a stable Asia-Pacific might rest better on other foundations have to admit to taking a leap in the dark. There is little or no evidence, for example, of past eras of genuinely cooperative Sino-Japanese relations at any time in the twentieth century. Beijing and Tokyo have rarely achieved more than a modicum of under-standing or approached equality in their dealings during the modern era, and to date the pointers to any satisfactory improvement are slender. Contemporary Japan remains anxious over the regional ambitions of the PRC and feels that the substantial contribution Tokyo's aid programmes have made to Chinese modernization has been slighted. China, no doubt unwilling to draw attention to its own economic and military dis-advantages, prefers to caution Japan against what it persists in viewing as excessively close political and security links to Washington. The entrails for substantial Sino-Japanese improvement are still difficult to read.

Those politicians and academics who feel that the Asia-Pacific area has yet to shed its hegemonic structure, based on the authority of the leading nations of the region, are surely correct. Many within Asia would automatically support the view of the late Professor Kanno Takehiko that 'Asian Pacific international circumstances, still dominated by power politics, or the politics of force, should be transformed into an inter-dependence regime of multilateral co-operation and competition without the exercise of force, such as in the European region'. Yet the evidence of the past half-century strongly suggests that such aspirations are most unlikely to be even partly fulfilled, unless the major nation-states were to substantially alter their conception of international relations and their subsequent conduct. It is far from likely that the post-Cold War era will be able to provide an incentive to work for a region of mutual respect, greater transparency and confidence-building measures, which their advocates invariably invoke when surveying its present condition. The hope after all that the 1990s would be the first decade where novel arrangements might begin to dissolve the antagonisms of the past was rarely realized. The region still has to live with two Koreas, two Chinas, nuclear and conventional weaponry on a massive scale and the absence of a Russo-Japanese peace treaty. The opening paragraph of the reputable *Asia Pacific Security Outlook* for 1999, for example, begins with the ominous sentence: 'By most conventional standards, the socio-economic environment for security in Asia Pacific could hardly be worse'. The same statement concludes by acknowledging that, while the economic crisis of 1997 had not seemingly wrecked the regional political system, 'the security outlook in the coming years remains uncertain, and multilateral security co-operation, in particular, faces significant challenges'.

Faced with potential crises in East Asia, decision-makers in Washington will increasingly need to attempt better coordination of policies among the regional allies of the United States. This is not merely a question of sensitive diplomacy in the field but, as in the vital question of how to deal with North Korea where there may be a host of nations all trying to negotiate with Pyongyang simultaneously, of greater attention from the highest levels of government. Since South Korea and Japan, to say nothing of the PRC and the Russian Federation, are constantly sounding out North Korea and responding in kind, the difficulties are formidable. The United States may have the greatest political impact on Pyongyang but North Korea's neighbours have to live with the consequences of Washington's behaviour and will necessarily expect their voices to be heard and respected. The fact that the United States relinquished operational control of South Korean military forces in the early 1990s and also removed its tactical nuclear weapons from the peninsula has served to strengthen Seoul's sovereignty and improved its negotiating position towards North Korea.

Similar caution and coordination will also have to be exercised by future US administrations when it engages the People's Republic of China. The entire region will be increasingly involved in dealing with a more ambitious and yet dissatisfied Communist state, since China still recalls the humiliations of the nineteenth century when it was 'sliced' like a melon among rival imperialists and still shares disputed land and sea borders with many countries. Since even a more substantial era of Chinese military modernization would leave Beijing much inferior to that of its Pacific rival, it is unlikely that the path will be smooth. The United States will attempt to work jointly with as many of its allies as possible to persuade the PRC that greater cooperation and transparency can enhance the region's security and be to Beijing's advantage. No doubt the thesis will be much in evidence that the PRC sorely needs economic and financial links to the United States and the entire Asia-Pacific region to keep up its economic momentum and thereby safeguard its political stability. It would be false comfort, however, to reckon that gaining China's trust will be easy in a region where the United States' power will continue to predominate to the chagrin of Beijing and its long-held anti-hegemonic stance. The United States remains the wielder of what the PRC regards as arbitrary and excessive force, which serves to undermine what it senses to be the region's desire for a more equitable distribution of power. It is far from clear how the Chinese civilian and military authorities will respond over the next generation to what is likely to remain a huge discrepancy in military and economic status between themselves and the United States, particularly as Beijing has also to factor in the military weight of US allies such as Japan. Some optimists assume that China's domestic modernization will present more than enough challenges for the successors to President Jiang Zemin and Prime Minister Zhu Rongji, while others envisage a more dire scenario with an accelerating arms race and an increasingly divided region that may leave Beijing almost friendless. Prospects for genuine détente between the United States and the PRC look decidedly remote today, particularly when Washington may well decide to deploy a theatre missile defence system bitterly opposed by China and the Taiwan question remains little nearer solution.

It should, too, be noted that China's intended modernization will, if at least reasonably successful over the next generation, provide fresh foreign policy choices for Beijing. Clearly the greater the future economic and financial transformation of the PRC, the greater the opportunities this presents for Beijing to assert itself both politically and militarily. The long-term consequence of Deng Xiaoping's economic programmes and the ending of the Cold War should result, to employ Helmut Schmidt's phrase of November 1994, in China winning 'a much freer hand than ever in this century or in the nineteenth century'. This re-emergence of China, if continued economically and reinforced in turn by approximate political and social stability at home, will earn it the right to claim an ever louder voice, first in regional and then surely in global affairs. Beijing after all has long been immensely proud of its membership of both the nuclear club and its permanent seat on the UN Security Council. It remains to be seen whether this evolution will approximate to the definition of a superpower, as claimed by its friends abroad but publicly disavowed by Chinese officials. Were this eventuality to occur, it would most certainly require considerable adjustment in the behaviour of all states within the Asia-Pacific region, not least in the policies of the United States

Optimists continue to suggest that a trilateral scheme composed of the United States, Japan and China might be a better alternative to the present polarization. Such advocates reckon that the opportunities for stability deserve to be emphasized and that the easy assumption of hostility between the existing US–Japan alliance and the emergent power of the PRC is unwarranted. Yet this thesis is hardly supported by the American desire to encourage the shifting Japanese cabinets in the 1990s to appreciate and respond to the potential dangers in East Asia from a stronger PRC. Equally, the sense of threat, or at the very least strong unease, displayed within Japan at the behaviour of Beijing in the mid and late 1990s discourages moves towards greater Sino-Japanese understanding. Mutual concern over the increased strengths of each nation's military is growing, and the view that the United States can effortlessly control such Asian rivalries is not particularly plausible. It is, of course, possible that a genuinely cooperative triad could evolve, but a more probable scenario remains one of a distancing of Beijing from an already long-established US–Japan partnership.

The United States deserves to take the Asia-Pacific region more seriously, if the rhetoric of presidential and official statements on the importance of US security and economic interests are to be fully fleshed out. It is hard for observers in Tokyo and Seoul, for example, not to gain the impression that Northeast Asia frequently waxes and wanes on the mental maps of US administrations, instead of being treated with the consistent attention that it warrants. No doubt similar complaints can be heard from allied capitals in other regions, but successive US governments may have tended to take their authority in Asia for granted. As Asian states continue to be accorded greater international status, more commensurate with their newly acquired political, military and economic strengths, it is clear that further adjustment to such trends will have to be made by the United States. We should be hearing more of cooperative Pacific partnerships and rather less of US initiatives and unilateral leadership. Moves towards effective regionalism would require new attitudes on all sides. If the United States were to encourage greater interdependence in the Asia-Pacific region, Washington would have to place less emphasis on established bilateral and vertical relations, while Asian states would then be expected to accept larger and more responsible roles in the same process. Over time it might be possible to reckon with the establishment of novel institutions that could better represent a less unequal regional power scheme, though such incrementalism will be difficult to orchestrate, given the hesitancies of some major powers and the overt ambitions of others.

For the foreseeable future, the hopes of advocates of a new world order in the Asia-Pacific are more likely to be realized by piecemeal change than by seismic shifts. One area where a modest start might be made is the institution of a conventional arms register and troop reduction proposals, though measures contributing towards a reduction of nuclear armaments in Asia would probably fail, given the extreme reluctance of the United States and China to be parties to any such scheme. Equally, preparations for more concerted efforts to stabilize currencies and the organization of a regional approach to combat future economic turmoil would pose major challenges, though preparatory discussions have begun. Yet the present instinct shared by many in the region of looking to the United States for salvation in good times and bad is not about to change. Recognition is based on the fact that many Asian economies remain particularly dependent on the American market for export-led growth and on the cold reality that Washington continues through its presence in Northeast Asia, the South China Sea and the western Pacific to be seen as the sole military hegemon. The United States' forward deployment policies have served as insurance against aggression and reassurance to its allies that it would fulfil its commitments in a crisis. Any substantial reduction in US personnel in the Asia-Pacific region would be seen as a serious weakening of American political resolve and would be regarded by many as an opportunity for other Asian states, such as the PRC and possibly Japan, to step forward to fill the resulting power vacuum. Few observers believe that once US troops are withdrawn from the continent there is any real prospect of a subsequent return to earlier force levels.

While the increasing importance of the PRC is widely recognized by the United States, there remains a considerable wariness throughout the region as to what changes may flow from further improvement in Beijing's position. To date the response from other powers has been more a case of watching and waiting than rejoicing. Hesitancy still rules. The instinctive move has been to shore up existing alliance structures and to note that the present dangers continue to preclude more than a modicum of warmth. Implementation, for example, of wider economic and security cooperation between the United States and Japan, which would certainly reinforce the Washington–Tokyo partnership, is probable in the next decade, even though this in turn could generate fresh regional instability if it led to renewed complaints from China. Attempts to fashion a more open and less militarized structure for what some might wish to term an embryonic Asian 'community', while laudable at first sight, would require immense dexterity to have much chance of success. Confidence-building in a region that possesses little confidence in the ambitions and behaviour of its neighbours is fated to be an uncomfortable and lengthy exercise. Since trust in Asia is in such short supply, this has inevitably left many foreign ministries willing to take their cue from Washington. Critics who point to the reluctance of successive US administrations to rethink their Asia-Pacific strategies deserve a measured response, but the consequences of radical change might well prove to be disadvantageous both to the stability of the region and to America's present dominance. If more frequent and more organized meetings were held by the major leaders of the region, the habit could generate new understandings and tentatively evolve towards novel associations. Whether such activities would work to the detriment of the United States might depend in part on the astuteness of US diplomacy and the manner in which its leadership responded to any such future pan-Asian movement. American diplomacy would then be required to work more intensely on a twin-track system that continues to maintain existing bilateral ties but is also prepared to accept measures that could promote both greater trilateralism with Tokyo and Beijing and a still wider regional-based multilateralism

Yet the era that began with Imperial Japan's surrender in Tokyo Bay on board the USS *Missouri* is far from over. Despite major errors that led to prolonged agony on the battlefield and the mishandling of relations with close friends, the past half-century has amply demonstrated the determination of the United States to remain committed to the Pacific Rim. As a record of generally constructive effort that has made possible the transformation of the lives of entire societies, it has few parallels. During the postwar occupation of Japan, Douglas MacArthur once remarked that his nation's sway in the Asia-Pacific region might endure for a hundred years. On the evidence to date, he may well be proved right.

8   Conclusions

Asia has replaced Europe as the principal area of instability and
potential conflict.
>   Samuel Huntington, *Daily Yomiuri* (Tokyo), 6 January 1999

The security order of the Asia-Pacific is caught between an
anachronistic Cold War framework and embryonic, untested
regional approaches.
>   Ramesh Thakor, *Asahi Evening News* (Tokyo), 10 October 2000

Today's international security requires economic peacekeeping as
well as traditional military peacekeeping.
>   Akio Morita, *The Atlantic*, June 1993

For over half a century the United States has remained at the heart of
Asian-Pacific affairs. Its impact on the entire area has been vast and
continuous, thereby ensuring that American behaviour has had a major
impact on the foreign policies of every state in the vast region. While
it would be difficult to point to any one single moment or document
that might provide an over-arching design for the entire enterprise,
it is perhaps permissible to review some of the salient points along
this remarkable journey. The United States had been recognized as
the predominant Western power in the Asia-Pacific region from at
least the 1930s onwards, if not earlier, given its active role in securing
the Washington naval treaties of 1921–22 and its efforts to restrain the
continental expansion of Imperial Japan. It was only to be expected,
therefore, that having won the Pacific War, the United States would
wish to secure the region against future aggression and attempt to revive its economic fortunes to ensure political and social stability in a
devastated and demoralized Asia. During the bitter years of fighting
against Imperial Japan, a handful of bureaucrats in Washington had
considered what might form at least the basis for a new, more liberal,
regional order in the Asia-Pacific region, once Tokyo had been forced
to surrender.

The Asia-Pacific, 2000

It was, of course, only possible to map out the general outlines of US strategy, but it was understood that the region, unlike the situation in Europe, was one where the views of the other major powers might impinge less on areas assumed to be under American influence. The State Department had already insisted in April 1944 that after the liberation of the region,

> our task will be that of making the Pacific and eastern Asia safe – safe for the United States, safe for our Allies, safe for all peace-loving peoples. Once there is peace and security, the Pacific and the Far East will be areas of great opportunity – for their own peoples, for us, for all who seek honest and mutually profitable relationships on a basis of reciprocal fair treatment.

By September 1945 the United States had earned the right to assume moral and international responsibility, through such strenuous political, military and economic means as it judged fit, to determine that there would be no possibility of a second Pearl Harbor. National interest and the call for regional leadership were seen to coincide. Naval and air bases would be acquired to criss-cross the Western Pacific, US troops might be deployed on the edges of Asia as the situation on the continent determined, and above all else, the United States should insist that it be granted a relatively free hand in occupied Japan. This was intended to ensure that it could impose a new design on its discredited ex-enemy and parts of its former empire. The manner, though, in which Douglas MacArthur seized his opportunity to graft parallel American and universal values on an alien society owed little to the agendas of lesser mortals. SCAP's belief in the righteousness of his own mission led to the transformation of postwar Japan and laid the foundations for a later relationship that has remained critical to US foreign policy in the Asia-Pacific region. American friendship with Tokyo during the occupation may have been composed of heady idealism, an element perhaps of guilt and a portion of early Cold War pragmatism, but the controversial mixture worked. The conservative Japanese cabinets from 1945 onwards have heartily disliked the bloodless revolution inflicted on their nation, yet they saw how limited the options were if Japan were to be fully protected and its economy reinvigorated. It has paid to stay with the United States.

What few US officials could hardly have anticipated in the autumn of 1945 was the rapidity with which the international rivalries between the United States and countries friendly to the Soviet Union would spread throughout the region. The emergence, however, of Mao Tse-tung's brand of Communism as the probable victor in the Chinese civil war long before 1949 and the parallel growth of indigenous Communist movements within both Northeast and Southeast Asia quickly led to a less benign view of Asia's prospects. Insurrections in Malaya, Indo-China, the Philippines and concerns over an already divided Korea were warning lights that the Western portions of the entire region were at best unstable and possibly at serious risk. Yet while some in Washington viewed the Asia-Pacific region as an intrinsic part of a global contest before the outbreak of the Korean war, it would be poor history to suggest that the United States had any particularly clear, coordinated Cold War strategy in place before the vicious fighting on the Korean Peninsula from 1950 to 1953. The United States, after all, had encouraged occupied Japan to enact a pacifist constitution that prohibits, at least on paper, a Japanese military establishment. It had also elected to keep out of the Chinese civil war and had withdrawn all American combat troops from South Korea by 1949. None of these actions suggest a particularly robust opposition to Communism in Northeast Asia. Equally, the exclusion of Korea and Taiwan from Secretary of State Acheson's speech on the extent of American responsibilities for the Asia-Pacific region in January 1950 underlines the hesitancies of the Truman administration. It took the outbreak of the Korean War to produce an immediate and far stronger American determination to resist and repel the infection across Asia. The war in Korea appeared to confirm the fears of the United States and its European allies on the global dangers they faced from hydra-headed Communism. The number of US military personnel more than doubled during the Korean War to 3 550 000 servicemen and thereafter remained considerably higher than pre-1950 levels. Once the Korean stalemate had been formally recognized, through protracted and convoluted armistice negotiations, the Asia-Pacific region was left as divided as Cold War Europe, with the United States committed to the seemingly unrewarding and interminable defence of its Pacific Rim allies from the Sino-Soviet bloc. Washington elected to garrison the frontiers to protect its interests, much in the manner that Imperial Britain had for long watched from the foothills of the Himalayas and policed the Indian Ocean and the South China Sea.

After the Korean conflict, the United States was not about to lower its guard a second time. Indeed, commentators have frequently noted that in its anxiety to oppose Communism in the region from the mid-1950s, the United States gravitated to the opposite extreme. By first instituting a complex series of bilateral, if invariably unequal, security pacts along the Pacific Rim and by then gradually extending commitments to South Vietnam, successive US administrations were eager to prove their leadership in the contest against Communism wherever it might appear in the region. The fact that Asian Communism was closely linked to Asian nationalism made no difference. The red tide had to be stopped and the United States had to be seen to be taking the fight to the enemy. This would serve both to mollify domestic critics, who were ever vigilant against any administration that appeared to be 'soft' on Communism, and demonstrate to American allies in the region that Washington meant what it said. South Vietnam was viewed as a test case for American resolve in Asia against the People's Republic of China. The United States felt that, in association with as many of its new allies in 'free' Asia as possible, it had to balance the growing power of the PRC. Memories of the intervention of the PRC in the Korean war and distrust for its activities in the region led to what the British Foreign Office aptly defined in 1960 as an American policy of 'containment plus isolation' towards Beijing. This would require 'the continuation of American support for the Nationalists in Formosa, of American refusal to contemplate the recognition of China or her admission to the United Nations, and of American chairmanship of the United Nations cause in Korea'. Many of these stances disappointed successive British governments, who had hoped that a more positive approach by the West might weaken Sino-Soviet links, lead to an expansion of trade and ensure the safety of Hong Kong.

Internal memorandums circulated within the Kennedy White House were also suggesting in 1963 that the existence of the Sino-Soviet split presented opportunities for the United States to persuade both Beijing and Moscow of the advantages that might accrue if the parties were to exhibit responsible behaviour in international affairs. Nearly a decade later, President Nixon and Secretary Kissinger were to act precisely as Kennedy's staff had then urged on their champion, though it would require a rare exhibition of statesmanship and the highest diplomacy to succeed. For Nixon and Kissinger – they ought to be ranked in this order though both the press and the wider public would sometimes be faulted for reversing their seniority – what mattered was attention to national interest. They intended to ensure that the United States start negotiations with its Communist adversaries, particularly as both might have much to offer Washington, in exchange for American support against the background of severe Sino-Soviet antagonism.

Such manoeuvrings, however, only followed the disastrous Vietnam policies of President Lyndon Johnson. The events can hardly be rehearsed here in detail, but suffice it to say that whatever the American intentions, the government of the United States failed totally in its war in Vietnam. Thirty years after successfully compelling Imperial Japan to accept unconditional surrender, the United States, for all its troop levels and technology, was itself required to bow before the military and political accomplishments of one of the poorest and smallest nations in Asia. It was a stunning reversal of fortunes. Yet the consequences for American foreign policy in the region were far less than had initially been assumed. Despite defeat, Washington was able to rebound in Asia, due in part to a widening Sino-Soviet split and also to the resilience of America's allies, whose governments had no wish to be subject either to collectivization on the Chinese model or to political control from Moscow.

President Nixon might proclaim in his Guam Doctrine of July 1969 that future support for American protégés in the Asia-Pacific region was contingent on at least a degree of allied self-help, but the United States did not scuttle back to Honolulu and San Diego. Its offshore security pacts held firm, refuting in the process both the widespread Asian view that the American century was ending and the suspicion that pro-Western governments in the region would be reluctant to begin to arm in depth. The fall of Saigon in 1975 led to few tremors beyond Indo-China. Despite the qualifications built into the Nixon Doctrine and the belief of many American liberals that the lesson of Vietnam was that massive intervention in Asia would become a thing of the past, the United States persisted with its Cold War strategic view of the region. American doubts over the conduct of the People's Republic of China and substantial US military and economic support for counter-revolutionary regimes in the Asia-Pacific region continued. Once the Vietnam War had been lost and the peace settlements signed, the future of American foreign policy in Asia turned out to be not too dissimilar to the recent past.

By the 1980s the pro-Western portions of the region were enjoying unprecedented prosperity. The phrase 'economic miracle' was suddenly being applied to nation-states that had only recently escaped from poverty and colonialism. The role of the United States as the guarantor of security for the Asia-Pacific region persisted, but its vital trading function and its provision of investment finance through its own institutions or international organizations now took precedence in Asian eyes. The United States was the market for the bulk of the finished products shipped from the 'tiger' economies, since Japan was reluctant to further weaken its own less competitive industrial sectors by welcoming cheap East Asian exports. Evidence of increasing US commercial involvement was greeted with enthusiasm on both sides of the Pacific as announcements were made with considerable fanfare by American and Asian trade officials that US trade flows across the Pacific had first equalled and then quickly surpassed those with Europe. The stronger countries such as South Korea, Taiwan, Malaysia, Singapore and Indonesia became economically, the greater the prospect for both more open governmental systems at home and the less the likelihood of external Communist powers gaining influence over their affairs. In the decade before the disintegration of the Soviet empire in eastern Europe, it was demonstrably the case that the United States was already 'winning' the political battle in support of its allies in Asia.

Yet equally, the decade following the end of Communism in Moscow's sphere of influence did not witness the collapse of the Asian states that claimed officially to be Marxist. Familiar structures did not disappear.

Whatever the many strains that these governments may be under, it remains true in the spring of 2001 that the People's Republic of China, North Korea, Vietnam and Laos have not been found guilty of apostasy. Despite widespread and confident predictions of the demise of North Korea, in particular, the Socialist states are still in business. It would be foolish to insist that their internal destruction is assured in the next decade. Pyongyang has been written off too many times in the recent past, by those who stated categorically that economic mismanagement, political repression and crop failures would assuredly reduce the country to famine, chaos and ultimate disintegration, for observers not to be highly suspicious of all such predictions.

What can perhaps be more confidently suggested is that the inauguration of the George W. Bush administration is unlikely to see major changes in the broad conduct of American foreign policy in the Asia-Pacific. The overall direction of US affairs in the region will almost certainly continue to centre on managing relations with China, Japan and the two Koreas. Events in Southeast Asia should present fewer difficulties and therefore will receive correspondingly less official attention. This prognosis, however, is conditional on a degree of political and economic stability in nations such as Indonesia, Thailand and the Philippines, where concern has been growing that military intervention might follow from the ineptitude and corruption of weak civilian governments. By the spring of 2001 it can no longer be assumed that the widening of the democratic process in Southeast Asia provides any firm guarantee against a return to the authoritarianism of the past. Yet given the strong support that earlier pro-military regimes, such as those of President Suharto in Indonesia and President Marcos in the Philippines, long received from the United States, no future US administration would readily wish to disassociate itself from its well-established ties to these nations.

The People's Republic of China is certain to be awarded priority, not out of any innate bond of trans-Pacific friendship but because of the increased power of Beijing and the continuing difficulties that face Sino-American relations. Few would question the assertion that China matters immensely and that efforts should be made to persuade Beijing to discuss issues of mutual concern. This might lead eventually to laying the groundwork for some future multilateral security organization in Northeast Asia, but at present this appears a remote prospect. Whether the PRC will be able to substantiate its rhetoric that it is committed to the existing international order depends equally on its domestic civil and military leadership and the responses of the United States to an emerging Great Power with whom its past relationship has frequently been dismal. It is easy to claim that Sino-American ties are the key to regional stability in the twenty-first century but immensely difficult to describe with any confidence how events over the next two decades may unfold. Senior US diplomat Richard Holbrooke, for example, suggested in January 2001 that the next 'large, overriding' historical cycle 'for the first half of the new century will be the relationship between the US and China'. He then added, perhaps a little optimistically after his active involvement in the lengthy Balkans imbroglio of the 1990s, that in his view at least it did not need to 'be a struggle that one has to win and the other has to lose'. He preferred instead to predict that Sino-American relations 'will be a search for co-existence, in a way in which each country respects the other'.

Evaluation of China's existing and potential strengths poses its own problems that may contribute to the American public's awareness of a significant threat to its national interests. Chinese commentators will frequently deplore the negative perceptions of their country conveyed in the American media and supported by the US Congress. The temptation, however, exhibited also with disturbing frequency in Japan when it too is faced with overseas criticism, to resort to statements of 'misunderstandings' by the other party should be discouraged. Similarly, it hardly dispels Western perceptions that China may possibly in the longer term equal or exceed the United States as an economic power to dismiss the anxieties of others as merely misplaced. What appears probable is that long before any such eventuality might be reached, there may well be serious trade friction between the United States and the PRC. Indeed, Chalmers Johnson has suggested recently that the 'economic challenge of China is likely to be the most difficult test not just for American economic policy but for its foreign policy in general in the first quarter of the twenty-first century'. The risk, as in an earlier phase of American–Japanese relations, is that the probable Sino-American trade and financial difficulties ahead could coincide with regional security disputes. Any unhappy amalgam of such twin issues would make attempts to discover a satisfactory resolution of either subject a lot harder.

Alliance partners also face considerable difficulties in policy co-ordination in Northeast Asia. In the case of China, the United States has traditionally taken the leading role in confronting Communism in the recent past and in engaging the PRC as at present. The instinct of any hegemonic power, however, to disregard or at least play down the views of other nations in the region should be resisted. China's many neighbours may disagree among themselves over the appropriate manner with which to respond to China's strengths, but they obviously have to live with the emerging power on their doorsteps. Such states may often be intimidated by Beijing but they possess only a fraction of the United States' ability to counter threats and taunts from the other side. Smaller Asian nations are obliged to get along with China or face potentially unpleasant repercussions, though the same countries may adopt similar cooperative policies towards the United States as well in order to insure themselves with both protagonists. It remains infinitely easier to adopt a tough response to China when diplomacy has the luxury of being backed by a far larger defence budget and more advanced military technology than that possessed by one's adversary.

Beijing, it has been widely suggested by regional analysts, is unlikely to be over-persuaded that the United States necessarily means what it says in wishing to engage constructively with China. The cold fact that Washington remains committed to bilateral security pacts in the region offering protection against the PRC is inevitably regarded by Beijing as a military reality that is felt to threaten it. There is, as the commanding officer of the US Seventh Fleet bluntly put it in keeping with the traditions of his service in December 2000, recognition internationally that his men were ready to 'stand up and stand against intimidation'. Vice-Admiral James Metzger noted that the Seventh Fleet served as a '911 force' ready to act in the case of regional emergencies, clearly implying an immediate response, if Beijing were to countenance possible Chinese moves against Taiwan. Yet as we have seen, there are limits to what the Chinese authorities can do to counterbalance the self-evident geopolitical strengths of the United States in the region. It would take at least a generation to realize a substantial shift in the relative strengths of the two sides, assuming that the PRC can manage its economy competently enough to continue with its military modernization schemes and that the United States may begin to scale back its own defence programmes.

Significant changes to the international political situation in the Asia-Pacific region may occur in Northeast Asia. The future of the Korean Peninsula is clearly an issue of the greatest importance to its neighbours and the wider world that will be immensely difficult to resolve. It is almost certain to be a protracted business where the first stage would be the establishment of full diplomatic ties between Pyongyang and its former opponents. This could be followed by the even steeper hurdle of working towards the possible reunification of Korea. Analysts have suggested that the two-step process might require a generation of painstaking negotiations in unknown waters. Any prospect of eventual success is highly contingent on factors that at this stage can hardly be foreseen, though it would appear that restraining North Korea's nuclear programmes in return for substantial economic packages would be among the critical questions that would have to be resolved before normalization.

All predictions on the possible shape of the Asia-Pacific region in the years ahead will depend on whether the United States is prepared to remain both the bulwark of Asia and the initiator of gradual moves to obtain a wider regional interdependence. The suggestion has also to be considered that any satisfactory outcome to the reunification of Korea would lead first to a reduction and then to an eventual withdrawal of US forces from the peninsula. It may well be that such measures would act to destabilize the Korean area by adding fresh competition from outside parties. It is difficult, however, to envisage any future US government long remaining in force in Korea if a peaceful reunification process were at some stage to be accomplished. The range of uncertainties over the outlook for Northeast Asia is clearly immense; all that is probable is that tension between the two Koreas is likely to be gradually reduced and replaced by measures contributing to greater understanding and co-operation. In the meantime, it is vital that the United States be seen to act as the main guarantor of peace and security in the region. Events thereafter are too remote at present for anything but imprecise guesswork, though achieving satisfactory settlements in Korea and over Taiwan can be assumed to be a process requiring possibly a generation of patient and difficult negotiations.

Equally, it remains highly problematic to envisage an Asia-Pacific region of genuine cooperation and mutual respect for all its members, whether large or small. Certainly participants at Asian academic conferences are discussing the possibility of a regional security community, much as their predecessors had successfully encouraged governments to build a Pacific-wide economic structure that eventually resulted in APEC, but the political realities still appear discouraging. Continental Asia never experienced the long peace that some historians have seen as the main characteristic of the Cold War era. The mutual advantages of increased pan-Pacific trade are easier to enumerate than abstract and amorphous ideas on confidence-building measures. The creation of a common future would require decades of painstaking diplomacy among rival states that to date have found it immensely difficult to work together. The achievements of ASEAN may be taken by some as evidence that contradicts this pessimism, but the future directions of any solidarity within Southeast Asia is itself in doubt and does not offer particular proof of progress. By the end of the twentieth century it was hard to mistake the doubts within ASEAN or to ignore the frequent commentaries that even questioned whether the organization could expect to survive for very much longer.

The overall American political position in the contemporary Asia-Pacific is being further enhanced by its cultural status. As the process of globalization accelerates and the economic well-being of Asia increases, the cultural impact of the United States on the region can be readily seen across the spectrum. The region's receptivity to news sources such as CNN is clearly apparent; so also is the popularity of Hollywood block-busters and vast Disney World theme parks. Critics in Asia, as has long been the case in Europe and Latin America, are quick to deplore portions of what is frequently portrayed as tasteless trivia, but the tide is unlikely to be halted. Pap for the semi-literate it may be, but over much of the twentieth century this has been the main avenue of increasing Asia's awareness of the outside world. Prewar Shanghai, Tokyo and Manila had a voracious appetite for American movies, and the present receptivity of the region's youth to American popular culture simply continues this long-established trend. The very first movies I saw as a boy in Hong Kong in the 1950s were the Cecil B. de Mille extravaganzas that played for week after week in the jam-packed cinemas of a city-state that was otherwise almost bereft of Western-style entertainment. In its early post-war years Hong Kong was more intent on producing accountants than the acrobatic action pictures and challenging art films characteristic of a later era. Throughout Asia, American movies, motor cars and consumer gadgetry were widely seen to symbolize an impossibly remote dream of individual freedom, affluence and mobility. If, as Reinhold Wagnleitner would claim in assessing US cultural hegemony in postwar Europe, 'film history is world history', it is also the case that from its birth, Asian television has fed imported American soap operas to curious audiences. Equally, US publishers of everything from lurid comics and crime novels to the works of Mailer, Bellow and Updike have been attracted by the potential size of the Asian market.

The influence of American culture is apparent at different levels and to different degrees in different societies, but the overall impact of the United States on a wealthier, more technologically advanced region can only grow. It is somewhat artificial, however, to imagine that cultural phenomena should be strictly portioned out in any exact manner. It is surely erroneous to suggest that those who admire Presley have no interest in the abstract expressionism of Jackson Pollock and Rothko or to reckon that the ever loyal fans of the ever touring Bob Dylan might be unreceptive to other musical forms. The popularity of professional basketball and baseball, the determination to master English and the attention to show-biz gossip all underline the wide appeal of the United States. American culture encompasses the trivial, the bland and the highest artistic endeavour. It forms part of the mental horizons of the affluent segments of Asian societies. Its influence is seen in accessibility to the Voice of America and American forces networks, the expansion of the Starbucks coffee chain and the ready availability of ATMs and US financial services. In the process, globalization is frequently equated with Americanization. The fact that a sizeable proportion of the electorate in the United States views globalization as a threat to its own livelihood is far less known overseas than the impact of American-based multinational corporations on Asian lifestyles.

What is clear is that American culture at both the popular and the highest intellectual levels is prospering in the Asia region. Readier access to instant communications has by its very success led several governments to attempt to censor websites and ban associated political, pornographic, and on-line gambling channels, but such defences are always likely to be subverted by the battering ram of still newer technologies. It should be noted, though, that the Asia-Pacific is only the latest of a long list of regions that have had serious reservations over what France in the 1960s deplored as the 'American invasion' and what would in the 1990s engender an unattractive campaign against fast-food restaurants. In similar vein, the British cabinet in the spring of 1963 spent part of a weekend cloistered at the Prime Minister's country residence complaining that the British contribution to global security and cultural affairs, defined as the 'part Britain plays in the world', risked being neglected. What the British ministers did note with some prescience, however, was that the 'great unfulfilled demand for consumer goods' was working against the USSR's side in the Cold War. 'The growing interest in the Soviet Union in bourgeois comforts' and the 'insidious effect of Western "culture", pop records, and the like', which was contributing to the 'rise and fall of Communism', would later dig a similar pit under Asian societies, almost regardless of their established national ideologies. By century's end, consumer capitalism, in whatever modified forms it would take in the different social and historical environments of an increasingly prosperous Asia-Pacific, was king.

At the quasi-official level, the cultural diplomacy associated with federally funded US centres in major cities throughout the Asia-Pacific and the increasing academic exchanges between American institutions and their counterparts in the region is also working to Washington's advantage. The Fulbright programme, named after the US senator who sponsored an imaginative scheme during the early days of the Cold War to allow foreign scholars and artists the opportunity in an era of widespread poverty to visit the United States, continues to enhance the influence of American higher learning overseas. What began as an attempt to wean Asian intellectuals and artists from the lure of Communism has, in some instances, been reversed; Japanese academia, for example, now encourages US figures to lecture on its campuses. In the early 1950s the pioneer Japanese Fulbrighters were given intensive lessons in Western table manners by the American ambassador's wife before boarding ship at Yokohama; now it is their American counterparts who have to learn to wrestle with chopsticks. While the successes and failures of government and privately funded activities by the likes of the Ford, Rockefeller and Asia Foundations can hardly be quantified, it is probable that their long-term impact has been considerable in the educational and professional fields. The fact that contemporary Japan has itself deployed generous corporate philanthropy overseas and instituted the Japan Foundation as the cultural arm of its diplomacy suggests that the American example has in its turn influenced other states in the region.

Perverse evidence of the success of the United States' official and semi-official cultural activity is seen through the overt opposition it has prompted on occasion. Although the days of marching on the local American centre to register anger at US foreign policy in Asia are likely to be behind us, the anger exhibited in recent May Day rallies against globalization trends serves to qualify this statement. Vocal protests in front of US embassies to jeer at what some see as the exploitative tentacles of American-dominated global capitalism is a reminder of the criticism that exists of multinational corporate behaviour. In several nations it is also probable that many who once protested at Yankee imperialism later went on to study at American academic institutions. In admittedly the most extreme instances, at least three-quarters of the current teaching staff at the University of the Philippines earned post-graduate degrees in the United States and recent Taiwanese cabinets have been awash with American MBAs and PhDs.

The reverse of this trend is evident in the greatly increased American interest in and knowledge of what might be loosely termed 'things Asian'. Evidence from the American press in the spring of 2001 indicates that the Asia-Pacific is receiving close, at times even continuous, attention from the American print media. Shortly after the US spy plane episode at Hainan had been resolved, the entire front pages of major newspapers were taken up with reporting the accession of yet another Japanese prime minister, the possible shift by President Bush over established American policy towards the defence of Taiwan, and the revelation that former Senator Kerrey had, when serving as a junior officer in South Vietnam, fired on unarmed civilians. Commentators are doubtless correct to stress that this two-way learning process remains mightily unequal, but the increase in the United States' general awareness of the Asia-Pacific region has surely been explosive over the past two generations. Discussion of Quality Control circles, Pulitzer prize works on Emperor Hirohito and post-surrender Japan, the popularity of Asian martial arts and Thai cooking all illustrate the public interest. Debate over the débâcle in Vietnam, Zen Buddhism, the so-called Confucian work ethic, 'Korea Inc.', concern over Chinese espionage and the detention of American citizens, Kuala Lumpur's boast of the tallest skyscraper in the world, and fashion design by the likes of Issey Miyake, are also random pieces of the Asian cultural jigsaw known in the United States.

It may never add up to a satisfactory whole but it is surely a vast improvement on the days before Pearl Harbor when the US government and its peoples looked almost automatically across the Atlantic to Europe and many Asians were subject to direct or indirect European colonialism. Mass tourism, the establishment of enviable research institutions and the stronger political position of Asian-Americans virtually guarantees that this transformation will endure. Americans continue to go to Asia for every reason under the sun; for some it is the demands of official or private sector careers, while for others it is the dictates of conscience. Government employees, fortune-hunters, venture capitalists and pleasure-seekers represent the political, economic, sexual and cultural motivation of American society. The impact today of this constant two-way collective migration on Asia and the United States is surely more than mere scratches on the mind.

Yet, while the region has paid careful attention to the United States and recognized that all roads lead to Washington, it remains the case that accurate knowledge of other societies within Asia may be lower than outsiders may too readily assume. South Korea, for example, whose leader was the first foreign visitor to the White House after George W. Bush's inauguration, frequently complains that Japan ignores both the impact of the Korean War on Japan's economic transformation and the important security role played by the South Koreans and the United States in defending Northeast Asia throughout the protracted Cold War era. Newspapers from Jakarta to Beijing are equally quick to remonstrate with Japan for ignoring its wartime barbarism in Asia or for doctoring its textbooks to produce a less 'masochistic' version of history to suit what some sense to be a new and dangerous nationalism in contemporary Japan. Asian students often much prefer to enter American universities than transfer to campuses within the region, in the same manner that open access to US advanced technology once brought eager Asian businessmen and scientists across the Pacific to inspect IBM and Bell laboratories or, more recently, today's Silicon Valley.

It would appear that trans-Pacific links to the United States still remain in the forefront of the thinking of many Asian states and that the impetus for greater regionalism will eventually have to transcend what is often a firmly entrenched dependence on American leadership. Loose talk within the region of the Pacific century and Asian values is hardly an adequate substitute for the development of closer links between Pacific Rim societies that have long stressed their dissimilarities with neighbouring nations. Reputable Asian universities, for example, have been particularly slow to recruit senior staff from outside their own borders. There remains also the tendency to imagine that the United States is the holy grail when it comes to democratic government, human rights or market capitalism and to ignore the alternative British, European and Anglo-Pacific approaches to such issues. The faults of American society may be downplayed in this process and it may be useful to reflect on the human rights failures of the United States, such as its inability to abolish capital punishment or the severe strains of promoting multiculturalism, before rushing to embrace the 'American way' too heartily. Yet this tendency is in itself a clear reflection of the continuing cultural influence of the United States in postwar Asia. Chinese students, to give but one telling example, who are invariably the first to voice their anger at what they see as American imperialism in East Asia, will candidly explain to foreign reporters that this does not necessarily stop them applying to expensive American business schools.

Whatever the realities of supposed American omniscience and omni-potence may be, there can be little doubt that many in the Asia-Pacific continue to hold the view that successful modernization in most of its complex forms is best equated with Americanization. It remains the case that for most of Asia, it is economic advancement, rather than any strenuous interest in democratic forms of government or commitment to the observance of human rights, that has been at the heart of the American example. In what has been aptly termed 'the great ascent' of one Asian economy after another, the contribution of the military and political strength of the United States to this process can also be neglected. It is easy to overlook the fact that the United States Pacific Command deploys six aircraft carrier battle groups and that two-thirds of the total strength of the entire US marine corps is stationed in the area to provide a bedrock of stability. The region has wished instead to recall its own accomplishments throughout the half-century since the Pacific War and has been generally more eager to embrace prosperity than par-ticipatory democracy. Invariably, the defeat of poverty and the security of the state has been accorded priority over too scrupulous a respect for open government and the rule of law. Citizens from societies as diverse politically as Japan, China and Singapore have unwittingly, in this important instance, shared a common cause. The goal of American affluence has been the spur. It is jeans rather than Jefferson that attracts. When the undoubted lure of American plenty is combined with other, perhaps secondary, attributes of American civilization in the eyes of many Asians, the resulting amalgam is hard to deny. This presents the United States with an enviable asset that reflects the successes of the past two generations, and can only work to Washington's advantage in the decades ahead.

At century's end, the position of the United States in the Asia-Pacific region was stronger than at any time since the first triumphant months after Imperial Japan's surrender in 1945. Explanations for Asia's American half-century stem in part from the continuation of Washington's long-established security alliance structures and its formidable domestic economy, which makes possible both the military foundations of US power and the ready market for Asian goods. American dominance, however, is also a reflection of the relative lack of effective regional challenges to the United States. The disappearance of the European powers from Southeast Asia and then the decline of first the Soviet Union and now the Russian Federation on the periphery of Northeast Asia leaves only the People's Republic of China as a possible contender for the American laurels.

While it is problematic as to how the future Sino-American relationship can be best managed, few observers doubt that the United States is currently intent on clarifying its position with regard to the greater status of the PRC. The debate is under way and is certain to take many forms. The Pentagon is known to be placing greater stress on its Pacific capabilities as the post-Cold War situation in Europe – the Balkans excepted – permits a global reconfiguration of forces. War games are now in use that refer to the PRC as a 'peer competitor'. Press reports in May 2000 also suggested that planners are preparing more liberal base agreements with both South Korea and Japan in order to ensure that these key alliances can be retained through greater cooperative effort. For some it remains a crude ideological and military case of 'China versus America'. For others it is a plea for greater maturity, with the assumption that crises are only to be expected but equally that ties ought to be robust enough to deal with such occurrences, whether caused by trade disputes, territorial questions, human rights or how the United States ought to respond to threats to Taiwan. No one school is likely to possess all the answers, but a less antagonistic approach would appear to be the safest way forward. The hope must surely be that US–Chinese economic and financial links will be regarded as possessing sufficient priority for both nations that the ever difficult question of Taipei's fate can remain in limbo. In any cross-strait crisis, however, President George W. Bush and his successors will have to demonstrate to China not only that the US military has the regional muscle to act decisively but that the American administration is seen to possess the political will to readily deploy the available forces in an emergency. Planners in Washington are now presented with the daunting task of simultaneously restraining Taiwan from making a bid for independence and ensuring that the US military has the necessary weapon systems and Pacific Rim basing facilities required to carry out its mission. It should keep enough political and diplomatic channels open to maintain an adequate dialogue with the Chinese leadership, if a crisis were to erupt. Clearly regional policy-makers in the White House, State Department and Pentagon now have an unenviable series of challenges to wrestle with in order to prevent any direct future confrontation with an increasingly confident China. There may not be any great public support for the United States to embrace Beijing but, as President Clinton tried to show, emerging geopolitical and economic realities cannot be ignored. His administration worked, as all its predecessors since Richard Nixon had done, to encourage the PRC to cooperate in the global arena and to demonstrate military resolve when it was felt that Taiwan was being unnecessarily threatened as during the 1995–96 crisis. More recently, President George W. Bush, in keeping with the approaches adopted by his father when in the White House a decade earlier, has instituted measures to enhance Taiwan's defence forces under President Chen Shui-bian. The present Bush administration is looking to strengthen US ties with its regional allies to maintain a favourable balance of power in the Asia-Pacific, but it is highly probable that these efforts will be matched by parallel attention to the engagement of Beijing and a judicious respect for China's emergence once again as a Great Power.

This Sino-American analysis assumes, of course, that Japan, at least for the next generation, will want to stay safely moored to Washington and would only slip anchor if the United States should fail to live up to its bilateral and regional commitments. Given that the American embassy in Tokyo possesses more diplomatic staff than any other US mission abroad and that the US Navy uses its base at Yokosuka as the only permanent overseas homeport for an aircraft carrier, there are few indications that Washington is about to weaken its relationship with Japan. Indeed, the United States may wish to encourage Japan, now almost certain to be governed in the years ahead by a shifting combination of centre-right party coalitions, to play a larger role in the region and to move gradually from being largely an economic power to a more responsible and thereby less unequal defence partner. The concept itself was originally a legacy of the Vietnam War, but it has to be said that, even a generation on, it has yet to yield much fruit. Japanese resistance and American ambivalence would both have to be corrected before any genuine strategic alliance could be fashioned and deployed in the region.

For the moment the Asia-Pacific is less violent and more prosperous than at any time in living memory. The United States may feel entitled to pause and congratulate itself on the present outcome, but its officials are unlikely to assume that this represents the end of history. The setbacks and disappointments of the last half-century should serve as reminders that America's considerable achievements were bought at a price and should also act as a warning of the possibility of fresh perils to come. The past has its uses. What it cannot do, however, is chart more than a highly approximate future for the Asia-Pacific region. The first decades of the twenty-first century may prove less manageable and more turbulent than the later part of the previous century. It remains to be seen whether the next generation of leaders in the United States will wish to accept the responsibilities and the associated risks of continuing to be the dominant Asia-Pacific power. Any substantial American retreat could undermine the entire edifice and leave the region facing fresh instability. Anarchy is the unpleasant alternative to not staying on.

Select Bibliography

General Texts

Borthwick, Martin, *Pacific Century* (Boulder, CO, 1992)

Chan, Steve, *East Asian Dynamism: Growth, Order and Security in the Pacific Region* (Boulder, CO, 1993)

Cohen, Warren I. (ed.), *Pacific Passage: The Study of American-East Asian Relations on the Eve of the Twenty-First Century* (New York, 1996)

Diamond, Larry, and Marc F. Plattner (eds), *Democracy in East Asia* (Baltimore, MD, 1998)

Kissinger, Henry, *Diplomacy* (New York, 1994)

McMillen, Donald Hugh (ed.), *Asian Perspectives on International Security* (London, 1984)

Maidment, Richard, et al. (eds), *Governance in the Asia-Pacific* (London, 1998)

Morley, James, et al. (eds), *Driven by Growth: Political Change in the Asia-Pacific Region* (Armonk, NY, 1999)

Reynolds, David, *One World Divisible: A Global History since 1945* (New York, 2000)

Ross, Robert S. (ed.), *East Asia in Transition* (Armonk, NY, 1995)

Segal, Gerald, *Rethinking the Pacific* (Oxford, 1990)

Singham, A. W., and Shirley Hune, *Non-alignment in an Age of Alignments* (London, 1986)

Steinberg, David Joel (ed.), *In Search of Southeast Asia* (Honolulu, 1985)

Tarling, Nicholas (ed.), *The Cambridge History of Southeast Asia*, vol. 2 (Cambridge, 1993)

Thompson, Robert C., *The Pacific Basin since 1945* (London, 1994)

Yahuda, Michael, *The International Politics of the Asia-Pacific, 1945–1995* (London, 1996)

Young, John W., *Cold War and Détente, 1941–91* (London, 1993)

Cold War and After: General Texts

Alagappa Muthiah (ed.), *Asian Security Practice: Material and Ideational Influences* (Stanford, 1998)

Brands, H. W., *The Wages of Globalism: Lyndon Johnson and the Limits of American Power* (New York, 1995)

Brown, Michael E., et al. (eds), *The Rise of China* (Cambridge, MA, 2000)

Buckley, Roger, *Hong Kong: The Road to 1997* (Cambridge, 1997)

Bush, George, and Brent Scowcroft, *A World Transformed* (New York, 1998)

Clark, Donald C. (ed.), *Korea Briefing, 1993* (Boulder, CO, 1993)

Cohen, Warren I., and Akira Iriye (eds), *The Great Powers in Asia, 1953–1960* (New York, 1990)

Cohen, Warren I., and Nancy Bernkopf Tucker (eds), *Lyndon Johnson Confronts the World: American Foreign Policy, 1963–1968* (Cambridge, 1994)

Cumings, Bruce, *Parallax Visions: Making Sense of American–East Asian Relations at the End of the Century* (Durham, NC, 1999)

Deibel, Terry L., and John Lewis Gaddis (eds), *Containing the Soviet Union: A Critique of US Policy* (Washington, DC, 1987)

Dockrill, Saki, *Eisenhower's New-Look National Security Policy, 1953–61* (Basingstoke, UK, 1996)

Dower, John, *Embracing Defeat: Japan in the Wake of World War Two* (New York, 1999)

Finn, Richard B., *Winners in Peace: MacArthur, Yoshida, and Postwar Japan* (Berkeley, CA, 1992)

Gaddis, John Lewis, *Strategies of Containment* (Oxford, 1982)

Gittings, John, *The World and China, 1922–1972* (London, 1974)

Harding, Harry (ed.), *China's Foreign Relations in the 1980s* (New Haven, CT, 1984)

Harris, Stuart, and James Cotton (eds), *The End of the Cold War in Northeast Asia* (Boulder, CO, 1991)

Hogan, Michael J. (ed.), *America and the World: The Historiogaphy of American Foreign Relations since 1941* (Cambridge, 1995)

Inoguchi Takashi, *Japan's International Relations* (London, 1991)

Iriye, Akira, *The Cold War in Asia: A Historical Introduction* (Englewood Cliffs, NJ, 1974)

Irving, R. E. M., *The First Indochina War* (London, 1975)

Itoh Fumio (ed.), *China in the Twenty-first Century: Politics, Economics, and Society* (Tokyo, 1997)

Kim, Samuel S., *China and the World: Chinese Foreign Relations in the Post-Cold War Era* (Boulder, CO, 1994)

Lee, Chae-Jin, *Japan Faces China: Political and Economic Relations in the Postwar Era* (Baltimore, MD, 1976)

Nagai Yonosuke and Akira Iriye, *The Origins of the Cold War in Asia* (Tokyo, 1977)

Nishihara Masashi, *East Asian Security and the Trilateral Countries* (New York, 1985)

Oberdorfer, Don, *The Two Koreas: A Contemporary History* (Reading, MA, 1997)

Pandey, B. N., *South and South-East Asia: Problems and Policies* (London, 1980)

Scalapino, Robert A. (ed.), *The Communist Revolution in Asia* (Berkeley, CA, 1965)

Schell, Orville, *To Get Rich is Glorious: China in the 80s* (New York, 1986)

Schram, Stuart R., *The Political Thought of Mao Tse-tung* (Harmondsworth, 1969)

Segal, Gerald, *The Soviet Union and the Pacific* (London, 1990)

Soderberg, Marie, and Ian Reader (eds), *Japanese Influences and Presences in Asia* (Richmond, UK, 2000)

White, Tyrene (ed.), *China Briefing 2000: The Continuing Transformation* (Armonk, NY, 2000)

Zagoria, Donald S. (ed.), *Soviet Policy in East Asia* (New Haven, CT, 1982)

Zagoria, Donald S., *The Sino-Soviet Conflict, 1956–1961* (Princeton, NJ, 1962)

Zubok, Vladislav, and Constantine Pleshakov, *Inside the Kremlin's Cold War: From Stalin to Khrushchev* (Cambridge, MA, 1996)

The USA and Northeast Asia

Buckley, Roger, *US–Japan Alliance Diplomacy, 1945–1990* (Cambridge, 1992)

Calder, Kent E., *Pacific Defense: Arms, Energy, and America's Future in Asia* (New York, 1996)

Chang, Gordon H., *Friends and Enemies: The United States, China and the Soviet Union, 1948–1972* (Stanford, CA, 1990)

Cohen, Warren I., *America's Response to China* (New York, 1990)

Cumings, Bruce, *The Origins of the Korean War*, 2 vols (Princeton, NJ, 1981 and 1990)

Faust, John R, and Judith F. Kornberg, *China in World Politics* (Boulder, CO, 1995)

Foot, Rosemary, *The Wrong War: American Policy and the Dimensions of the Korean Conflict, 1950–1953* (Ithaca, NY, 1985)

Funabashi Yoichi, *Alliance Adrift* (New York, 1999)

Gourevitch, Peter, et al. (eds), *United States–Japan Relations and International Institutions After the Cold War* (La Jolla, CA, 1995)

Green, Michael J., and Patrick M. Cronin (eds), *The U.S.–Japan Alliance: Past, Present, and Future* (New York, 1999)

Harding, Harry, *A Fragile Relationship: The United States and China since 1972* (Washington, DC, 1992)

Johnson, Chalmers, *Blowback: The Costs and Consequences of American Empire* (New York, 2000)

Lasater, Martin L., *The Taiwan Conundrum in U.S. China Policy* (Boulder, CO, 2000)

Lowe, Peter, *The Origins of the Korean War* (Basingstoke, UK, 1997)

Mann, James, *About Face* (New York, 1999)

Nam, Joo-Hong, *America's Commitment to South Korea: The First Decade of the Nixon Doctrine* (Cambridge, 1986)

Oksenberg, Michael, and Robert B. Oxnam (eds), *Dragon and Eagle: United States–China Relations: Past and Future* (New York, 1978)

Robinson, Thomas W., and David Shambaugh (eds), *Chinese Foreign Policy: Theory and Practice* (Oxford, 1994)

Ross, Robert S., *The Indochina Triangle: China's Vietnam Policy* (New York, 1988)

Stueck, William, *The Korean War: An International History* (Princeton, NJ, 1995)

Tucker, Nancy Bernkopf, *Patterns in the Dust: Chinese–American Relations and the Recognition Controversy, 1949–1950* (New York, 1983)

Tucker, Nancy Bernkopf, *Taiwan, Hong Kong, and the United States, 1945–1992* (New York, 1994)

Tyler, Patrick, *A Great Wall: Six Presidents and China: An Investigative History* (New York, 1999)

Ward, Robert E. and Sakamoto Yoshikazu (eds), *Democratizing Japan: The Allied Occupation* (Honolulu, 1987)

Zhao, Suisheng (ed.), *Across the Taiwan Strait: Mainland China, Taiwan, and the 1995–1996 Crisis* (New York, 1999)

The USA and Southeast Asia

Aggarwal, Vinod K., and Charles E. Morrison, *Asia-Pacific Crossroads: Regime Creation and the Future of APEC* (New York, 1998)

Brady, Christopher, *United States Foreign Policy towards Cambodia: A Question of Realities* (Basingstoke, UK, 1999)

Colbert, Evelyn, *Southeast Asia in International Politics* (Ithaca, NY, 1977)

Harrison, James P., *The Endless War: Vietnam's Struggle for Independence* (New York, 1989)

Herring, George C., *America's Longest War: The United States and Vietnam, 1950–1975* (Philadelphia, PA, 1986)

Kaiser, David, *American Tragedy: Kennedy, Johnson, and the Origins of the Vietnam War* (Cambridge, MA, 2000)

Leifer, Michael, *ASEAN and the Security of South-East Asia* (London, 1989)

Logevall, Fredrik, *Choosing War* (Berkeley, CA, 1999)

McMahon, Robert J., *The Limits of Empire: the United States and Southeast Asia since World War II* (New York, 1999)

McNamara, Robert S., et al., *Argument Without End* (Washington, DC, 2000)

New York Times, The Pentagon Papers (1971)

O'Nan, Stewart, *The Vietnam Reader* (New York, 1998)

Short, Anthony, *The Origins of the Vietnam War* (London, 1989)

Smith, R. B., *An International History of the Vietnam War*, 2 vols (London, 1983 and 1985)

Economic Issues

Bergsten, C. Fred, et al., *American Multinationals and American Interests* (Washington, DC, 1978)

Burstein, Daniel, and Arne de Keijizer, *Big Dragon* (New York, 1998)

Forsberg, Aaron, *America and the Japanese Miracle: The Cold War Context of Japan's Economic Revival, 1950–1960* (Chapel Hill, NC, 2000)

Gilpin, Robert, *The Challenge of Global Capitalism: the World Economy in the 21st Century* (Princeton, NJ, 2000)

Korhonen, Pekka, *Japan and Asia Pacific Regionalism: Pacific Romances, 1968–1996* (London, 1998)

Lee, Hiro and David W. Roland-Hurst (eds), *Economic Development and Co-operation in the Pacific Basin* (Cambridge, 1998)

Lincoln, Edward J., *Troubled Times: US–Japan Trade Relations in the 1990s* (Washington, DC, 1999)

McLeod, Ross H., and Ross Garnaut (eds), *East Asia in Crisis: From Being a Miracle to Needing One?* (London, 1998)

Ohmae Kenichi, *The Borderless World* (London, 1990)

Taylor, Robert, *Greater China and Japan: Prospects for an Economic Partnership in East Asia* (London, 1996)

Vogel, Ezra, *The Four Little Dragons: The Spread of Industrialization in East Asia* (Cambridge, MA, 1997)

Memoirs

Carter, Jimmy, *Keeping Faith: Memoirs of a President* (New York, 1982)
Christopher, Warren, *In the Stream of History: Shaping Foreign Policy for a New Era* (Stanford, CA, 1998)
Eisenhower, Dwight D., *Mandate for Change* (Garden City, NY, 1963)
Johnson, Lyndon B., *The Vantage Point* (New York, 1971)
Kennan, George F., *Memoirs, 1950–1963* (New York, 1983)
Kissinger, Henry A., *White House Years* (New York, 1979)
Lee Kuan Yew, *The Singapore Story* (Singapore, 1999)
Nixon, Richard M., *RN: The Memoirs of Richard Nixon* (New York, 1978)
Truman, Harry S. *Memoirs*, 2 vols (New York, 1965)
Yoshida Shigeru, *Memoirs* (London, 1959)

Official Documents

Defense Agency, Japan, *Defense of Japan, 2000* (Tokyo, 2000)
Foreign Relations of the United States, multiple vols on the Asia-Pacific from 1945 (Washington, DC)
Kandiah, Michael David, et al. (eds), *Asia: Official British Documents 1945–65*, CD-ROM (London, 1999)
Ministry of Foreign Affairs, Japan, *Diplomatic Bluebook*, annual vols (Tokyo)
People's Republic of China, The Basic Law of the Hong Kong Special Administrative Region of the People's Republic of China (Hong Kong, 1992)
USSR, Security in the Asia-Pacific Region: The Soviet Approach (Moscow, 1988)

Presidential Libraries

Dwight D. Eisenhower, Abilene, KS
Lyndon B. Johnson, Austin, TX
J. F. Kennedy, Boston, MA
Harry S. Truman, Independence, MO

Journals

Asian Survey
China Quarterly
Current History
Diplomatic History
Foreign Affairs
International Affairs
International Security
Japan Echo
Japan Quarterly
Journal of Asian Studies
Modern Asian Studies
Pacific Review

Index

Lightning Source UK Ltd.
Milton Keynes UK
UKHW010945020820
367557UK00001B/1

9 780521 007252